Just for Today

Just for Today

❖ ❖ ❖

Daily Meditations
for Recovering Addicts

The Twelve Steps and Twelve Traditions reprinted
for adaptation by permission of AA World Services, Inc.

World Service Office
PO Box 9999
Van Nuys, CA 91409
Tel. (818) 773-9999
Fax (818) 700-0700
Website: www.na.org

World Service Office–CANADA
Mississauga, Ontario

World Service Office–EUROPE
Brussels, Belgium
Tel. +32/2/646-6012

World Service Office–IRAN
Tehran, Iran
www.na-iran.org

This is NA Fellowship-approved literature.

Narcotics Anonymous, , and The NA Way are registered
trademarks of Narcotics Anonymous World Services, Incorporated.

ISBN 978-1-55776-151-4   English   11/08

WSO Catalog Item No. EN-1112

Foreword

The book you have in your hands, *Just for Today,* is the culmination of almost a decade of work on the part of the NA Fellowship. Serious interest in creating a daily meditation book for NA members began shortly after the initial approval of our Basic Text in 1982. Between 1984 and 1989, nearly a thousand pages of source material were developed by hundreds of individual members and dozens of local literature subcommittees. In 1989 and 1990, the World Service Conference Literature Committee began experimenting with methods of processing that source material into daily book entries, finally settling on one in April 1991. The following month, the daily book project went into full swing. By November 1991, the book was complete.

The following is the statement of purpose developed by our committee in July 1990 to guide the work to be done on *Just for Today:*

> "The purpose of *Just for Today* is to offer a wide variety of meditational topics to recovering addicts. These topics will range from the nuts and bolts of recovery to the vast array of intangible spiritual concepts existent. The book is meant for those at any and all stages of recovery, regardless of clean time. We hope it will convey, encourage, and even inspire the joy inherent in recovery. By deliberately including a wide assortment of points of view, concepts, and issues, we hope it will encompass the diversity of our fellowship and offer each individual what he or she needs at any given time."

There are a number of ways this book can be used. Individual members are encouraged to use it as a part of their daily program of recovery. You can go through it by calendar date, from front to back, or however suits you best. We've also included a topic index at the back of the book so that, if you wish, you can focus your meditations on particular subjects.

Narcotics Anonymous groups may wish to include *Just for Today* as a regular part of their meeting formats. Some groups will have a member read the meditation for the day at the beginning of their meetings along with the White Booklet passages read by most groups. Other groups may wish to start *Just for Today* meetings at which the day's meditation, or an entry on a particular topic, is used to spark discussion.

Narcotics Anonymous is a spiritual program, seeking to connect powerless addicts with a Power greater than themselves. For that reason, you will find many references in this book to prayer, meditation, "God," "the God of our understanding," and a "Higher Power." However, please remember that each individual member's approach to spirituality is entirely up to that person.

Please note that Basic Text page numbers following most of the opening quotations refer to *Narcotics Anonymous,* Fifth Edition[1].

We are grateful to have been given the opportunity to be a part of this project. We hope that *Just for Today* will prove useful to you, your group, and the NA Fellowship as a whole in the years to come. Thanks for letting us be of service.

WSC Literature Committee
November 21, 1991

Just for Today quotations without a citation are from previous versions of NA literature that are no longer published.

---

[1] *Narcotics Anonymous,* Sixth Edition has replaced *Narcotics Anonymous,* Fifth Edition.

Just for Today

Just for today my thoughts will be on my recovery, living and enjoying life without the use of drugs.

Just for today I will have faith in someone in NA who believes in me and wants to help me in my recovery.

Just for today I will have a program. I will try to follow it to the best of my ability.

Just for today through NA I will try to get a better perspective on my life.

Just for today I will be unafraid, my thoughts will be on my new associations, people who are not using and who have found a new way of life. So long as I follow that way, I have nothing to fear.

❖ ❖ ❖

January

❖ ❖ ❖

"We keep what we have only with vigilance..."
Basic Text, p. 60

❖

How do we remain vigilant about our recovery? First, by realizing that we have a disease we will always have. No matter how long we've been clean, no matter how much better our lives have become, no matter what the extent of our spiritual healing, we are still addicts. Our disease waits patiently, ready to spring the trap if we give it the opportunity.

Vigilance is daily accomplishment. We strive to be constantly alert and ready to deal with signs of trouble. Not that we should live in irrational fear that something horrible will possess us if we drop our guard for an instant; we just take normal precautions. Daily prayer, regular meeting attendance, and choosing not to compromise spiritual principles for the easier way are acts of vigilance. We take inventory as necessary, share with others whenever we are asked, and carefully nurture our recovery. Above all, we stay aware!

We have a daily reprieve from our addiction as long as we remain vigilant. Each day, we carry the principles of recovery into all we do, and each night, we thank our Higher Power for another day clean.

❖

Just for today: I will be vigilant, doing everything necessary to guard my recovery.

*"Sometimes when we pray, a remarkable thing
happens: We find the means, ways, and energies to
perform tasks far beyond our capacities."*

Basic Text, p. 46

❖

Coping successfully with life's minor annoyances and frustrations is sometimes the most difficult skill we have to learn in recovery. We are faced with small inconveniences daily. From untangling the knots in our children's shoelaces to standing in line at the market, our days are filled with minor difficulties that we must somehow deal with.

If we're not careful, we may find ourselves dealing with these difficulties by bullying our way through each problem or grinding our teeth while giving ourselves a stern lecture about how we *should* handle them. These are extreme examples of poor coping skills, but even if we're not this bad, there's probably room for improvement.

Each time life presents us with another little setback to our daily plans, we can simply take a deep breath and talk to the God of our understanding. Knowing we can draw patience, tolerance, or whatever we need from that Power, we find ourselves coping better and smiling more often.

❖

Just for today: I will take a deep breath and talk to my God whenever I feel frustrated.

> *"We eventually redefine our beliefs and understanding
> to the point where we see that our greatest need
> is for knowledge of God's will for us and
> the strength to carry that out."*

Basic Text, p. 48

❖

When we first arrived in NA, we had all kinds of ideas of what we needed. Some of us set our sights on amassing personal possessions. We thought recovery equaled outward success. But recovery does *not* equal success. Today, we believe that our greatest need is for spiritual guidance and strength.

The greatest damage done to us by our addiction was the damage done to our spirituality. Our primary motivation was dictated by our disease: to get, to use, and to find ways and means to get more. Enslaved by our overwhelming need for drugs, our lives lacked purpose and connection. We were spiritually bankrupt.

Sooner or later, we realize that our greatest need in recovery is "for knowledge of God's will for us and the strength to carry that out." There, we find the direction and sense of purpose our addiction had hidden from us. In our God's will we find freedom from self-will. No longer driven only by our own needs, we are free to live with others on an equal footing.

There's nothing wrong with outward success. But without the spiritual connection offered by the NA program, our greatest need in recovery goes unmet, regardless of how "successful" we may be.

❖

Just for today: I will seek the fulfillment of my greatest need: a vital, guiding connection with the God of my understanding.

"Today, secure in the love of the fellowship, we can finally look another human being in the eye and be grateful for who we are."

Basic Text, p. 92

❖

When we were using, few of us could tolerate looking someone in the eye—we were ashamed of who we were. Our minds were not occupied with anything decent or healthy, and we knew it. Our time, money, and energy weren't spent building loving relationships, sharing with others, or seeking to better our communities. We were trapped in a spiral of obsession and compulsion that went only in one direction: downward.

In recovery, our journey down that spiral path has been cut short. But what is it that has turned us around, drawing us back upward into the open spaces of the wide, free world? The love of the fellowship has done this.

In the company of other addicts, we knew we would not be rejected. By the example of other addicts, we were shown how to begin taking a positive part in the life around us. When we were unsure which way to turn, when we stumbled, when we had to correct a wrong we'd done, we knew our fellow members were there to encourage us.

Slowly, we've gotten the feel of our freedom. No longer are we locked up in our disease; we are free to build and grow and share along with everyone else. And when we need support to take our next step, it is there. The security we've found in the love of the fellowship has made our new lives possible.

❖

Just for today: I can look anyone in the eye without shame. I am grateful for the loving support that has made this possible.

*"We can enjoy our families in a new way and
may become a credit to them instead of
an embarrassment or a burden."*

Basic Text, p. 104

❖

We're doing great in recovery, aren't we? We go to a meeting every day, we spend every evening with our friends in the fellowship, and every weekend we dash off to a service workshop. But if things are falling to pieces at home, we're not doing so great after all.

We expect our families to understand. After all, we're not using drugs anymore. Why don't they recognize our progress? Don't they understand how important our meetings, our service, and our involvement with the fellowship are?

Our families will not appreciate the change NA is working in our lives unless we show them. If we rush off to a meeting the same way we rushed off to use drugs, what has changed? If we continue to ignore the needs and desires of our partners and children, failing to accept our responsibilities at home, we aren't "practicing these principles in all our affairs."

We must live the program everywhere we go, in everything we do. If we want the spiritual life to be more than a theory, we have to *live* it at home. When we do this, the people we share our lives with are sure to notice the change and be grateful that we've found NA.

❖

Just for today: I will take my recovery home with me.

*"I used to think that I had all the answers,
but today I am glad that I don't."*

❖

What are the two favorite words of most addicts? *"I know!"*
Unfortunately, many of us arrive in NA thinking we have all the
answers. We have a lot of knowledge about what's wrong with
us. But in and of itself, knowledge never helped us stay clean for
any length of time.

Members who have achieved long-term recovery will be the first
to admit that the longer they are here, the more they have to learn.
But they do know one thing: By following this simple Twelve-Step
program, they have been able to stay clean. They no longer ask
"why"; they ask "how." The value of endless speculation pales in
comparison to the experience of addicts who've found a way to
stay clean and live clean.

This doesn't mean we don't ask "why" when it's appropriate.
We don't come to NA and stop thinking! But in the beginning, it's
often a very good idea to reword our questions. Instead of asking
"why," we ask "how." *How* do I work this step? *How* often should
I attend meetings? *How* do I stay clean?

❖

Just for today: I don't have all the answers, but I know where to
find the ones that matter. Today, I will ask another addict, "How
does it work?"

> *"Narcotics Anonymous offers addicts a program
> of recovery that is more than just a life without drugs.
> Not only is this way of life better than the hell we lived,
> it is better than any life that we have ever known."*

Basic Text, p. 107

❖

Few of us have any interest in "recovering" what we had before we started using. Many of us suffered severely from physical, sexual, and emotional abuse. Getting high and staying high seemed like the only possible way to cope with such abuse. Others suffered in less noticeable but equally painful ways before addiction took hold. We lacked direction and purpose. We were spiritually empty. We felt isolated, unable to empathize with others. We had none of the things that give life its sense and value. We took drugs in a vain attempt to fill the emptiness inside ourselves. Most of us wouldn't *want* to "recover" what we used to have.

Ultimately, the recovery we find in NA is something different: a chance at a new life. We've been given tools to clear the wreckage from our lives. We've been given support in courageously setting forth on a new path. And we've been given the gift of conscious contact with a Power greater than ourselves, providing us with the inner strength and direction we so sorely lacked in the past.

Recovering? Yes, in every way. We're recovering a whole new life, better than anything we ever dreamed possible. We are grateful.

❖

Just for today: I've recovered something I never had, something I never imagined possible: the life of a recovering addict. Thank you, Higher Power, in more than words can say.

> *"Our spiritual condition is the basis for a successful
> recovery that offers unlimited growth."*

Basic Text, p. 44

❖

When our members celebrate their recovery anniversaries, they often say that they've "grown up" in NA. *Well, then,* we think, *what does that mean?* We start to wonder if we're grownups yet. We check our lives and yes, all the trappings of adulthood are there: the checkbook, the children, the job, the responsibilities. On the inside, though, we often feel like children. We're still confused by life much of the time. We don't always know how to act. We sometimes wonder whether we're really grownups at all, or whether we're children who've somehow been put into adult bodies and given adult responsibilities.

Growth is not best measured by physical age or levels of responsibility. Our best measure of growth is our spiritual condition, the basis of our recovery. If we're still depending on people, places, and things to provide our inner satisfaction, like a child depending on its parents for everything, we do indeed have some growing to do. But if we stand secure on the foundation of our spiritual condition, considering its maintenance our most important responsibility, we can claim maturity. Upon that foundation, our opportunities for growth are limitless.

❖

Just for today: The measure of my maturity is the extent to which I take responsibility for the maintenance of my spiritual condition. Today, this will be my highest priority.

> *"Our earliest involvements with others often
> begin with our sponsor."*

Basic Text, p. 57

❖

Our sponsors can be abundant sources of recovery information, wisdom, and loving words. They've done so much for us. From the late night telephone calls to the hours spent listening to our recovery writing, they've believed in us and invested their time to prove it. They've lovingly and firmly shown us how to be honest. Their boundless compassion in times of turmoil has given us the strength to go on. Their way of helping has prompted us to seek our answers within ourselves, and we've become mature, responsible, confident individuals as a result.

Though our sponsor has given so generously and has never demanded repayment, there are things we can do to show our appreciation. We treat our sponsor with respect. They are not trash cans designed for us to dump our garbage in. They have their times of trial, just as we do, and sometimes need our support. They are human, have feelings, and appreciate our concern. Maybe they would like to receive a card in the mail or a phone call expressing our love.

Whatever we do to return our sponsor's kindness will enhance our personal recovery, not to mention the joy we'll bring to our sponsor.

❖

Just for today: My sponsor has cared for me when I couldn't care for myself. Today, I will do something nice for my sponsor.

"I'm very grateful to have come to believe."

IP No. 21, *The Loner*

❖

Belief in a Higher Power can make all the difference when the going gets tough! When things don't go our way in recovery, our sponsor may direct us to make a "gratitude list." When we do, we should include our faith in a Power greater than ourselves on the list. One of the greatest gifts we receive from the Twelve Steps is our belief in a God of our own understanding.

The Twelve Steps gently lead us toward a spiritual awakening. Just as our addiction progressed, so does our spiritual life develop in the course of working the program of Narcotics Anonymous. The steps are our path to a relationship with a God of our understanding. This Higher Power gives us strength when our road gets rough.

Are we grateful for our deepening relationship with a Higher Power? Do we remember to thank God for each day clean, no matter what has happened that day? Do we remember that, no matter how deep our despair or how great our joy, the God of our understanding is with us?

Our recovery is a gift, a gift that we sometimes take for granted. Each day we stay clean, we can rejoice in our Higher Power's care.

❖

Just for today: I am grateful for my relationship with a Higher Power that cares for me.

*"As we develop faith in our daily lives, we find that our
Higher Power supplies us with the strength
and guidance that we need."*

Basic Text, p. 94

❖

Some of us come into recovery very frightened and insecure.
We feel weak and alone. We are uncertain of our direction and
don't know where to go for answers. We are told that if we find
some faith in a Power greater than ourselves, we will find security
and guidance. We want that feeling of safety and strength. But
faith doesn't come overnight. It takes time and effort to grow.

The seed is planted when we ask our Higher Power for help
and then acknowledge the source of our help when it comes.
We nurture the tiny seed of faith with the sunlight of our prayers
each day. Our faith grows, a reward for living life on its own terms.
One day we realize our faith has become like a huge spreading
tree; it doesn't stop the storms of life, but we know that we are
safe in its shelter.

❖

Just for today: I know that faith in my Higher Power will not
calm the storms of life, but it will calm my heart. I will let my faith
shelter me in times of trouble.

*"Having had a spiritual awakening
as a result of these steps..."*

Step Twelve

❖

"How will I know when I have had a spiritual awakening?" For many of us, a spiritual awakening comes gradually. Perhaps our first spiritual awareness is as simple as a new appreciation for life. Maybe one day we'll suddenly discover the sound of birds singing early in the morning. The simple beauty of a flower may remind us that there is a Power greater than ourselves at work around us.

Often, our spiritual awakening is something that grows stronger over time. We can strive for more spiritual awareness simply by living our lives. We can persist in efforts to improve our conscious contact through prayer and meditation on a daily basis. We can listen within for the guidance we need. We can question other addicts about their experiences with spirituality. We can take time to appreciate the world around us.

❖

Just for today: I will reflect on the spiritual awakenings I have experienced. I will strive to be God-conscious. I will take time out in the day to appreciate my Higher Power's handiwork.

> *"Help for addicts begins only when we are able*
> *to admit complete defeat."*

Basic Text, p. 22

❖

Complete defeat—what a concept! That must mean surrender. Surrender—to give up absolutely. To quit with *no* reservations. To put up our hands and quit fighting. Maybe to put up our hand at our first meeting and admit we're addicts.

How do we know we've taken a First Step that will allow us to live drug-free? We know because, once we have taken that gigantic step, we never have to use again—just for today. That's it. It's not easy, but it's very simple.

We work the First Step. We accept that, yes, we are addicts. "One is too many, and a thousand never enough." We've proven that to ourselves enough times. We admit that we cannot handle drugs in any form. We admit it; we say it out loud, if necessary.

We take the First Step at the beginning of our day. For one day. This admission frees us, just for today, from the need to live out our addiction all over again. We've surrendered to this disease. We give up. We quit. But in quitting, we win. And that's the paradox of the First Step: We surrender to win, and by surrendering we gain a far greater power than we ever imagined possible.

❖

Just for today: I admit that I am powerless over my addiction. I will surrender to win.

---

*"Our understanding of a Higher Power is up to us....
The only suggested guidelines are that this Power be
loving, caring, and greater than ourselves."*

Basic Text, p. 24

❖

We've been told that we can believe in any kind of Higher
Power we want as long as it is loving and, of course, greater
than ourselves. Some of us, however, have trouble with these
requirements. We either believe in nothing *but* ourselves, or
we believe that anything that could be called "God" could only
be cold-hearted and unreasonable, sending us bad luck on a
whim.

Believing in a loving Power is quite a leap for some of us, for
many reasons. The thought of turning our will and lives over to
the care of something we think might hurt us is sure to fill us
with reluctance. If we come into the program believing that God
is judgmental and unforgiving, we must overcome those beliefs
before we can be truly comfortable with the Third Step.

Our positive experiences in recovery can help us come to
believe in a loving God of our own understanding. We've been
given relief from a disease that has afflicted us for a long time.
We've found the guidance and support we need to develop a new
way of life. We've begun to experience a fullness of spirit where
once there was only emptiness. These aspects of our recovery
have their source in a loving God, not a harsh, hateful one. And
the more we experience recovery, the more we'll trust that loving
Higher Power.

❖

Just for today: I will open my mind and my heart to believe that
God is loving, and trust my loving Higher Power to do for me
what I cannot do for myself.

"We grow to feel comfortable with our Higher Power as a source of strength. As we learn to trust this Power, we begin to overcome our fear of life."

Basic Text, p. 25

❖

Powerless as we are, living on self-will is a frightening, unmanageable experience. In recovery, we have turned our will and our lives safely over to the care of the God of our understanding. When we lapse in our program, when we lose conscious contact with our Higher Power, we begin to take control of our own lives again, refusing the care of the God of our understanding. If we do not make a daily decision to surrender our lives to the care of our Higher Power, we may become overwhelmed with our fear of life.

Through working the Twelve Steps, we've found that faith in a Power greater than ourselves helps relieve our fear. As we draw closer to a loving God, we become more conscious of our Higher Power. And the more conscious we are of God's care for us, the less our fears.

When we feel afraid, we ask ourselves, "Is this fear an indication of a lack of faith in my life? Have I taken control again, only to find my life still unmanageable?" If we answer yes to these questions, we can overcome our fear by turning our will and our lives back over to care of the God of our understanding.

❖

Just for today: I will rely on the care of my Higher Power to relieve my fear of life.

---

*"We feared that if we ever revealed ourselves as we
were, we would surely be rejected.... [But] our fellow
members do understand us."*

Basic Text, p. 32

❖

We need our fellow NA members—their experience, their
friendship, their laughter, their guidance, and much, much more.
Yet many of us hesitate to call our sponsor or visit our NA friends.
We don't want to impose on them. We think about phoning
someone, but we don't feel worthy of their time. We fear that if they
ever got to know us—really *know* us—they'd surely reject us.

We forget that our fellow NA members are just like us. There's
nothing we've done, no place we've been, no feeling we've felt that
other recovering addicts won't be able to identify with. The more
we let others get to know us, the more we'll hear, "You're in the
right place. You're among friends. You belong. Welcome!"

We also forget that, just as we need others, they need us. We're
not the only ones who want to feel like we belong, who want to
experience the warmth of friendship, who want someone to share
with. If we isolate ourselves from our fellow members, we deprive
them of something they need, something only we can give them:
our time, our company, our true selves.

In Narcotics Anonymous, recovering addicts care for one
another. What waits at the other end of the telephone is not
rejection, but the love, warmth, and identification of the NA
Fellowship. Make that call!

❖

Just for today: In NA, I am among friends. I will reach out to
others, giving and receiving in fellowship.

"As we realize our need to be forgiven, we tend to be more forgiving. At least we know that we are no longer intentionally making life miserable for people."

Basic Text, pp. 39–40

❖

In our addiction we often treated others badly, sometimes deliberately finding ways to make their lives miserable. In our recovery, we may still have a tendency to pass judgment on others' actions because we think we know how that person should behave. But as we progress in our recovery we often find that, to accept ourselves, we must accept those around us.

It may be difficult to watch as someone's insanity manifests itself. But if we detach ourselves from the problem, we can start living in the solution. And if we feel affected by another's actions, we can extend the principle of forgiveness.

❖

Just for today: I will strive to forgive rather than be forgiven. I will try to act in such a way that I feel worthy of self-love.

*"Continuing to take a personal inventory means that we
form a habit of looking at ourselves, our actions,
our attitudes, and our relationships on a regular basis."*

Basic Text, p. 42

❖

The daily inventory is a tool we can use to simplify our lives. The most complicated part of taking a regular inventory is deciding how to start. Should we write it out? What should we examine? In how much detail? And how do we know when we've finished? In no time, we've turned a simple exercise into a major project.

Here's one simple approach to the daily inventory. We set aside a few minutes at the close of each day to sit quietly and check out our feelings. Is there a knot, big or small, in our gut? Do we feel uncomfortable about the day we've just finished? What happened? What was our part in the affair? Do we owe any amends? If we could do it over again, what would we do differently?

We also want to monitor the positive aspects of our lives in our daily inventory. What has given us satisfaction today? Were we productive? Responsible? Kind? Loving? Did we give unselfishly of ourselves? Did we fully experience the love and beauty the day offered us? What did we do today that we would want to do again?

Our daily inventory doesn't have to be complicated to be effective. It is a very simple tool we can use to keep in daily touch with ourselves.

❖

Just for today: I want to keep in touch with the way I feel in living this life I've been given. At the end of this day, I will take a brief, simple inventory.

*"When we stop living in the here and now,
our problems become magnified unreasonably."*

Basic Text, p. 99

❖

Some of us seem to make mountains out of molehills with our problems. Even those of us who've found some measure of serenity have probably blown a problem far out of proportion at some time in our recovery—and if we haven't done so yet, we probably will before long!

When we find ourselves obsessed with a complication in our lives, we will do well to sharply remind ourselves of all that is going right. Perhaps we're afraid we won't be able to pay our bills for the month. Instead of sitting at the calculator, adding our financial liabilities over and over, we can take stock of our efforts to reduce expenses. Following this mini-inventory, we continue with the task at hand and remind ourselves that as long as we are doing the footwork, a loving Higher Power will care for our lives.

Mountain-sized problems happen sometimes, but we don't need to create them. Trust in a loving God of our understanding will put most of our problems in their proper perspective. We no longer need to create chaos to feel excited about our lives. Our recovery gives us countless real-life opportunities for excitement and drama.

❖

Just for today: I will take a realistic look at my problems and see that most of them are minor. I will leave them that way and enjoy my recovery.

*"Narcotics Anonymous offers only one promise,
and that is freedom from active addiction..."*

Basic Text, p. 106

❖

Imagine how it might be if we had arrived at the doors of Narcotics Anonymous, desperate, wanting to stop using drugs, only to be met by a sales pitch: "If you just work the steps and don't use drugs, you'll get married, live in the suburbs, have 2.6 children, and start wearing polyester. You will become a responsible, productive member of society and be fit company for kings and presidents. You will be rich and have a dynamic career." Most of us, greeted with such a heavy-handed spiel, would have shrieked and bolted for the door.

Instead of high-pressure nonsense and frightening predictions, we are greeted with a promise of hope: freedom from active addiction. We feel a blessed relief come over us when we hear that we never have to use drugs again. We aren't going to be forced to become anything!

Of course, after some time in recovery, good things start happening in our lives. We are given gifts—spiritual gifts, material gifts, gifts that we've always dreamed of but never dared hope we'd get. These, however, are truly gifts—they are not promised to us just because we become NA members. All we are *promised* is freedom from addiction—and it's more than enough!

❖

Just for today: I have been promised freedom from active addiction. The gifts I receive are the benefits of recovery.

"Unity is a must in Narcotics Anonymous."

Basic Text, p. 63

❖

Unity is not uniformity. Unity springs from the fact that we have unity of purpose—to recover, and to help others stay clean. Even so, we often find that while we strive to fulfill the same purpose, our means and methods may be radically different.

We can't impose our ideas of unity on others or confuse unity with uniformity. In fact, a big attraction of the NA program is the absence of uniformity. Unity springs from our common purpose, not from standards imposed on the group by a few well-meaning members. A group that has the unity which springs from the loving hearts of its members allows each addict to carry the message in his or her own unique way.

In our dealings with each other in NA, we sometimes disagree rather vocally. We must remember that the details of how we get things done isn't always important, so long as we keep our focus on the group's primary purpose. We can watch members who vehemently disagree over trivial things pull together when a newcomer reaches out for help. Someone was there for us when we got to the rooms of NA. Now it is our turn to be there for others. We need unity to help show the newcomer that this way of life works.

❖

Just for today: I will strive to be a part of unity. I know that unity does not equal uniformity.

"This is a program for learning."

Basic Text, p. 16

❖

Learning in recovery is hard work. The things we most need to know are often the hardest to learn. We study recovery to prepare ourselves for the experiences life will give us. As we listen to others share in meetings, we take mental notes we can refer to later. To be prepared, we study our notes and literature between "lessons." Just as students have the opportunity to apply their knowledge during tests, so do we have the opportunity to apply our recovery during times of crisis.

As always, we have a choice in how we will approach life's challenges. We can dread and avoid them as threats to our serenity, or we can gratefully accept them as opportunities for growth. By confirming the principles we've learned in recovery, life's challenges give us increased strength. Without such challenges, however, we could forget what we've learned and begin to stagnate. These are the opportunities that prod us to new spiritual awakenings.

We will find that there is often a period of rest after each crisis, giving us time to get accustomed to our new skills. Once we've reflected on our experience, we are called on to share our knowledge with someone who is studying what we've just learned. In the school of recovery, all of us are teachers as well as students.

❖

Just for today: I will be a student of recovery. I will welcome challenges, confident in what I've learned and eager to share it with others.

*"Lack of daily maintenance can show up
in many ways."*

Basic Text, p. 95

❖

Ever had a perfect stranger remark about how great the weather was, only to reply "It stinks"? When this happens, we are probably suffering from a lack of daily maintenance in our program.

In recovery, life can get pretty hectic. Maybe those added responsibilities at work have got you hopping. Maybe you haven't been to a meeting for awhile. Perhaps you've been too busy to meditate, or haven't been eating regularly or sleeping well. Whatever the reason, your serenity is slipping.

When this happens, it is crucial that we take action. We can't afford to let one "bad day," complete with a bad attitude, slip into two days, four days, or a week. Our recovery depends on our daily maintenance program. No matter what is happening in our lives, we can't afford to neglect the principles that have saved our lives.

There are many ways to recover our serenity. We can go to a meeting, phone our sponsor, meet another recovering addict for lunch, or try to carry the message to a newcomer. We can pray. We can take a moment to ask ourselves what simple things we *haven't* been doing. When our attitudes head downhill, we can avert a crash with simple solutions.

❖

Just for today: I will examine the maintenance of my daily program of recovery.

*"Our disease isolated us... Hostile, resentful,
self-centered, and self-seeking, we cut ourselves
off from the outside world."*

Basic Text, p. 4

❖

Addiction is an isolating disease, closing us off from society, family, and self. We hid. We lied. We scorned the lives we saw others living, surely beyond our grasp. Worst of all, we told ourselves there was nothing wrong with us, even though we knew we were desperately ill. Our connection with the world, and with reality itself, was severed. Our lives lost meaning, and we withdrew further and further from reality.

The NA program is designed especially for people like us. It helps reconnect us to the life we were meant to live, drawing us out of our isolation. We stop lying to ourselves about our condition; we admit our powerlessness and the unmanageability of our lives. We develop faith that our lives can improve, that recovery is possible, and that happiness is not permanently beyond our grasp. We get honest; we stop hiding; we "show up and tell the truth," no matter what. And as we do, we establish the ties that connect our individual lives to the larger life around us.

We addicts need not live lives of isolation. The Twelve Steps can restore our connection to life and living—if we work them.

❖

Just for today: I am a part of the life around me. I will practice my program to strengthen my connection to my world.

> *"We see it happening among us every day.*
> *This miraculous turnabout is evidence*
> *of a spiritual awakening."*

Basic Text, p. 51

❖

We watch them walk in to their first meeting defeated, their spirits broken. Their suffering is obvious, and their desire for help even more apparent. They collect a welcome chip and go back to their seats, shaken by the effort.

We see them again, and they seem a little more comfortable. They've found a sponsor and are attending meetings every night. They still won't meet our glance, but they nod their heads in recognition as we share. We notice a spark of hope in their eyes, and they smile uncertainly when we encourage them to keep coming back.

A few months later, they are standing straight. They've learned how to make eye contact. They're working the steps with their sponsor and are healing as a result. We listen to them sharing at meetings. We stack chairs with them afterward.

A few years later, they are speaking at a convention workshop. They've got a wonderful, humorous personality. They smile when they see us, they hug us, and they tell us they could never have done it without us. And they understand when we say, "nor could we, without you."

❖

Just for today: I will find joy in witnessing the recovery of another.

> *"The spiritual part of our disease is our*
> *total self-centeredness."*

Basic Text, p. 20

❖

What is self-centeredness? It is our belief that the world revolves around us. Our wishes, our demands are the only ones worth consideration. Our self-centered minds believe they are capable of getting everything they want if only they would be left to their own devices. Self-centeredness assumes total self-sufficiency.

We say that self-centeredness is the spiritual part of our disease because the self-centered mind cannot conceive of anything greater or more important than itself. But there is a spiritual solution to our spiritual malady: the Twelve Steps of Narcotics Anonymous. The steps lead us away from self-centeredness and toward God-centeredness.

We strip away our delusion of self-sufficiency by admitting our own powerlessness and seeking the aid of a Power greater than ourselves. We acknowledge the bankruptcy of our self-righteousness by admitting we've been wrong, making amends, and seeking knowledge of what's right from the God our understanding. And we deflate our overwhelming sense of self-importance by seeking to serve others, not only ourselves.

The self-centeredness afflicting our spirit can be treated with a spiritual solution: the Twelve Steps.

❖

Just for today: My guidance and my strength comes from a Higher Power, not from my own self. I will practice the Twelve Steps to become more God-centered and less self-centered.

*"We learn new ways to live. We are no longer
limited to our old ideas."*

Basic Text, p. 56

We may or may not have been taught right from wrong and other basics of life as children. No matter, by the time we found recovery, most of us had only the vaguest idea of how to live. Our isolation from the rest of society had caused us to ignore basic human responsibilities and develop bizarre survival skills to cope with the world we lived in.

Some of us didn't know how to tell the truth; others were so frank we wounded everyone we talked to. Some of us couldn't cope with the simplest of personal problems, while others attempted solving the problems of the whole world. Some of us never got angry, even when receiving unfair treatment; others busily lodged complaints against everyone and everything.

Whatever our problems, no matter how extreme, we all have a chance in Narcotics Anonymous to learn how to live anew. Perhaps we need to learn kindness and how to care about others. Perhaps we need to accept personal responsibilities. Or maybe we need to overcome fear and take some risks. We can be certain of one thing: Each day, simply by living life, we'll learn something new.

Just for today: I know more about how to live than I did yesterday, but not as much as I'll know tomorrow. Today, I'll learn something new.

> *"We can never fully recover,*
> *no matter how long we stay clean."*

Basic Text, p. 84

❖

After getting a little time in the program, some of us begin to think we have been cured. We've learned everything NA has to teach us; we've grown bored with the meetings; and our sponsor keeps droning the same old refrain: "The steps—the steps—the *steps!*" We decide it is time to get on with our lives, cut way back on meetings, and try to make up for the years we have lost to active addiction. We do this, however, at the peril of our recovery.

Those of us who have relapsed after such an episode often try to go to as many meetings as we can—some of us go to a meeting every day for several years. It may take that long for us to understand that we will always be addicts. We may feel well some days and sick on other days, but we are addicts *every day.* At any time, we are subject to delusion, denial, rationalization, justification, insanity—all the hallmarks of the typical addict's way of thinking. If we want to continue living and enjoying life without the use of drugs, we must practice an active program of recovery each day.

❖

Just for today: I am an addict every day, but today I have the choice to be a *recovering* addict. I will make that choice by practicing my program.

> *"Do we understand that we have no real control over drugs?"*

Basic Text, p. 18

❖

At first, many of us may have thought the First Step required no action—we just surrender and go on to Step Two. But Step One *does* require action!

The action we take in the First Step will be evident in the way we live, even from our first day clean. If we truly believe that we are powerless over our addiction, we will not choose to be around drugs. To continue to live with or associate with practicing addicts may indicate a reservation in our program. An absolute belief that the First Step applies to us will insure that we clear our homes of all drugs and paraphernalia.

As time goes on, we'll not only continue with the basics but add new actions to our First Step repertoire. We'll learn to feel our feelings rather than trying to control them. We'll stop trying to be our own and only guides on our recovery journey; self-sponsorship will cease. We'll begin looking to a Power greater than ourselves more and more for spiritual satisfaction rather than trying to fill that void with something else.

Surrender is only the beginning. Once we surrender, we need to learn how to live in the peace we have found.

❖

Just for today: I will take all the action necessary to practice the First Step. I truly believe it applies to me.

*"We must give freely and gratefully that which has been
freely and gratefully given to us."*

Basic Text, p. 49

❖

In recovery, we receive many gifts. Perhaps one of the greatest
of these gifts is the spiritual awakening that begins when we stop
using, growing stronger each day we apply the steps in our lives.
The new spark of life within is a direct result of our new relationship
with a Higher Power, a relationship initiated and developed by living
the Twelve Steps. Slowly, as we pursue our program, the radiance
of recovery dispels the darkness of our disease.

One of the ways we express our gratitude for the gifts of
recovery is to help others find what we've found. We can do
this in any number of ways: by sharing in meetings, making
Twelfth Step calls, accepting a commitment to sponsorship, or
volunteering for H&I or phoneline duty. The spiritual life given to
us in recovery asks for expression, for "we can only keep what
we have by giving it away."

❖

Just for today: The gift of recovery grows when I share it. I will
find someone with whom to share it.

"Just for today I will have faith in someone in NA who believes in me and wants to help me in my recovery."

Basic Text, p. 93

Learning to trust is a risky proposition. Our past experience as using addicts has taught us that our companions could not be trusted. Most of all, we couldn't trust ourselves.

Now that we're in recovery, trust is essential. We need something to hang onto, believe in, and give us hope in our recovery. For some of us, the first thing we can trust is the words of other members sharing in meetings; we feel the truth in their words.

Finding someone we can trust makes it easier to ask for help. And as we grow to trust in their recovery, we learn to trust our own.

Just for today: I will decide to trust someone. I will act on that trust.

February

"We felt different.... Only after surrender are we able to overcome the alienation of addiction."

Basic Text, p. 22

❖

"But you don't understand!" we spluttered, trying to cover up. "I'm different! I've *really* got it rough!" We used these lines over and over in our active addiction, either trying to escape the consequences of our actions or avoid following the rules that applied to everyone else. We may have cried them at our first meeting. Perhaps we've even caught ourselves whining them recently.

So many of us feel different or unique. As addicts, we can use almost anything to alienate ourselves. But there's no excuse for missing out on recovery, nothing that can make us ineligible for the program—not a life-threatening illness, not poverty, not anything. There are thousands of addicts who have found recovery despite the real hardships they've faced. Through working the program, their spiritual awareness has grown, in spite of—or perhaps in response to—those hardships.

Our individual circumstances and differences are irrelevant when it comes to recovery. By letting go of our uniqueness and surrendering to this simple way of life, we're bound to find that we feel a part of something. And feeling a part of something gives us the strength to walk through life, hardships and all.

❖

Just for today: I will let go of my uniqueness and embrace the principles of recovery I have in common with so many others. My hardships do not exclude me from recovery; rather, they draw me into it.

"Goodwill is best exemplified in service; proper service is 'Doing the right thing for the right reason.'"

Basic Text, p. xv

❖

The spiritual core of our disease is self-centeredness. In dealing with others, the only motive our addiction taught us was selfishness—we wanted what we wanted when we wanted it. Obsession with self was rooted in the very ground of our lives. In recovery, how do we root self-obsession out?

We reverse the effects of our disease by applying a few very simple spiritual principles. To counteract the self-centeredness of our addiction, we learn to apply the principle of *goodwill*. Rather than seeking to serve only ourselves, we begin serving others. Rather than thinking only about what we can get out of a situation, we learn to think first of the welfare of others. When faced with a moral choice, we learn to stop, recall spiritual principles, and act appropriately.

As we begin "doing the right thing for the right reason," we can detect a change in ourselves. Where once we were ruled by self-will, now we are guided by our goodwill for others. The chronic self-centeredness of addiction is losing its hold on us. We are learning to "practice these principles in all our affairs"; we are living in our recovery, not in our disease.

❖

Just for today: Wherever I am, whatever I do, I will seek to serve others, not just myself. When faced with a dilemma, I will try to do the right thing for the right reason.

"Anyone may join us, regardless of age, race, sexual identity, creed, religion, or lack of religion."

Basic Text, p. 9

❖

Addiction closed our minds to anything new or different. We didn't need anyone or anything, we thought. There was nothing of value to be found in anyone from a different neighborhood, a different racial or ethnic background, or a different social or economic class. We may have thought that if it was different, it was bad.

In recovery, we can't afford such attitudes. We came to NA because our very best thinking had gotten us nowhere. We must open our minds to experience what works, no matter where it comes from, if we hope to grow in our recovery.

Regardless of our personal backgrounds, we all have two things in common with one another in NA that we share with no one else: our disease, and our recovery. We depend on one another for our shared experience—and the broader that experience, the better. We need every bit of experience, every different angle on our program we can find to meet the many challenges of living clean.

Recovery often isn't easy. The strength we need to recover, we draw from our fellow NA members. Today, we are grateful for the diversity of our group's membership, for in that diversity we find our strength.

❖

Just for today: I know that the more diverse my group's experience is, the better able my group will be to offer me support in the different circumstances I find myself facing. Today, I welcome addicts from all backgrounds to my home group.

"For us, recovery is more than just pleasure."

Basic Text, p. 43

❖

In our active addiction, most of us knew exactly how we were going to feel from one day to the next. All we had to do was read the label on the bottle or know what was in the bag. We planned our feelings, and our goal for each day was to feel good.

In recovery, we're liable to feel *anything* from one day to the next, even from one minute to the next. We may feel energetic and happy in the morning, then strangely let down and sad in the afternoon. Because we no longer plan our feelings for the day each morning, we could end up having feelings that are somewhat inconvenient, like feeling tired in the morning and wide-awake at bedtime.

Of course, there's always the possibility we *could* feel good, but that isn't the point. Today, our main concern is not feeling good but learning to understand and deal with our feelings, no matter what they are. We do this by working the steps and sharing our feelings with others.

❖

Just for today: I will accept my feelings, whatever they may be, just as they are. I will practice the program and learn to live with my feelings.

> *"We are grateful that we were made so welcome at
> meetings that we felt comfortable."*

Basic Text, p. 83

❖

Remember how scared we were when we walked into our first
NA meeting? Even if we walked in with a friend, most of us recall
how difficult it was to attend that first meeting. What was it that
kept us coming back? Most of us have grateful memories of the
welcome we were given and how comfortable that made us feel.
When we raised our hand as a newcomer, we opened the door
for other members to approach us and welcome us.

Sometimes the difference between those addicts who walk
back out the door of their first meeting, never to return to NA,
and the addicts who stay to seek recovery is the simple hug of an
NA member. When we have been clean awhile, it's easy to step
back from the procession of newcomers—after all, we've seen so
many people come and go. But members with some clean time
can make the difference between the addict who doesn't return
and the addict who keeps coming back. By offering our phone
numbers, a hug, or just a warm welcome, we extend the hand of
Narcotics Anonymous to the addict who still suffers.

❖

Just for today: I remember the welcome I was given when I first
came to NA. Today, I will express my gratitude by offering a hug
to a newcomer.

*"We had convinced ourselves that we could make it
alone and proceeded to live life on that basis.
The results were disastrous and, in the end, each of us
had to admit that self-sufficiency was a lie."*

Basic Text, p. 62

❖

"I can't, but we can." This simple but profound truth applies
initially to our first need as NA members: Together, we can stay
clean, but when we isolate ourselves, we're in bad company. To
recover, we need the support of other addicts.

Self-sufficiency impedes more than just our ability to stay
clean. With or without drugs, living on self-will inevitably leads to
disaster. We depend on other people for everything from goods
and services to love and companionship, yet self-will puts us in
constant conflict with those very people. To live a fulfilling life, we
need harmony with others.

Other addicts and others in our communities are not the only
ones we depend on. Power is not a human attribute, yet we need
power to live. We find it in a Power greater than ourselves which
provides the guidance and strength we lack on our own. When
we pretend to be self-sufficient, we isolate ourselves from the one
source of power sufficient to effectively guide us through life: our
Higher Power.

Self-sufficiency doesn't work. We need other addicts; we need
other people; and, to live fully, we need a Power greater than our
own.

❖

Just for today: I will seek the support of other recovering addicts; harmony with others in my community; and the care of
my Higher Power. *I can't, but we can.*

*"... we have found a loving, personal God to whom
we can turn."*

Basic Text, p. 27

❖

Some of us come into recovery with the impression that
life's hardships are a series of cosmic tests designed to teach
us something. This belief is readily apparent when something
traumatic happens and we wail, "My Higher Power is testing me!"
We're convinced that it's a test of our recovery when someone
offers us drugs, or a test of our character when faced with a
situation where we could do something unprincipled without
getting caught. We may even think it's a test of our faith when
we're in great pain over a tragedy in our lives.

But a loving Higher Power doesn't test our recovery, our
character, or our faith. Life just happens, and sometimes it hurts.
Many of us have lost love through no fault of our own. Some
of us have lost all of our material wealth. A few of us have even
grieved the loss of our own children. Life can be terribly painful
at times, but the pain is not inflicted on us by our Higher Power.
Rather, that Power is constantly by our sides, ready to carry us if
we can't walk by ourselves. There is no harm that life can do us
that the God of our understanding can't heal.

❖

Just for today: I will have faith that my Higher Power's will for
me is good, and that I am loved. I will seek my Higher Power's
help in times of need.

"…an NA sponsor is a member of Narcotics Anonymous, living our program of recovery, who is willing to build a special, supportive, one-on-one relationship with us."

IP No. 11, *Sponsorship*, Revised

❖

What is a sponsor? You know: That nice person with whom you had coffee after your first meeting. That generous soul who keeps sharing recovery experience free of charge. The one who keeps amazing you with stunning insight regarding your character defects. The one who keeps reminding you to finish your Fourth Step, who listens to your Fifth Step, and who doesn't tell anyone how weird you are.

It's pretty easy to start taking all this stuff for granted once we're used to someone being there for us. We may run wild for a while and tell ourselves, "I'll call my sponsor later, but right now I have to clean the house, go shopping, chase that attractive..." And so we end up in trouble, wondering where we went wrong.

Our sponsor can't read minds. It's up to us to reach out and ask for help. Whether we need help with our steps, a reality check to help us straighten out our screwy thinking, or just a friend, it's our job to make the request. Sponsors are warm, wise, wonderful people, and their experience with recovery is ours—all we have to do is ask.

❖

Just for today: I'm grateful for the time, the love, and the experience my sponsor has shared with me. Today, I will call my sponsor.

"When we accept ourselves, we can accept others into our lives, unconditionally, probably for the first time."

IP No. 19, *Self-Acceptance*

❖

From our earliest memories, many of us felt like we never belonged. No matter how big the gathering, we always felt apart from the crowd. We had a hard time "fitting in." Deep down, we believed that if we really let others get to know us, they would reject us. Perhaps our addiction began to germinate in this climate of self-centeredness.

Many of us hid the pain of our alienation with an attitude of defiance. In effect, we told the world, "You don't need me? Well, I don't need any of you, either. I've got my drugs and I can take care of myself!" The further our addiction progressed, the higher the walls we built around ourselves.

Those walls begin to fall when we start finding acceptance from other recovering addicts. With this acceptance from others, we begin to learn the important principle of *self*-acceptance. And when we start to accept ourselves, we can allow others to take part in our lives without fear of rejection.

❖

Just for today: I am accepted in NA; I fit in. Today, it's safe to start letting others into my life.

"In recovery, our ideas of fun change."
Basic Text, p. 107

❖

In retrospect, many of us realize that when we used, our ideas of fun were rather bizarre. Some of us would get dressed up and head for the local club. We would dance, drink, and do other drugs until the sun rose. On more than one occasion, gun battles broke out. What we then called fun, we now call insanity.

Today, our notion of fun has changed. Fun to us today is a walk along the ocean, watching the dolphins frolic as the sun sets behind them. Fun is going to an NA picnic, or attending the comedy show at an NA convention. Fun is getting dressed up to go to the banquet and not worrying about any gun battles breaking out over who did what to whom.

Through the grace of a Higher Power and the Fellowship of Narcotics Anonymous, our ideas of fun have changed radically. Today when we are up to see the sun rise, it's usually because we went to bed early the night before, not because we left a club at six in the morning, eyes bleary from a night of drug use. And if that's all we have received from Narcotics Anonymous, that would be enough.

❖

Just for today: I will have *fun* in my recovery!

> *"We have become very grateful in the course of our recovery.... We have a disease, but we do recover."*

Basic Text, p. 8

Active addiction was no picnic; many of us barely came out of it alive. But ranting against the disease, lamenting what it has done to us, pitying ourselves for the condition it has left us in—these things can only keep us locked in the spirit of bitterness and resentment. The path to freedom and spiritual growth begins where bitterness ends, with acceptance.

There is no denying the suffering brought by addiction. Yet it was this disease that brought us to Narcotics Anonymous; without it, we would neither have sought nor found the blessing of recovery. In isolating us, it forced us to seek fellowship. In causing us to suffer, it gave us the experience needed to help others, help no one else was so uniquely suited to offer. In forcing us to our knees, addiction gave us the opportunity to surrender to the care of a loving Higher Power.

We would not wish the disease of addiction on anyone. But the fact remains that we addicts already have this disease—and further, that without this disease we may never have embarked on our spiritual journey. Thousands of people search their whole lives for what we have found in Narcotics Anonymous: fellowship, a sense of purpose, and conscious contact with a Higher Power. Today, we are grateful for everything that has brought us this blessing.

Just for today: I will accept the fact of my disease, and pursue the blessing of my recovery.

"We regretted the past, dreaded the future, and weren't too thrilled about the present."

Basic Text, p. 7

❖

Until we experience the healing that happens when we work the Twelve Steps, it is doubtful that we can find a statement more true than the quote above. Most of us come to NA hanging our heads in shame, thinking about the past and wishing we could go back and change it. Our fantasies and expectations about the future may be so extreme that, on our first date with someone, we find ourselves wondering which lawyer we'll use for the divorce. Almost every experience causes us to remember something from the past or begin projecting into the future.

At first, it's difficult to stay in the moment. It seems as though our minds won't stop. We have a hard time just enjoying ourselves. Each time we realize that our thoughts are not focused on what's happening right now, we can pray and ask a loving God to help us get out of ourselves. If we regret the past, we make amends by living differently today; if we dread the future, we work on living responsibly today.

When we work the steps and pray each time we discover we're not living in the present, we'll notice that those times aren't occurring as often as they used to. Our faith will help us live just for today. We'll have hours, even days, when our full attention is focused on the current moment in time, not the regrettable past or fearful future.

❖

Just for today: When I live fully in each moment, I open myself to joys that might otherwise escape me. If I am having trouble, I will ask a loving God for help.

> *"As long as the ties that bind us together are stronger*
> *than those that would tear us apart, all will be well."*

Basic Text, p. 60

❖

Many of us feel that without NA we would surely have died from our disease. Hence, its existence is our very lifeline. However, disunity is an occasional fact of life in Narcotics Anonymous; we must learn to respond in a constructive way to the destructive influences that sometimes arise in our fellowship. If we decide to be part of the solution instead of the problem, we are headed in the right direction.

Our personal recovery and the growth of NA is contingent upon maintaining an atmosphere of recovery in our meetings. Are we willing to help our group deal constructively with conflict? As group members, do we strive to work out difficulties openly, honestly, and fairly? Do we seek to promote the common welfare of all our members rather than our own agenda? And, as trusted servants, do we take into consideration the effect our actions might have on newcomers?

Service can bring out both the best and the worst in us. But it is often through service that we begin to get in touch with some of our more pressing defects of character. Do we shrink from service commitments rather than face what we might find out about ourselves? If we bear in mind the strength of the ties that bind us together—our recovery from active addiction—all *will* be well.

❖

Just for today: I will strive to be of service to our fellowship. I will be unafraid to discover who I am.

*"The right to a God of your understanding is total
and without any catches. Because we have this right,
it is necessary to be honest about our belief
if we are to grow spiritually."*

Basic Text, pp. 25–26

❖

In meetings, over refreshments, in talks with our sponsor, we hear our NA friends talking about the way they understand their Higher Power. It would be easy to "go with the flow," adopting someone else's beliefs. But just as no one else can recover for us, so no one else's spirituality can substitute for our own. We must honestly search for an understanding of God that truly works for us.

Many of us begin that search with prayer and meditation, and continue with our experiences in recovery. Have there been instances where we have been given power beyond our own to face life's challenges? When we have quietly sought direction in times of trouble, have we found it? What kind of Power do we believe has guided and strengthened us? What kind of Power do we seek? With the answers to these questions, we will understand our Higher Power well enough to feel safe and confident about asking it to care for our will and lives.

A borrowed understanding of God may do on a short haul. But in the long run, we must come to our own understanding of a Higher Power, for it is that Power which will carry us through our recovery.

❖

Just for today: I seek a Power greater than myself that can help me grow spiritually. Today, I will examine my beliefs honestly and come to my own understanding of God.

> *"The last thing we expected was*
> *an awakening of the spirit."*

Basic Text, p. 49

❖

Few of us came to our first Narcotics Anonymous meeting aching to take a personal inventory or believing that a spiritual void existed in our souls. We had no inkling that we were about to embark on a journey which would awaken our sleeping spirits.

Like a loud alarm clock, the First Step brings us to semi-consciousness—although at this point, we may not be sure whether we want to climb out of bed or maybe sleep for just five more minutes. The gentle hand shaking our shoulders as we apply the Second and Third Steps causes us to stand up, stretch, and yawn. We need to wipe the sleep from our eyes to write the Fourth Step and share our Fifth. But as we work the Sixth, Seventh, Eighth, and Ninth Steps, we begin noticing a spring in our step and the start of a smile on our lips. Our spirits sing in the shower as we take the Tenth and Eleventh Steps. And then we practice the Twelfth, leaving the house in search of others to awaken.

We don't have to spend the rest of our lives in a spiritual coma. We may not like to get up in the morning but, once out of bed, we're almost always glad we did.

❖

Just for today: To awaken my sleepy spirit, I will use the Twelve Steps.

"When we refuse to accept the reality of today,
we are denying faith in our Higher Power.
This can only bring more suffering."

IP No. 8, *Just for Today*

❖

Some days just aren't the way we wish they would be. Our problems may be as simple as a broken shoelace or having to stand in line at the supermarket. Or we may experience something far more serious, such as the loss of a job, a home, or a loved one. Either way, we often end up looking for a way to avoid our feelings instead of simply acknowledging that those feelings are painful.

No one promises us that everything will go our way when we stop using. In fact, we can be sure that life will go on whether we're using or not. We will face good days and bad days, comfortable feelings and painful feelings. But we don't have to run from any of them any longer.

We can experience pain, grief, sadness, anger, frustration—all those feelings we once avoided with drugs. We find that we can get through those emotions clean. We won't die and the world won't come to an end just because we have uncomfortable feelings. We learn to trust that we can survive what each day brings.

❖

Just for today: I will demonstrate my trust in God by experiencing this day just as it is.

"They can be analyzed, counseled, reasoned with, prayed over, threatened, beaten, or locked up, but they will not stop until they want to stop."

Basic Text, p. 65

❖

Perhaps one of the most difficult truths we must face in our recovery is that we are as powerless over another's addiction as we are over our own. We may think that because we've had a spiritual awakening in our own lives we should be able to persuade another addict to find recovery. But there are limits to what we can do to help another addict.

We cannot force them to stop using. We cannot give them the results of the steps or grow for them. We cannot take away their loneliness or their pain. There is nothing we can say to convince a scared addict to surrender the familiar misery of addiction for the frightening uncertainty of recovery. We cannot jump inside other peoples' skins, shift their goals, or decide for them what is best for them.

However, if we refuse to try to exert this power over another's addiction, we may help them. They may grow if we allow them to face reality, painful though it may be. They may become more productive, by their own definition, as long as we don't try and do it for them. They can become the authority on their own lives, provided we are only authorities on our own. If we can accept all this, we can become what we were meant to be—carriers of the message, not the addict.

❖

Just for today: I will accept that I am powerless not only over my own addiction but also over everyone else's. I will carry the message, not the addict.

*"As long as I take it easy and make a commitment with
my Higher Power to do the best I can, I know I will be
taken care of today."*

❖

Many of us feel that our fundamental commitment in recovery
is to our Higher Power. Knowing that we lack the power to stay
clean and find recovery on our own, we enter into a partnership
with a Power greater than we are. We make a commitment to
live in the care of our Higher Power and, in return, our Higher
Power guides us.

This partnership is vital to staying clean. Making it through
the early days of recovery often feels like the hardest thing we've
ever done. But the strength of our commitment to recovery and
the power of God's care is sufficient to carry us through, just for
today.

Our part in this partnership is to do the very best we can
each day, showing up for life and doing what's put in front of us,
applying the principles of recovery to the best of our ability. We
promise to do the *best* we can—not to fake it, not to pretend to
be superhuman, but simply to do the footwork of recovery. In
fulfilling our part of the recovery partnership, we experience the
care our Higher Power has provided us.

❖

Just for today: I will honor my commitment to a partnership
with my Higher Power.

> *"Relapse is never an accident. Relapse is a sign*
> *that we have a reservation in our program."*
>
> **Basic Text, p. 79**

❖

A reservation is something we set aside for future use. In our case, a reservation is the expectation that, if such-and-such happens, we will surely relapse. What event do we expect will be too painful to bear? Maybe we think that if a spouse or lover leaves us, we will have to get high. If we lose our job, surely, we think, we will use. Or maybe it's the death of a loved one that we expect to be unbearable. In any case, the reservations we harbor give us permission to use when they come true—as they often do.

We can prepare ourselves for success instead of relapse by examining our expectations and altering them where we can. Most of us carry within us a catalog of anticipated misery closely related to our fears. We can learn how to survive pain by watching other members live through similar pain. We can apply their lessons to our own expectations. Instead of telling ourselves we will have to get high if *this* happens, we can quietly reassure ourselves that we, too, can stay clean through whatever life brings us today.

❖

Just for today: I will check for any reservations that may endanger my recovery and share them with another addict.

*"Through our inability to accept personal
responsibilities we were actually creating
our own problems."*

Basic Text, p. 13

❖

When we refuse to take responsibility for our lives, we give away all of our personal power. We need to remember that we are powerless over our addiction, not our personal behavior.

Many of us have misused the concept of powerlessness to avoid making decisions or to hold onto things we had outgrown. We have claimed powerlessness over our own actions. We have blamed others for our circumstances rather than taking positive action to change those circumstances. If we continue to avoid responsibility by claiming that we are "powerless," we set ourselves up for the same despair and misery we experienced in our active addiction. The potential for spending our recovery years feeling like victims is very real.

Instead of living our lives by default, we can learn how to make responsible choices and take risks. We may make mistakes, but we can learn from these mistakes. A heightened awareness of ourselves and an increased willingness to accept personal responsibility gives us the freedom to change, to make choices, and to grow.

❖

Just for today: My feelings, actions, and choices are mine. I will accept responsibility for them.

*"Self-pity is one of the most destructive of defects;
it will drain us of all positive energy."*

Basic Text, p. 80

❖

In active addiction, many of us used self-pity as a survival mechanism. We didn't believe there was an alternative to living in our disease—or perhaps we didn't want to believe. As long as we could feel sorry for ourselves and blame someone else for our troubles, we didn't have to accept the consequences of our actions; believing ourselves powerless to change, we didn't have to accept the need for change. Using this "survival mechanism" kept us from entering recovery and led us closer, day by day, to self-destruction. Self-pity is a tool of our disease; we need to stop using it and learn instead to use the new tools we find in the NA program.

We have come to believe that effective help is available for us; when we seek that help, finding it in the NA program, self-pity is displaced by gratitude. Many tools are at our disposal: the Twelve Steps, the support of our sponsor, the fellowship of other recovering addicts, and the care of our Higher Power. The availability of all these tools is more than enough reason to be grateful. We no longer live in isolation, without hope; we have certain help at hand for anything we may face. The surest way to become grateful is to take advantage of the help available to us in the NA program and to experience the improvement the program will bring in our lives.

❖

Just for today: I will be grateful for the hope NA has given me. I will cultivate my recovery and stop cultivating self-pity.

> *"We continued to take personal inventory and*
> *when we were wrong promptly admitted it."*

Step Ten

❖

In Narcotics Anonymous, we've found that the more we live in harmony with our Higher Power's will for us, the greater the harmony in our lives. We use the Tenth Step to help us maintain that harmony. On a daily basis, we take time to look at our behavior. Some of us measure each action with a very simple question: "God's will, or mine?"

In many cases, we find that our actions have been in tune with our Higher Power's will for us, and we in turn have been in tune with the world around us. In some cases, however, we will discover inconsistencies between our behavior and our values. We've been acting on our own will, not God's, and the result has been dissonance in our lives.

When we discover such inconsistencies, we admit we've been wrong and take corrective action. With greater awareness of what we believe God's will for us to be in such situations, we are less likely to repeat those actions. And we are more likely to live in greater concord with our Higher Power's will for us and with the world around us.

❖

Just for today: I wish to live in harmony with my world. Today, I will examine my actions, asking, "God's will, or mine?"

> *"Anonymity is the spiritual foundation of*
> *all our traditions, ever reminding us to place*
> *principles before personalities."*

Tradition Twelve

❖

The Twelfth Tradition reminds us of the importance of putting "principles before personalities." In recovery meetings, this might be paraphrased, "don't shoot the messenger." We often get the message confused with the messenger, and negate what someone shares at a meeting because we have personality conflicts with the person speaking.

If we are having problems with what certain people have to share at meetings, we might want to seek the guidance of our sponsor. Our sponsor can help us concentrate on what's being said rather than who's saying it. Our sponsor can also help us address the resentments that may be keeping us from acknowledging the value of some particular person's recovery experience. It is surprising how much more we can get out of meetings when we allow ourselves to do as our Twelfth Tradition suggests, focusing on recovery principles rather than personalities.

❖

Just for today: I will practice the principle of anonymity in today's NA meeting. I will focus on the message of recovery, not the personality of the messenger.

"Personality change was what we really needed.
Change from self-destructive patterns of life
became necessary."

Basic Text, p. 15

❖

In early life, most of us were capable of joy and wonder, of giving and receiving unconditional love. When we started using, we introduced an influence into our lives that slowly drove us away from those things. The further we were pushed down the path of addiction, the further we withdrew from joy, wonder, and love.

That journey was not taken overnight. But however long it took, we arrived at the doors of NA with more than just a drug problem. The influence of addiction had warped our whole pattern of living beyond recognition.

The Twelve Steps work miracles, it's true, but not many of them are worked overnight. Our disease slowly influenced our spiritual development for the worse. Recovery introduces a new influence to our lives, a source of fellowship and spiritual strength slowly impelling us into new, healthy patterns of living.

This change, of course, doesn't "just happen." But if we cooperate with the new influence NA has brought to our lives, over time we will experience the personality change we call recovery. The Twelve Steps provide us with a program for the kind of cooperation required to restore joy, wonder, and love to our lives.

❖

Just for today: I will cooperate with the new influence of fellowship and spiritual strength NA has introduced to my life. I will work the next step in my program.

*"It would be tragic to write [out an inventory only to]
shove it in a drawer. These defects grow in the dark
and die in the light of exposure."*

Basic Text, p. 32

❖

How many times have we heard it said that we are only as sick as our secrets? While many members choose not to use meetings to share the intimate details of their lives, it is important that we each discover what works best for us. What about those behaviors we have carried into our recovery that, if discovered, would cause us shame? How much are we comfortable disclosing, and to whom? If we are uncomfortable sharing some details of our lives in meetings, to whom do we turn?

We have found the answer to these questions in sponsorship. Although a relationship with a sponsor takes time to build, it is important that we come to trust our sponsor enough to be completely honest. Our defects only have power as long as they stay hidden. If we want to be free of those defects, we must uncover them. Secrets are only secrets until we share them with another human being.

❖

Just for today: I will uncover my secrets. I will practice being honest with my sponsor.

> *"The Eighth Step offers a big change from a life
> dominated by guilt and remorse."*

Basic Text, p. 39

❖

Remorse was one of the feelings that kept us using. We had stumbled our way through active addiction, leaving a trail of heartbreak and devastation too painful to consider. Our remorse was often intensified by our perception that we couldn't do anything about the damage we had caused; there was no way to make it right.

We remove some of the power of remorse when we face it squarely. We begin the Eighth Step by actually making a list of all the people we have harmed. We own our part in our painful past.

But the Eighth Step does not ask us to make right all of our mistakes, merely to become *willing* to make amends to all those people. As we become willing to clean up the damage we've caused, we acknowledge our readiness to change. We affirm the healing process of recovery.

Remorse is no longer an instrument we use to torture ourselves. Remorse has become a tool we can use to achieve self-forgiveness.

❖

Just for today: I will use any feelings of remorse I may have as a stepping-stone to healing through the Twelve Steps.

> *"We examine our actions, reactions, and motives.*
> *We often find that we've been doing better*
> *than we've been feeling."*

Basic Text, p. 43

❖

Imagine a daily meditation book with this kind of message: "When you wake up in the morning, before you rise from your bed, take a moment for reflection. Lie back, gather your thoughts, and consider your plans for the day. One by one, review the motives behind those plans. If your motives are not entirely pure, roll over and go back to sleep." Nonsense, isn't it?

No matter how long we've been clean, almost all of us have mixed motives behind almost everything we do. However, that's no reason to put our lives on hold. We don't have to wait for our motives to become perfectly pure before we can start living our recovery.

As the program works its way into our lives, we begin acting less frequently on our more questionable motives. We regularly examine ourselves, and we talk with our sponsor about what we find. We pray for knowledge of our Higher Power's will for us, and we seek the power to act on the knowledge we're given. The result? We don't get perfect, but we do get better.

We've begun working a spiritual program. We won't ever become spiritual giants. But if we look at ourselves realistically, we'll probably realize that we've been doing better than we've been feeling.

❖

Just for today: I will examine myself realistically. I will seek the power to act on my best motives, and not to act on my worst.

*"Our newly found faith serves as a firm foundation
for courage in the future."*

Basic Text, p. 96

❖

When we begin coming to meetings, we hear other addicts
talking about the gifts they have received as a result of this
program, things we never thought of as gifts before. One such
gift is the renewed ability to feel the emotions we had deadened
for so long with drugs. It's not difficult to think of love, joy, and
happiness as gifts, even if it's been a long time since we've felt
them. But what about "bad" feelings like anger, sadness, fear,
and loneliness? Such emotions can't be seen as gifts, we tell
ourselves. After all, how can we be thankful for things we want
to run from?!

We can become grateful for these emotions in our lives if we
place them in their proper perspective. We need to remember
that we've come to believe in a loving Higher Power, and we've
asked that Power to care for us—and our Higher Power doesn't
make mistakes. The feelings we're given, "good" or "bad," are
given to us for a reason. With this in mind, we come to realize
that there are no bad feelings, only lessons to be learned. Our
faith and our Higher Power's care give us the courage we need
to face whatever feelings may come up on a daily basis.

As we heard early in recovery, "Your Higher Power won't give
you more than you can handle in just one day." And the ability to
feel our emotions is one of the greatest gifts of recovery.

❖

Just for today: I will try to welcome my feelings, firm in the
belief that I have the courage to face whatever emotions may
come up in my life.

> *"Our disease has been arrested, and now anything*
> *is possible. We become increasingly open-minded*
> *and open to new ideas in all areas of our lives."*

Basic Text, p. 106

❖

For many of us, our first few months or years in NA are a wonderful time. We're willing to try anything, and our eyes are constantly opened to new joys and new horizons. Finally freed from active addiction, our recovery young and fresh, anything seems possible.

With a little time clean under our belts, however, there may be less urgency to our program. We might not be quite as willing as we once were to put to use the experience of others. We may have encountered a few seemingly intractable defects in our character, whittling away at the boundless optimism of our early recovery. We know too much to believe that anything is possible.

How do we restore enthusiasm to our recovery? We pray about it; we share about it; and we seek out the enthusiasm we are lacking. There are members—some with more time clean than ourselves, some with less—who have the enthusiasm we seek, and who will be happy to share it with us if we ask them to. To gain the benefit of their experience, however, we must practice open-mindedness and become teachable again. When we become open to new ideas and willing to try them out we'll find that, once more, anything seems possible.

❖

Just for today: There is always more to learn and someone to learn from in my recovery. Today, I will be open to new ideas and willing to try them out. As long as I am, I know that anything is possible.

❖ ❖ ❖
March
❖ ❖ ❖

> *"[The] Power that brought us to this program is still with us and will continue to guide us if we allow it."*

Basic Text, p. 27

❖

Ever had a panic attack? Everywhere we turn, life's demands overwhelm us. We're paralyzed, and we don't know what to do about it. How do we break an anxiety attack?

First, we stop. We can't deal with everything at once, so we stop for a moment to let things settle. Then we take a "spot inventory" of the things that are bothering us. We examine each item, asking ourselves this question: "How important is it, really?" In most cases, we'll find that most of our fears and concerns don't need our immediate attention. We can put those aside, and focus on the issues that really need to be resolved right away.

Then we stop again and ask ourselves, "Who's in control here, anyway?" This helps remind us that our Higher Power is in control. We seek our Higher Power's will for the situation, whatever it is. We can do this in any number of ways: through prayer, talks with our sponsor or NA friends, or by attending a meeting and asking others to share their experience. When our Higher Power's will becomes clear to us, we pray for the ability to carry it out. Finally, we take action.

Anxiety attacks need not paralyze us. We can utilize the resources of the NA program to deal with anything that comes our way.

❖

Just for today: My Higher Power has not brought me all this way in recovery only to abandon me! When anxiety strikes, I will take specific steps to seek God's continuing care and guidance.

"Any form of success was frightening and unfamiliar."

Basic Text, p. 14

❖

Before coming to NA, few of us had much experience with success. Every attempt to stop using on our own had ended in failure. We had begun to give up hope of finding any relief from active addiction. We had grown accustomed to failure, expecting it, accepting it, thinking it was just part of our makeup.

When we stay clean, we begin to experience success in our lives. We begin to take pride in our accomplishments. We start to take healthy risks. We may take some knocks in the process, but even these can be counted as successes if we learn from them.

Sometimes when we fulfill a goal, we hesitate to "pat ourselves on the back" for fear that we will seem arrogant. But our Higher Power wants us to succeed, and wants us to share with our loved ones the pride we take in our accomplishments. When we share our successes with others in NA, they often begin to believe that they can achieve their goals as well. When we succeed, we help lay the groundwork for others who follow in our path.

❖

Just for today: I will take time to savor my successes. I will share my victories with an "attitude of gratitude."

*"There will be times, however, when we really feel
like using. We want to run, and we feel lousy.
We need to be reminded of where we came from
and that it will be worse this time. This is when
we need the program the most."*

Basic Text, p. 81

❖

If we're contemplating a relapse, we should think our using through to the bitter ends. For many of us, those ends would include severe medical problems, imprisonment, or even death. How many of us have known people who relapsed after many years clean, only to die from their disease?

But there is a death that accompanies a return to active addiction that may be worse than physical death. That is the spiritual death we experience when we are separated from our Higher Power. If we use, the spiritual relationship we have nurtured over the years will weaken and perhaps disappear. We will feel truly alone.

There is no doubt that we have periods of darkness in our recovery. There is only one way we can make it through those troubling times: with faith. If we believe that our Higher Power is with us, then we know that all will be well.

No matter how badly we may feel in our recovery, a relapse is never the answer. Together, we find recovery. If we stay clean, the darkness will lift and we will find a deeper connection to our Higher Power.

❖

Just for today: I thank my Higher Power for the gift of NA. I know that relapse is not the way out. Whatever challenges I face, I will face them with the God of my understanding.

*"This program has become a part of me.... I understand
more clearly the things that are happening in my life
today. I no longer fight the process."*

Basic Text, p. 127

❖

In active addiction, things happened seemingly without rhyme
or reason. We just "did things," often without knowing why or what
the results would be. Life had little value or meaning.

The Twelve-Step process gives meaning to our lives; in working
the steps, we come to accept both the dark and the bright
sides of ourselves. We strip away the denial that kept us from
comprehending addiction's affect on us. We honestly examine
ourselves, picking out the patterns in our thoughts, our feelings,
and our behavior. We gain humility and perspective by fully
disclosing ourselves to another human being. In seeking to have
our shortcomings removed, we develop a working appreciation
of our own powerlessness and the strength provided by a
Power greater than we are. With our enhanced understanding
of ourselves, we gain greater insight into and acceptance of
others.

The Twelve Steps are the key to a process we call "life." In
working the steps, they become a part of us—and we become a
part of the life around us. Our world is no longer meaningless; we
understand more about what happens in our lives today. We no
longer fight the process. Today, in working the steps, we live it.

❖

Just for today: Life is a process; the Twelve Steps are the key.
Today, I will use the steps to participate in that process, understanding and enjoying myself and my recovery.

"When a need arises for us to admit our powerlessness,
we may first look for ways to exert power against it.
After exhausting these ways, we begin sharing
with others and find hope."

Basic Text, p. 82

We've sometimes heard it said in our meetings that "rude awakenings lead to spiritual awakenings." What kind of rude awakenings do we have in recovery? Such an awakening might occur when some undesirable bit of our behavior that we thought safely hidden away is suddenly revealed for all the world to see. Or our sponsor might provoke such an awakening by informing us that, just like everyone else, we have to work the steps if we expect to stay clean and recover.

Most of us hate to have our covers pulled; we don't like being laid naked in full view. The experience delivers a strong dose of humility. Our first reaction to such a disclosure is usually shock and anger, yet we recognize the truth when we hear it. What we are having is a rude awakening.

Such awakenings often disclose barriers that block us from making spiritual progress in our recovery. Once those barriers are exposed, we can work the steps to begin removing them from our lives. We can begin experiencing the healing and serenity which are the preludes to a renewed awakening of the spirit.

Just for today: I will recognize the rude awakenings I have as opportunities to grow toward spiritual awakening.

"As a result of the Twelve Steps, I'm not able to hold on to old ways of deceiving myself."

❖

We all rationalize. Sometimes we know we are rationalizing, admit we are rationalizing, yet continue to behave according to our rationalizations! Recovery can become very painful when we decide that, for one reason or another, the simple principles of the program don't apply to us.

With the help of our sponsor and others in NA, we can begin to look at the excuses we use for our behavior. Do we find that some principles just don't apply to us? Do we believe that we know more than everyone else in Narcotics Anonymous, even those who have been clean for many years? What makes us think that we're so special?

There is no doubt, we can successfully rationalize our way through part of our recovery. But, eventually, we must squarely face the truth and start acting accordingly. The principles in the Twelve Steps guide us to a new life in recovery. There is little room for rationalization there.

❖

Just for today: I cannot work the steps and also continue deceiving myself. I will examine my thinking for rationalizations, reveal them to my sponsor, and be rid of them.

*"The good times can also be a trap; the danger is that
we may forget that our first priority is to stay clean."*

Basic Text, p. 43

❖

Things can get really good in our recovery. Perhaps we've found
our "soul mate," built a rewarding career, started a family. Maybe
our relationships with our family members have healed. Things are
going so well, we barely have time to attend meetings. Perhaps
we begin to reintegrate into society so successfully that we forget
that we don't always react to situations like others do.

Maybe, just maybe, we've put some priorities ahead of
themselves. Is meeting attendance still a priority with us? Do
we still sponsor? Do we phone *our* sponsor? What step are we
working? Are we still willing to drag ourselves out of bed at some
ungodly hour for a Twelfth Step call? Do we remember to practice
principles in *all* our affairs? If others in NA reach out to us, are
we available? Do we remember where we came from, or have the
"good times" allowed us to forget?

To stay clean, we must remember that we are only one drug
away from our past. We stay grateful for the good times, but we
don't let them divert us from our continuing recovery in Narcotics
Anonymous.

❖

Just for today: I'm grateful for the good times, but I've not forgotten from where I've come. Today, my first priority is staying
clean and growing in my recovery.

"What we want most is to feel good about ourselves."

Basic Text, p. 101

❖

"We'll love you until you can learn to love yourself." These words, heard so often in our meetings, promise a day we look forward to eagerly—the day when we'll know how to love ourselves.

Self-esteem—we all want this elusive quality as soon as we hear about it. Some of us seem to stumble upon it accidentally, while others embark on a course of action complete with affirmations made to our reflections in the mirror. But fix-it-yourself techniques and trendy psychological cures can only take us so far.

There are some definite, practical steps we can take to show love for ourselves, whether we "feel" that love or not. We can take care of our personal responsibilities. We can do nice things for ourselves, as we would for a lover or a friend. We can start paying attention to our own needs. We can even pay attention to the qualities that we cherish in our friends—qualities like intelligence and humor—and look for those same qualities in ourselves. We're sure to find that we really are lovable people, and once we do that, we're well on our way.

❖

Just for today: I will do something today that helps me recognize and feel love for myself.

"In the past, we made simple situations into problems; we made mountains out of molehills."

Basic Text, p. 90

❖

Making mountains out of molehills seems to be our specialty. Have you heard it said that to an addict, a flat tire is a traumatic event? Or how about those of us who forget all pretense of principle when confronted with a bad driver? And what about that can opener that won't work—you know, the one you just threw out the second story window? We can relate when we hear others share, "God, grant me patience *right now!*"

No, it's not the major setbacks that drive us to distraction. The big things—divorce, death, serious illness, the loss of a job—will throw us, but we survive them. We've learned from experience that we must reach out to our Higher Power and others to make it through life's major crises. It's the small things, the constant day-to-day challenges of living life without the use of drugs, that seem to affect most addicts most strongly in recovery.

When the little things get to us, the Serenity Prayer can help us regain our perspective. We can all remember that "turning over" these small matters to the care of our Higher Power results in peace of mind and a refreshed perspective on life.

❖

Just for today: I will work on patience. I will try to keep from blowing things out of proportion, and walk with my Higher Power through my day.

*"The steps are our solution. They are our survival kit.
They are our defense against addiction, a deadly disease.
Our steps are the principles that make
our recovery possible."*

Basic Text, p. 19

❖

There's lots to like in Narcotics Anonymous. The meetings, for one, are great. We get to see our friends, hear some inspiring stories, share some practical experience, maybe even hook up with our sponsor. The campouts, the conventions, the dances are all wonderful, clean fun in the company of other recovering addicts. But the heart of our recovery program is the Twelve Steps—in fact, they *are* the program!

We've heard it said that we can't stay clean by osmosis—in other words, we can't just attend meetings, no matter how many, and expect to breath recovery in through the pores of our skin. Recovery, as another saying goes, is an inside job. And the tools we use in working that "inside job" are the Twelve Steps. Hearing endlessly about acceptance is one thing; working the First Step for ourselves is something very different. Stories about making amends may be inspiring, yet nothing will give us the freedom from remorse that taking the Ninth Step ourselves will give. The same applies to all Twelve Steps.

There's much to appreciate about NA, but to get the most from our recovery we must work the Twelve Steps for ourselves.

❖

Just for today: I want everything my personal program has to offer. I will work the steps for myself.

> *"It will not make us better people to judge*
> *the faults of another. It will make us feel better*
> *to clean up our lives..."*

Basic Text, p. 38

❖

Sometimes we need something tangible to help us understand what holding a resentment is doing to us. We may not be aware of how destructive resentments actually are. We think, "So what, I have a right to be angry," or, "I might be nursing a grudge or two, but I don't see the harm."

To see more clearly the effect that holding resentments is having in our lives, we might try imagining that we are carrying a rock for each resentment. A small grudge, such as anger at someone driving badly, might be represented by a pebble. Harboring ill will toward an entire group of people might be represented by a enormous boulder. If we actually had to carry stones for each resentment, we would surely tire of the weight. In fact, the more cumbersome our burden, the more sincere our efforts to unload it would be.

The weight of our resentments hinders our spiritual development. If we truly desire freedom, we will seek to rid ourselves of as much extra weight as possible. As we lighten up, we'll notice an increased ability to forgive our fellow human beings for their mistakes, and to forgive ourselves for our own. We'll nourish our spirits with good thoughts, kind words, and service to others.

❖

Just for today: I will seek to have the burden of resentments removed from my spirit.

> *"Many times in our recovery, the old bugaboos*
> *will haunt us. Life may again become*
> *meaningless, monotonous, and boring."*

Basic Text, p. 78

❖

Sometimes it seems as though nothing changes. We get up and go to the same job every day. We eat dinner at the same time every night. We attend the same meetings each week. This morning's rituals were identical to the ones we performed yesterday, and the day before that, and the day before that. After the hell of our addiction and the roller-coaster craziness of early recovery, the stable life may have some appeal—for a while. But, eventually, we realize we want something more. Sooner or later, we become turned off to the creeping monotony and boredom in our lives.

There are sure to be times when we feel vaguely dissatisfied with our recovery. We feel as though we're missing something for some reason, but we don't know what or why. We draw up our gratitude lists and find literally hundreds of things to be grateful for. All our needs are being met; our lives are fuller than we had ever hoped they'd be. So what's up?

Maybe it's time to stretch our potential to its fullest. Our possibilities are only limited by what we can dream. We can learn something new, set a new goal, help another newcomer, or make a new friend. We're sure to find something challenging if we look hard enough, and life will again become meaningful, varied, and fulfilling.

❖

Just for today: I'll take a break from the routine and stretch my potential to its fullest.

"A sponsor is not necessarily a friend, but may be someone in whom we confide. We can share things with our sponsor that we might not be comfortable sharing in a meeting."

IP No. 11, *Sponsorship*, Revised

❖

We've asked someone to sponsor us, and the reasons we have for asking that particular person are as many as the grains of sand on a beach. Perhaps we heard them share at a speaker meeting and thought they were funny or inspiring. Perhaps we thought they had a great car and we would get one by working the same program they work. Or maybe we live in a small town and they were the only person who had the time available to help.

Whatever our initial reasons for getting the sponsor we have, we're sure to find that our reasons for keeping them are quite different. Suddenly they'll amaze us with some stunning insight, making us wonder whether they've been sneaking peeks at our Fourth Step. Or maybe we're going through some sort of life crisis, and their experience with the same problem helps us in ways we never dreamed possible. We call them in pain, and they come up with a special combination of caring words that provide genuine comfort.

None of these remarkable feats on the part of our sponsor are mere coincidence. They've simply walked the same path before us. A Higher Power has placed that one special person in our lives, and we are grateful for their presence.

❖

Just for today: I will appreciate that one special person in my life—my sponsor.

> *"Also, our inventories usually include
> material on relationships."*
>
> **Basic Text, p. 29**

❖

What an understatement this is! Especially in later recovery, entire inventories may focus on our relationships with others. Our lives have been filled with relationships with lovers, friends, parents, coworkers, children, and others with whom we come in contact. A look at these associations can tell us much about our essential character.

Often our inventories catalog the resentments that arise from our day-to-day interactions with others. We strive to look at our part in these frictions. Are we placing unrealistic expectations on other people? Do we impose our standards on others? Are we sometimes downright intolerant?

Often just the writing of our inventory will release some of the pressure that a troubled relationship can produce. But we must also share this inventory with another human being. That way, we get some needed perspective on our part in the problem and how we can work toward a solution.

The inventory is a tool that allows us to begin healing our relationships. We learn that today, with the help of an inventory, we can start to enjoy our relationships with others.

❖

Just for today: I will inventory the part I play in my relationships. I will seek to play a richer, more responsible part in those relationships.

> *"The get-togethers after our meetings are good*
> *opportunities to share things that we didn't get to*
> *discuss during the meeting."*

Basic Text, p. 98

❖

Active addiction set us apart from society, isolating us. Fear was at the core of that alienation. We believed that if we let others get to know us, they would only find out how terribly flawed we were. Rejection would be only a short step away.

When we come to our first NA meeting, we are usually impressed by the familiarity and friendliness we see other recovering addicts share. We, too, can quickly become a part of this fellowship, if we allow ourselves to. One way to start is by tagging along to the local coffee shop after the meeting.

At these gatherings, we can let down the walls that separate us from others and discover things about ourselves and other NA members. One on one, we can sometimes disclose things that we may be reluctant to share at the group level. We learn to make small talk at many of these late-night gatherings and forge deep, strong friendships as well.

With our newfound friends in NA, we no longer have to live lives of isolation. We can become a part of the greater whole, the Fellowship of Narcotics Anonymous.

❖

Just for today: I will break free of isolation. I will strive to feel a part of the NA Fellowship.

> *"The purpose of a searching and fearless moral inventory is to sort through the confusion and the contradiction of our lives so that we can find out who we really are."*

Basic Text, p. 27

❖

Using addicts are a confused and confusing bunch of people. It's hard to tell from one minute to the next what they're going to do or who they're going to be. Usually, the addict is just as surprised as anyone else.

When we used, our behavior was dictated by the needs of our addiction. Many of us still identify our personalities closely with the behavior we practiced while using, leading us to feel shame and despair. Today, we don't have to be the people we once were, shaped by our addiction; recovery has allowed us to change.

We can use the Fourth Step inventory to see past the needs of the old using life and find out who we want to be today. Writing about our behavior and noticing how we *feel* about that behavior helps us understand who we want to be. Our inventory helps us see beyond the demands of active addiction, beyond our desire to be loved and accepted—we find out who we are at the root. We begin to understand what's appropriate for us, and what we want our lives to be like. This is the beginning of becoming who we really are.

❖

Just for today: If I want to find out who I am, I'll look at who I've been and who I want to be.

*"Those who make it through these times show
a courage not their own."*

Basic Text, p. 86

❖

Before coming to NA, many of us thought we were brave simply because we had never experienced fear. We had drugged all our feelings, fear among them, until we had convinced ourselves that we were tough, courageous people who wouldn't crack under any circumstances.

But finding our courage in drugs has nothing to do with the way we live our lives today. Clean and in recovery, we are bound to feel frightened at times. When we first realize we are feeling frightened, we may think we are cowards. We're afraid to pick up the phone because the person on the other end might not understand. We're afraid to ask someone to sponsor us because they might say no. We're afraid to look for a job. We're afraid to be honest with our friends. But all of these fears are natural, even healthy. What's not healthy is allowing fear to paralyze us.

When we permit our fear to stop our growth, we will be defeated. True courage is not the absence of fear, but rather the willingness to walk through it.

❖

Just for today: I will be courageous today. When I'm afraid, I'll do what I need to do to grow in recovery.

> *"There is a special feeling for addicts when*
> *they discover that there are other people who*
> *share their difficulties, past and present."*

Basic Text, pp. 55–56

❖

The wealth of our recovery is too good to keep to ourselves. Some of us believe that when we talk in meetings, we should "remember the newcomer" and always try and carry a positive message. But sometimes the most positive message we can carry is that we are going through difficult times in our recovery and are staying clean in spite of them!

Yes, it's gratifying to send out a strong message of hope to our newer members. After all, no one likes a whiner. But distressing things happen, and life on life's terms can send shock waves even through the recovery of long-time members of Narcotics Anonymous. If we are equipped with the tools of the program, we can walk through such turmoil and stay clean to tell the tale.

Recovery doesn't happen all at once; it is an ongoing process, sometimes a struggle. When we dilute the fullness of our message by neglecting to share about the tough times we may walk through on our journey, we fail to allow newcomers the chance to see that they, too, can stay clean, no matter what. If we share the full message of our recovery, we may not know who benefits, but we can be sure *someone* will.

❖

Just for today: I will honestly share both the good times and the difficult times of my recovery. I will remember that my experience in walking through adversity may benefit another member.

> *"A simple, honest message of recovery*
> *from addiction rings true."*

Basic Text, p. 51

❖

You're in a meeting. The sharing has been going on for some time. One or two members have described their spiritual experiences in an especially meaningful way. Another has had us all rolling in the aisles with entertaining stories. And then the leader calls on you... *gulp.* You shyly introduce yourself, apologetically stammer out a few lines, thank everyone for listening, and sit out the rest of the meeting in embarrassed silence. Sound familiar? Well, you're not alone.

We've all had times when we've felt that what we had to share wasn't spiritual enough, wasn't entertaining enough, wasn't *something* enough. But sharing is not a competitive sport. The meat of our meetings is identification and experience, something all of us have in abundance. When we share from our hearts the truth of our experience, other addicts feel they can trust us because they know we're just like them. When we simply share what's been effective in our lives, we can be sure that our message will be helpful to others.

Our sharing doesn't have to be either fancy or funny to ring true. Every addict working an honest program that brings meaningful recovery has something of immense value to share, something no one else can give: his or her own experience.

❖

Just for today: I have something valuable to share. I will attend a meeting today and share my experience in recovery from addiction.

81

"Most of us have no trouble admitting that addiction had become a destructive force in our lives. Our best efforts resulted in ever greater destruction and despair. At some point, we realized that we needed the help of some Power greater than our addiction."

Basic Text, p. 24

❖

Most of us know without a doubt that our lives have been filled with destruction. Learning that we have a disease called addiction helps us understand the source or cause of this destruction. We can recognize addiction as a power that has worked devastation in our lives. When we take the First Step, we admit that the destructive force of addiction is bigger than we are. We are powerless over it.

At this point, our only hope is to find some Power greater than the force of our addiction—a Power bent on preserving life, not ending it. We don't have to understand it or even name it; we only have to believe that there *could* be such a Higher Power. The belief that a benevolent Power greater than our addiction just might exist gives us enough hope to stay clean, a day at a time.

❖

Just for today: I believe in the possibility of some Power that's bigger than my addiction.

> *"Addiction is a disease that involves more than
> the use of drugs."*

Basic Text, p. 3

❖

At our first meeting, we may have been taken aback at the way members shared about how the disease of addiction had affected their lives. We thought to ourselves, "Disease? I've just got a drug problem! What in the world are they talking about?"

After some time in the program, we began to see that our addiction ran deeper than our obsessive, compulsive drug use. We saw that we suffered from a chronic illness that affected many areas of our lives. We didn't know where we'd "caught" this disease, but in examining ourselves we realized that it had been present in us for many years.

Just as the disease of addiction affects every area of our lives, so does the NA program. We attend our first meeting with all the symptoms present: the spiritual void, the emotional agony, the powerlessness, the unmanageability.

Treating our illness involves much more than mere abstinence. We use the Twelve Steps, and though they don't "cure" our illness, they do begin to heal us. And as we recover, we experience the gift of life.

❖

Just for today: I will treat my illness with the Twelve Steps.

"In our addiction, we were dependent upon people, places, and things. We looked to them to support us and supply the things we found lacking in ourselves."

Basic Text, pp. 70–71

❖

In the animal kingdom, there is a creature that thrives on others. It is called a leech. It attaches itself to people and takes what it needs. When one victim brushes the leech off, it simply goes to the next.

In our active addiction, we behaved similarly. We drained our families, our friends, and our communities. Consciously or unconsciously, we sought to get something for nothing from virtually everyone we encountered.

When we saw the basket passed at our first meeting we may have thought, "Self-support! Now what kind of odd notion is this?" As we watched, we noticed something. These self-supporting addicts were free. By paying their own way, they had earned the privilege of making their own decisions.

By applying the principle of self-support in our personal lives, we gain for ourselves the same kind of freedom. No longer does anyone have the right to tell us where to live, because we pay our own rent. We can eat, wear, or drive whatever we choose, because we provide it for ourselves.

Unlike the leech, we don't have to depend on others for our sustenance. The more responsibility we assume, the more freedom we'll gain.

❖

Just for today: There are no limits to the freedom I can earn by supporting myself. I will accept personal responsibility and pay my own way today.

*"We do the footwork and accept what's being given
to us freely on a daily basis."*

Basic Text, p. 47

❖

Our relationship with our Higher Power is a two-way street. In prayer, we speak and God listens. When we meditate, we do our best to listen for the will of our Higher Power. We know that we are responsible for our part of the relationship. If we do not pray and listen, we shut our Higher Power out of our lives.

When we think about our relationship with our Higher Power, it's important to remember which one we are: the powerless one. We can ask for guidance; we can ask for willingness or strength; we can ask for knowledge of our Higher Power's will—but we cannot make demands. The God of our understanding—the one with the power—will fulfill that half of the relationship by giving us exactly what we need, when we need it.

We need to take action every day to keep our relationship with a Higher Power alive. One way we do this is by applying the Eleventh Step. Then we remember our own powerlessness and accept the will of a Power greater than ourselves.

❖

Just for today: In my relationship with my Higher Power, I am the powerless one. Remembering who I am, today I will humbly accept the gifts of the God I understand.

*"It is not where we were that counts,
but where we are going."*

Basic Text, p. 23

❖

When we first find recovery, some of us feel shame or despair at calling ourselves "addicts." In the early days, we may be filled with both fear and hope as we struggle to find new meaning in our lives. The past may seem inescapable and overpowering. It may be hard to think of ourselves in any way other than the way we always have.

While memories of the past can serve as reminders of what's waiting for us if we use again, they can also keep us stuck in a nightmare of shame and fear. Though it may be difficult to let go of those memories, each day in recovery can bring us that much farther away from our active addiction. Each day, we can find more to look forward to and less to punish ourselves for.

In recovery, all doors are open to us. We have many choices. Our new life is rich and full of promise. While we cannot forget the past, we don't have to live in it. We can move on.

❖

Just for today: I will pack my bags and move out of my past into a present filled with hope.

*"From the isolation of our addiction, we find a
fellowship of people with a common bond...
Our faith, strength, and hope come from people
sharing their recovery..."*

Basic Text, p. 98

❖

Admit no weakness, conceal all shortcomings, deny every failure, go it alone—that was the creed many of us followed. We denied that we were powerless over our addiction, that our lives had become unmanageable, despite all evidence to the contrary. Many of us would not surrender without the assurance there was something worth surrendering *to*. Many of us took our First Step only when we had evidence that addicts could recover in Narcotics Anonymous.

In NA, we find others who've been in the same predicament, with the same needs, who've found tools that work for them. These addicts are willing to share those tools with us and give us the emotional support we need as we learn to use them. Recovering addicts know how important the help of others can be because they've been given that help themselves. When we become a part of Narcotics Anonymous, we join a society of addicts like ourselves, a group of people who know that we help one another recover.

❖

Just for today: I will join in the bond of recovery. I will find the experience, strength, and hope I need in the Fellowship of Narcotics Anonymous.

*"In seeking a sponsor, most members look for
someone they feel they can learn to trust,
someone who seems compassionate..."*

IP No. 11, *Sponsorship*, Revised

❖

The idea of sponsorship may be new to us. We have spent many years without direction, relying only on self-interest, suspecting everyone, trusting no one. Now that we're learning to live in recovery, we find we need help. We can't do it alone anymore; we must take the risk of trusting another human being. Often, the first person we take that risk with is our sponsor—someone we respect, someone we identify with, someone we have reason to trust.

As we open up to our sponsor, a bond develops between us. We disclose our secrets and develop confidence in our sponsor's discretion. We share our concerns and learn to value our sponsor's experience. We share our pain and are met with empathy. We get to know one another, respect one another, love one another. The more we trust our sponsor, the more we learn to trust ourselves.

Trust helps us move away from a life of fear, confusion, suspicion, and indirection. In the beginning, it feels risky to trust another addict. But that trust is the same principle we apply in our relationship with a Higher Power—risky or not, our experience tells us we can't do without it. And the more we take the risk of trusting our sponsor, the more open we will feel about our lives.

❖

Just for today: I want to grow and change. I will risk trusting my sponsor and find the rewards of sharing.

*"In accordance with the principles of recovery, we try
not to judge, stereotype, or moralize with each other."*

Basic Text, p. 11

❖

How many times in our recovery have we misunderstood the behavior of another, immediately formed a judgment, applied a label, and neatly tucked the individual into a pigeonhole? Perhaps they had developed a different understanding of a Power greater than themselves than we had, so we concluded their beliefs were unspiritual. Or maybe we saw a couple having an argument; we assumed their relationship was sick, only to find out later that their marriage had prospered for many years.

Thoughtlessly tossing our fellows into categories saves us the effort of finding out anything about them. Every time we judge the behavior of another, we cease to see them as potential friends and fellow travelers on the road to recovery.

If we happened to ask those we are judging if they appreciate being stereotyped, we would receive a resounding "no" in response. Would we feel slighted if this were done to us? Yes, indeed. Our best qualities are what we want others to notice. In the same way, our fellow recovering addicts want to be well thought of. Our program of recovery asks us to look positively at life. The more we concentrate on the positive qualities in others, the more we'll notice them in ourselves.

❖

Just for today: I will set aside my negative judgments of others, and concentrate instead on appreciating the favorable qualities in all.

*"We may fear that being in touch with our feelings
will trigger an overwhelming chain reaction
of pain and panic."*

Basic Text, p. 30

❖

While we were using, many of us were unable or unwilling to feel many emotions. If we were happy, we used to make us happier. If we were angry or depressed, we used to mask those feelings. In continuing this pattern throughout our active addiction, we became so emotionally confused that we weren't sure what normal emotions were anymore.

After being in recovery for some time, we find that the emotions we had suppressed suddenly begin to surface. We may find that we do not know how to identify our feelings. What we may be feeling as rage may only be frustration. What we perceive as suicidal depression may simply be sadness. These are the times when we need to seek the assistance of our sponsor or other members of NA. Going to a meeting and talking about what is happening in our lives can help us to face our feelings instead of running from them in fear.

❖

Just for today: I will not run from the uncomfortable emotions I may experience. I will use the support of my friends in recovery to help me face my emotions.

"...God's will for us consists of the very things we most value. God's will... becomes our own true will for ourselves."

Basic Text, p. 48

❖

It's human nature to want something for nothing. We may be ecstatic when a store cashier gives us back change for a twenty though we only paid with a ten. We tend to think that, if no one knows, one small deception won't make any difference. But someone *does* know—*we* do. And it *does* make a difference.

What worked for us when we used frequently doesn't work long in recovery. As we progress spiritually by working the Twelve Steps, we begin to develop new values and standards. We begin to feel uncomfortable when we take advantage of situations that, when we used, would have left us gloating about what we had gotten away with.

In the past, we may have victimized others. However, as we draw closer to our Higher Power, our values change. God's will becomes more important than getting away with something.

When our values change, our lives change, too. Guided by an inner knowledge given us by our Higher Power, we *want* to live out our newfound values. We have internalized our Higher Power's will for us—in fact, God's will has become our own true will for ourselves.

❖

Just for today: By improving my conscious contact with God, my values have changed. Today, I will practice God's will, my own true will.

> *"Gradually, as we become more God-centered than*
> *self-centered, our despair turns to hope."*

Basic Text, p. 95

❖

What a glorious thing to have hope! Before coming to Narcotics Anonymous, many of us lived lives of utter hopelessness. We believed we were destined to die from our disease.

Many members speak of being on a "pink cloud" their first months in the program. We've stopped using, made some friends, and life looks promising. Things are going great. Then reality sets in. Life is still life—we still lose jobs, our partners still leave us, friends still die, we still get sick. Abstinence is no guarantee that life will always go our way.

When the reality of life on its own terms sets in, we turn to our Higher Power and remember that life happens the way life happens. But no matter what occurs in our recovery we need not despair, for there is always hope. That hope lies in our relationship with our Higher Power.

This relationship, as expressed by the thought in our text, develops over time: *"Gradually,* we become more God-centered." As we rely more and more on the strength of our Higher Power, life's struggles don't have to drag us into the sea of despair. As we focus more on God, we focus less on ourselves.

❖

Just for today: I will rely on my Higher Power. I will accept that, regardless of what happens, my Higher Power will provide me with the resources to live with it.

"Our real value is in being ourselves."

Basic Text, p. 105

❖

As we work the steps, we're bound to discover some basic truths about ourselves. The process of uncovering our secrets, exposing them, and searching our characters reveals our true nature. As we become acquainted with ourselves, we'll need to make a decision to be just who we are.

We may want to take a look at what we present to our fellow addicts and the world and see if it matches up with what we've discovered inside. Do we pretend that nothing bothers us when, in truth, we're very sensitive? Do we cover our insecurities with obnoxious jokes, or do we share our fears with someone? Do we dress like a teenager when we're approaching forty and are basically conservative?

We may want to take another look at those things which we thought "weren't us." Maybe we've avoided NA activities because we "don't like crowds." Or maybe we have a secret dream of changing careers but have put off taking action because our dream "wasn't really right" for us. As we attain a new understanding of ourselves, we'll want to adjust our behavior accordingly. We want to be genuine examples of who we are.

❖

Just for today: I will check my outsides to make sure they match my insides. I will try to act on the growth I have experienced in recovery.

❖ ❖ ❖

April

❖ ❖ ❖

> *"Some of us first saw the effects of addiction on
> the people closest to us. We were very dependent
> on them to carry us through life. We felt angry,
> disappointed, and hurt when they found
> other interests, friends, and loved ones."*

Basic Text, p. 7

❖

Addiction affected every area of our lives. Just as we sought the drug that would make everything alright, so we sought people to fix us. We made impossible demands, driving away those who had anything of worth to offer us. Often, the only people left were those who were themselves too needy to be capable of denying our unrealistic expectations. It's no wonder that we were unable to establish and maintain healthy intimate relationships in our addiction.

Today, in recovery, we've stopped expecting drugs to fix us. If we still expect people to fix us, perhaps it's time to extend our recovery program to our relationships. We begin by admitting we have a problem—that we don't know the first thing about how to have healthy intimate relationships. We seek out members who've had similar problems and have found relief. We talk with them and listen to what they share about this aspect of their recovery. We apply the program to all our affairs, seeking the same kind of freedom in our relationships that we find throughout our recovery.

❖

Just for today: Loving relationships are within my reach. Today, I will examine the effects of addiction on my relationships so that I can begin seeking recovery.

*"Our public image consists of what we have to offer:
a successful, proven way of maintaining
a drug-free lifestyle."*

Basic Text, p. 75

❖

Yes, we are attracting new members. More and more addicts are finding Narcotics Anonymous. But how do we treat our newest members when they arrive, worn out from their struggles with addiction? Do we reach out to newcomers who are standing by themselves at our meetings, confused and uncertain? Are we willing to give them rides to meetings? Do we still work one-on-one with the addict who suffers? Do we give out our phone numbers? Are we eager to go on a Twelfth Step call, even if it means getting up from our comfortable beds in the middle of the night? Will we work with someone who has a different sexual orientation or is from another culture? Are we generous with the gift of our time?

No doubt we were met with love and acceptance by our fellow addicts. What attracted many of us to Narcotics Anonymous was the feeling that we had finally found a place where we belonged. Are we offering that same sense of belonging to our newer members? We cannot promote Narcotics Anonymous. But when we put principles into action in our lives, we attract newer members to the NA way, just as we were attracted to recovery.

❖

Just for today: I will work with a newcomer. I will remember that I was once a newcomer myself. I will seek to attract others with the same sense of belonging I've found in NA.

> *"The idea of a spiritual awakening takes many
> different forms in the different personalities that
> we find in the fellowship."*

Basic Text, p. 49

❖

Though we all work the same steps, each of us experiences the spiritual awakening resulting from them in our own way. The shape that spiritual awakening takes in our lives will vary, depending on who we are.

For some of us, the spiritual awakening promised in the Twelfth Step will result in a renewed interest in religion or mysticism. Others will awaken to an understanding of the lives of those around them, experiencing empathy perhaps for the first time. Still others will realize that the steps have awakened them to their own moral or ethical principles. Most of us experience our spiritual awakening as a combination of these things, each combination as unique as the individual who's been awakened.

If there are so many different varieties of spiritual awakenings, how do we know if we've truly had one? The Twelfth Step provides us with two signs: We've found principles capable of guiding us well, the kind of principles we want to practice in all our affairs. And we've begun to care enough about other addicts to freely share with them the experience we've had. No matter what the details of our awakenings are like, we all are given the guidance and the love we need to live fulfilling, spiritually oriented lives.

❖

Just for today: Regardless of its particular shape, my spiritual awakening has helped me fill my place in the world with love and life. For that, I am grateful.

*"Remember that we... are ultimately responsible for
our recovery and our decisions."*

Basic Text, p. 103

❖

Most of us will face choices that challenge our recovery. If we find ourselves in extreme physical pain, for example, we will have to decide whether or not we will take medication. We will have to be very honest with ourselves about the severity of our pain, honest with our doctor about our addiction and our recovery, and honest with our sponsor. In the end, however, the decision is ours, for we are the ones who must live with the consequences.

Another common challenge is the choice of attending a party where alcohol will be served. Again, we should consider our own spiritual state. If someone who supports our recovery can attend the event with us, so much the better. However, if we don't feel up to such a challenge, we should probably decline the invitation. Today, we know that preserving our recovery is more important than saving face.

All such decisions are tough ones, requiring not only our careful consideration but the guidance of our sponsor and complete surrender to a Higher Power. Using all of these resources, we make the best decision we can. Ultimately, however, the decision is ours. Today, we are responsible for our own recovery.

❖

Just for today: When faced with a decision that may challenge my recovery, I will consult all the resources at my disposal before I make my choice.

*"Someone finally knew the crazy thoughts that I had
and the crazy things I'd done."*

❖

Addicts often feel terminally unique. We're sure that no one used drugs like we did or had to do the things that we did to get them. Feeling that no one really understands us can keep us from recovery for many years.

But once we come to the rooms of Narcotics Anonymous, we begin to lose that feeling of being "the worst" or "the craziest." We listen as members share their experiences. We discover that others have walked the same twisted path that we've walked and still have been able to find recovery. We begin to believe that recovery is available to us, too.

As we progress in our own recovery, sometimes our thinking is still insane. However, we find that when we share the hard time we may be having, others identify, sharing how they have dealt with such difficulties. No matter how troubled our thinking seems, we find hope when others relate to us, passing along the solutions they've found. We begin to believe that we can survive whatever we're going through to continue on in our recovery.

The gift of Narcotics Anonymous is that we learn we are not alone. We can get clean and stay clean by sharing our experience, our strength, and even our crazy thinking with other members. When we do, we open ourselves to the solutions others have found to the challenges we face.

❖

Just for today: I am grateful that I can identify with others. Today, I will listen as they share their experience, and I'll share mine with them.

*"On a practical level, changes occur
because what's appropriate to one phase of recovery
may not be for another."*

Basic Text, p. 105

❖

When we first came to Narcotics Anonymous, many of us had no legitimate occupation. Not all of us suddenly decide we're going to become honest and productive model citizens the moment we arrive in NA. But we soon find, in recovery, that we are not so comfortable doing many of the things we once did without a second thought when we were using.

As we grow in our recovery, we begin to be honest in matters that probably hadn't bothered us when we used. We start returning extra change a cashier may have given us by mistake, or admitting when we hit a parked car. We find that if we can begin to be honest in these small ways, the bigger tests of our honesty become much easier to handle.

Many of us came here with very little capacity to be honest. But we find that as we work the Twelve Steps, our lives begin to change. We are no longer comfortable when we benefit at the expense of others. And we can feel good about our newfound honesty.

❖

Just for today: I will examine the level of honesty in my life and see if I'm comfortable with it.

> *"This firsthand experience in all phases of illness
> and recovery is of unparalleled therapeutic value.
> We are here to share it freely with any addict
> who wants to recover."*

Basic Text, p. 10

❖

Most of us came into the program with some serious regrets. We had never finished high school, or we had missed going to college. We had destroyed friendships and marriages. We had lost jobs. And we knew that we couldn't change any of it. We may have thought that we'd always be regretful and simply have to find a way to live with our regrets.

On the contrary, we find that our past represents an untapped gold mine the first time we are called on to share it with a struggling newcomer. As we listen to someone share their Fifth Step with us, we can give a special form of comfort that no one else could provide—our own experience. We've done the same things. We've had the same feelings of shame and remorse. We've suffered in the ways only an addict can suffer. We can relate—and so can they.

Our past is valuable—in fact, priceless—because we can use all of it to help the addict who still suffers. Our Higher Power can work through us when we share our past. That possibility is why we are here, and its fulfillment is the most important goal we have to accomplish.

❖

Just for today: I no longer regret my past because, with it, I can share with other addicts, perhaps averting the pain or even death of another.

"We come to know happiness, joy, and freedom."

Basic Text, p. 91

❖

If someone stopped you on the street today and asked if you were happy, what would you say? "Well, gee, let's see... I have a place to live, food in the refrigerator, a job, my car is running... Well, yes, I guess I'm happy," you might respond. These are outward examples of things that many of us have traditionally associated with happiness. We often forget, however, that happiness is a choice; no one can *make* us happy.

Happiness is what we find in our involvement with Narcotics Anonymous. The happiness we derive from a life focused on service to the addict who still suffers is great indeed. When we place service to others ahead of our own desires, we find that we take the focus off ourselves. As a result, we live a more contented, harmonious life. In being of service to others, we find our own needs more than fulfilled.

Happiness. What is it, really? We can think of happiness as contentment and satisfaction. Both of these states of mind seem to come to us when we least strive for them. As we live just for today, carrying the message to the addict who still suffers, we find contentment, happiness, and a deeply meaningful life.

❖

Just for today: I am going to be happy. I will find my happiness by being of service to others.

> *"We learn to experience feelings and realize*
> *they can do us no harm unless we act on them."*
>
> **IP No. 16, *For the Newcomer***

❖

Many of us came to Narcotics Anonymous with something less than an overwhelming desire to stop using. Sure, the drugs were causing us problems, and we wanted to be rid of the problems, but we didn't want to stop getting high. Eventually, though, we saw that we couldn't have one without the other. Even though we really wanted to get loaded, we didn't use; we weren't willing to pay the price anymore. The longer we stayed clean and worked the program, the more freedom we experienced. Sooner or later, the compulsion to use was lifted from us completely, and we stayed clean because we wanted to live clean.

The same principles apply to other negative impulses that may plague us. We may feel like doing something destructive, just because we want to. We've done it before, and sometimes we think we've gotten away with it, but sometimes we haven't. If we're not willing to pay the price for acting on such feelings, we don't have to act on them.

It may be hard, maybe even as hard as it was to stay clean in the beginning. But others have felt the same way and have found the freedom not to act on their negative impulses. By sharing about it and seeking the help of other recovering people and a Power greater than ourselves, we can find the direction, the support, and the strength we need to abstain from *any* destructive compulsion.

❖

Just for today: It's okay to feel my feelings. With the help of my sponsor, my NA friends, and my Higher Power, I am free not to act out my negative feelings.

> *"We must use what we learn or we will lose it,*
> *no matter how long we have been clean."*

Basic Text, p. 85

❖

After putting some clean time together, some of us have a tendency to forget what our most important priority is. Once a week or less we say, "I've gotta get to a meeting tonight. It's been..." We've been caught up in other things, important for sure, but no more so than our continued participation in Narcotics Anonymous.

It happens gradually. We get jobs. We reunite with our families. We're raising children, the dog is sick, or we're going to school at night. The house needs to be cleaned. The lawn needs to be mowed. We have to work late. We're tired. There's a good show at the theater tonight. And all of a sudden, we notice that we haven't called our sponsor, been to a meeting, spoken to a newcomer, or even talked to God in quite a while.

What do we do at this point? Well, we either renew our commitment to our recovery, or we continue being too busy to recover until something happens and our lives become unmanageable. Quite a choice! Our best bet is to put more of our energy into maintaining the foundation of recovery on which our lives are built. That foundation makes everything else possible, and it will surely crumble if we get too busy with everything else.

❖

Just for today: I can't afford to be too busy to recover. I will do something today that sustains my recovery.

> *"A new idea cannot be grafted onto a closed mind....*
> *Open-mindedness leads us to the very insights*
> *that have eluded us during our lives."*

Basic Text, p. 96

❖

We arrived in NA at the lowest point in our lives. We'd just about run out of ideas. What we needed most when we got here were new ideas, new ways of living, shared from the experience of people who'd seen those ideas work. Yet our closed minds prevented us from taking in the very ideas we needed to live.

Denial keeps us from appreciating just how badly we really need new ideas and new direction. By admitting our powerlessness and recognizing how truly unmanageable our lives have become, we allow ourselves to see how much we need what NA has to offer.

Self-dependence and self-will can keep us from admitting even the possibility of the existence of a Power greater than ourselves. However, when we admit the sorry state self-will has gotten us into, we open our eyes and our minds to new possibilities. When others tell us of a Power that has brought sanity to their lives, we begin to believe that such a Power may do the same for us.

A tree stripped of its branches will die unless new branches can be grafted onto its trunk. In the same way, addiction stripped us of whatever direction we had. To grow or even to *survive,* we must open our minds and allow new ideas to be grafted onto our lives.

❖

Just for today: I will ask my Higher Power to open my mind to the new ideas of recovery.

> *"All spiritual awakenings have some things in common.*
> *Common elements include an end to loneliness*
> *and a sense of direction in our lives."*

Basic Text, p. 50

❖

Some kinds of spiritual experiences take place when we confront something larger than we are. We suspect that forces beyond our understanding are operating. We see a fleeting glimpse of the big picture and find humility in that moment.

Our journey through the Twelve Steps will bring about a spiritual experience of the same nature, only more profound and lasting. We undergo a continual process of ego-deflation, while at the same time we become more conscious of the larger perspective. Our view of the world expands to the point where we no longer possess an exaggerated sense of our own importance.

Through our new awareness, we no longer feel isolated from the rest of the human race. We may not understand why the world is the way it is or why people sometimes treat one another so savagely. But we do understand suffering and, in recovery, we can do our best to alleviate it. When our individual contribution is combined with others, we become an essential part of a grand design. We are connected at last.

❖

Just for today: I am but one person in the entire scheme of things. I humbly accept my place in the big picture.

*"...approval-seeking behavior carried us further
into our addiction...."*

Basic Text, p. 14

❖

When others approve of what we do or say, we feel good; when they disapprove, we feel bad. Their opinions of us, and how those opinions make us feel, can have positive value. By making us feel good about steering a straight course, they encourage us to continue doing so. "People-pleasing" is something else entirely. We "people-please" when we do things, right or wrong, solely to gain another person's approval.

Low self-esteem can make us think we need someone else's approval to feel okay about ourselves. We do whatever we think it will take to make them tell us we're okay. We feel good for awhile. Then we start hurting. In trying to please another person, we've diminished ourselves and our values. We realize that the approval of others will not fill the emptiness inside us.

The inner satisfaction we seek can be found in doing the right things for the right reasons. We break the people-pleasing cycle when we stop acting merely to gain others' approval and start acting on our Higher Power's will for us. When we do, we may be pleasantly surprised to find that the people who really count in our lives will approve all the more of our behavior. Most importantly, though, *we* will approve of ourselves.

❖

Just for today: Higher Power, help me live in accordance with spiritual principles. Only then can I approve of myself.

> *"Do we really want to be rid of our resentments,*
> *our anger, our fear?"*

Basic Text, p. 34

❖

Why do we call them "shortcomings"? Perhaps they should be called "long-goings," because that's often what it takes for them to fade from our lives. Some of us feel that our shortcomings are the very characteristics that saved our lives when we used. If this is true, then it is little wonder that we sometimes cling to them like old, dear friends.

If we are having trouble with resentment, anger, or fear, we may want to envision what our lives could be like without these troubling defects. Asking ourselves *why* we react in a certain manner can sometimes root out the fear at the core of our conduct. "Why am I afraid to step beyond these aspects of my personality?" we ask ourselves. "Am I afraid of who I will be without these attributes?"

Once we have uncovered our fear, we are able to move beyond it. We try to imagine what our lives could be like without some of our more glaring shortcomings. This gives us a feeling for what lies past our fear, providing the motivation we need to push through it. Our Higher Power offers us a new vision for our lives, free of our defects. That vision is the essence of our own best, brightest dreams for ourselves. We need not fear that vision.

❖

Just for today: I will imagine what my life would be like without my character defects. I will ask for the willingness to have God remove my shortcomings.

*"We have come to enjoy living clean and want more
of the good things that the NA Fellowship holds for us."*

Basic Text, p. 27

Can you remember a time when you looked at the addicts recovering in NA and wondered, "If they aren't using drugs, what on earth do they have to laugh about?" Did you believe that the fun stopped when the using stopped? So many of us did; we were certain that we were leaving the "good life" behind. Today, many of us can laugh at that misconception because we know how full our life in recovery can be.

Many of the things we enjoy so much in recovery are gained by actively participating in the Fellowship of NA. We begin to find true companionship, friends who understand and care about us just for ourselves. We find a place where we can be useful to others. There are recovery meetings, service activities, and fellowship gatherings to fill our time and occupy our interests. The fellowship can be a mirror to reflect back to us a more accurate image of who we are. We find teachers, helpers, friends, love, care, and support. The fellowship always has more to offer us, as long as we keep coming back.

❖

Just for today: I know where the "good life" is. I'll keep coming back.

"Today, we seek solutions, not problems. We try what we have learned on an experimental basis."

Basic Text, p. 58

❖

The first time we heard that we should "act as if," many of us exclaimed, "But that's not honest! I thought we were always supposed to be honest about our feelings in Narcotics Anonymous."

Perhaps we can reflect on when we first came into the program. We may not have believed in God, but we prayed anyway. Or maybe we weren't sure the program would work for us, but we kept coming to meetings regardless of what we thought. The same applies as we progress in recovery. We may be terrified of crowds, but if we act confidently and extend our hand, we'll not only feel better about ourselves, we'll find that we are no longer so frightened of large gatherings.

Each action we take in this vein brings us closer to becoming the people we were meant to be. Each positive change we make builds our self-esteem. Through acting differently, we will realize that we are beginning to think differently. We are living ourselves into right thinking by "acting as if."

❖

Just for today: I will take the opportunity to act as if I can accept a situation I used to run from.

*"I initially felt that it would be impossible
to attend more than one or two meetings a week.
It just wouldn't fit in with my busy schedule. I later
learned that my priorities were [180] degrees reversed.
It was the everything else that would have to fit
into my meeting schedule."*

❖

Some of us attended meetings infrequently when we first came to Narcotics Anonymous, then wondered why we couldn't stay clean. What we soon learned was that if we wanted to stay clean, we had to make meeting attendance our priority.

So we began again. Following our sponsor's suggestion, we made a commitment to attend ninety meetings in ninety days. We identified ourselves as newcomers for our first thirty days so that others could get to know us. At our sponsor's direction, we stopped talking long enough to learn to listen. We soon began to look forward to meetings. And we began to stay clean.

Today, we attend meetings for a variety of reasons. Sometimes we go to meetings to share our experience, strength, and hope with newer members. Sometimes we go to see our friends. And sometimes we go just because we need a hug. Occasionally we leave a meeting and realize that we haven't really heard a word that's been said—but we still *feel* better. The atmosphere of love and joy that fills our meetings has kept us clean another day. No matter how hectic our schedule, we make meeting attendance our priority.

❖

Just for today: In my heart, I know that meetings benefit me in all kinds of ways. Today, I want what's good for me. I will attend a meeting.

"We humbly asked Him to remove our shortcomings."

Step Seven

❖

Once we are entirely ready to have our character defects removed, many of us are *entirely* ready! Ironically, that's when the trouble really starts. The more we struggle to rid ourselves of a particular defect, the stronger that shortcoming seems to become. It is truly humbling to realize that not only are we powerless over our addiction, but even over our own defects of character.

Finally, it clicks. The Seventh Step doesn't suggest that we rid ourselves of our shortcomings, but that we ask our Higher Power to rid us of them. The focus of our daily prayers begins to shift. Admitting our inability to perfect ourselves, we plead with our Higher Power to do for us what we cannot do for ourselves. And we wait.

For many days, our program may stay on Step Seven. We may experience no sudden, total relief from defects—but we often do experience a subtle shift in our perceptions of ourselves and others. Through the eyes of the Seventh Step, we begin to see those around us in a less critical way. We know that, just like us, many of them are struggling with shortcomings they would dearly love to be rid of. We know that, just like us, they are powerless over their own defects. We wonder if they, too, humbly pray to have their defects removed.

We begin evaluating others as we have learned to evaluate ourselves, with an empathy born of humility. As we watch others, and as we keep watch on ourselves, we can finally say, "I understand."

❖

Just for today: God, help me see through the eyes of Step Seven. Help me understand.

*"So many times, addicts have sought the rewards
of hard work without the labor."*

Basic Text, p. 34

❖

When we first came to NA, some of us wanted everything, and right away. We wanted the serenity, the cars, the happy relationships, the friends, the closeness with our sponsor—all the things other people had gotten after months and years of working the steps and living life on life's terms.

We learned the hard way that serenity comes only from working the steps. A new car comes from showing up on the job every day and trying to "practice these principles in all our affairs," including our employment. Healthy relationships come as a result of lots of hard work and a new willingness to communicate. Friendship with our sponsor comes as a result of reaching out during the good times as well as the bad.

In Narcotics Anonymous, we have found the path to a better way of life. To reach our destination, however, we must do the footwork.

❖

Just for today: I want a better life. I will make an inventory of what I want, find out how to get it, talk with my sponsor about it, and do the necessary footwork.

113

> *"Addiction is a family disease,*
> *but we could only change ourselves."*

❖

Many of us come from severely damaged families. At times, the insanity that reigns among our relatives feels overwhelming. Sometimes we feel like packing our bags and moving far, far away.

We pray that our family members will join us in recovery but, to our great sadness, this does not always happen. Sometimes, despite our best efforts to carry the message, we find that we cannot help those we hold most dear. Our group experience has taught us that, frequently, we are too close to our relatives to help them. We learn it is better to leave them in our Higher Power's care.

We have found that when we stop trying to settle the problems of family members, we give them the room they need to work things out in their own lives. By reminding them that we are not able to solve their problems for them, we give ourselves the freedom to live our own lives. We have faith that God will help our relatives. Often, the best thing we can give our loved ones is the example of our own ongoing recovery. For the sake of our family's sanity and our own, we must let our relatives find their own ways to recover.

❖

Just for today: I will seek to work my own program and leave my family in the care of a Higher Power.

*"We have found that we had no choice except
to completely change our old ways of thinking
or go back to using."*

Basic Text, p. 22

❖

Many of us find that our old ways of thinking were dominated by fear. We were afraid that we wouldn't be able to get our drugs or that there wouldn't be enough. We feared discovery, arrest, and incarceration. Further down the list were fears of financial problems, homelessness, overdose, and illness. And our fear controlled our actions.

The early days of recovery weren't a great deal different for many of us; then, too, fear dominated our thinking. "What if staying clean hurts too much?" we asked ourselves. "What if I can't make it? What if the people in NA don't like me? What if NA doesn't work?" The fear behind these thoughts can still control our behavior, keeping us from taking the risks necessary to stay clean and grow. It may seem easier to resign ourselves to certain failure, giving up before we start, than to risk everything on a slim hope. But that kind of thinking leads only to relapse.

To stay clean, we must find the willingness to change our old ways of thinking. What has worked for other addicts can work for us—but we must be willing to try it. We must trade in our old cynical doubts for new affirmations of hope. When we do, we'll find it's worth the risk.

❖

Just for today: I pray for the willingness to change my old ways of thinking, and for the ability to overcome my fears.

"This is our road to spiritual growth."

Basic Text, p. 37

❖

When we arrived at our first NA meeting, it looked like the end of the road to many of us. We weren't going to be able to use anymore. We were spiritually bankrupt. Most of us were totally isolated and didn't think we had much to live for. Little did we realize that, as we began our program of recovery, we were stepping onto a road of unlimited possibilities.

At first, just not using was tough enough. Yet, as we watched other addicts working the steps and applying those principles in their lives, we began to see that recovery was more than just not using. The lives of our NA friends had changed. They had a relationship with the God of their understanding. They were responsible members of the fellowship and of society. They had a reason to live. We began to believe these things were possible for us, too.

As we continue our recovery journey, we can get sidetracked by complacency, intolerance, or dishonesty. When we do, we need to recognize the signs quickly and get back on our path— the open road to freedom and growth.

❖

Just for today: I am continuing to develop my spiritual, social, and general living skills by applying the principles of my program. I can travel as far as I wish on the open road of recovery.

> *"Many of us understand God to be simply*
> *whatever force keeps us clean."*

Basic Text, p. 25

❖

Some of us enter recovery with a working understanding of a Higher Power. For a lot of us, however, "God" is a troublesome word. We may doubt the existence of *any* sort of Power greater than ourselves. Or we may remember uncomfortable experiences with religion and shy away from "the God stuff."

Starting over in recovery means we can start over in our spiritual life, too. If we're not comfortable with what we learned when we were growing up, we can try a different approach to our spirituality. We don't have to understand everything all at once or find the answers to all our questions right away. Sometimes it's enough just to know that other NA members believe and that their belief helps keep them clean.

❖

Just for today: All I have to know right now about my Higher Power is that it is the Power that helps keep me clean.

*"Through abstinence and through working
the Twelve Steps of Narcotics Anonymous,
our lives have become useful."*

Basic Text, p. 8

❖

Before coming to Narcotics Anonymous, our lives were centered around using. For the most part, we had very little energy left over for jobs, relationships, or other activities. We served only our addiction.

The Twelve Steps of Narcotics Anonymous provide a simple way to turn our lives around. We start by staying clean, a day at a time. When our energy is no longer channeled into our addiction, we find that we have the energy to pursue other interests. As we grow in recovery, we become able to sustain healthy relationships. We become trustworthy employees. Hobbies and recreation seem more inviting. Through participation in Narcotics Anonymous, we help others.

Narcotics Anonymous does not promise us that we will find good jobs, loving relationships, or a fulfilling life. But when we work the Twelve Steps to the best of our ability, we find that we can become the type of people who are *capable* of finding employment, sustaining loving relationships, and helping others. We stop serving our disease, and begin serving God and others. The Twelve Steps are the key to transforming our lives.

❖

Just for today: I will have the wisdom to use the Twelve Steps in my life, and the courage to grow in my recovery. I will practice my program to become a responsible, productive member of society.

"Recovery is a reality for us today."

Basic Text, p. 101

❖

Pain and misery were realities in our using lives. We were unwilling either to accept our living situation or to change what was unacceptable in our lives. We attempted to escape life's pain by taking drugs, but using only compounded our troubles. Our altered sense of reality became a nightmare.

Through living the program of Narcotics Anonymous, we learn that our dreams can replace our nightmares. We grow and change. We acquire the freedom of choice. We are able to give and receive love. We can share honestly about ourselves, no longer magnifying or minimizing the truth. We accept the challenges real life offers us, facing them in a mature, responsible way.

Although recovery does not give us immunity from the realities of life, in the NA Fellowship we can find the support, genuine care, and concern we need to face those realities. We need never hide from reality by using drugs again, for our unity with other recovering addicts gives us strength. Today, the support, the care, and the empathy of recovery give us a clean, clear window through which to view, experience, and appreciate reality as it is.

❖

Just for today: A gift of my recovery is living and enjoying life as it truly is. Today, I will embrace reality.

"The most effective means of achieving self-acceptance is through applying the Twelve Steps of recovery."

IP No. 19, *Self-Acceptance*

❖

Most of us came to Narcotics Anonymous without much self-acceptance. We looked at the havoc we had wreaked in our active addiction, and we loathed ourselves. We had difficulty accepting our past and the self-image produced by it.

Self-acceptance comes more quickly when we first accept that we have a disease called *addiction*, because it's easier to accept ourselves as sick people than as bad people. And the easier it is to accept ourselves, the easier it becomes to accept responsibility for ourselves.

We achieve self-acceptance through the process of ongoing recovery. Working the Twelve Steps of Narcotics Anonymous teaches us to accept ourselves and our lives. Spiritual principles like surrender, honesty, faith, and humility help relieve us of the burden of our past mistakes. Our attitude changes with the application of these principles in our daily lives. Self-acceptance grows as we grow in recovery.

❖

Just for today: Self-acceptance is a process set in motion by the Twelve Steps. Today, I will trust the process, practice the steps, and learn to better accept myself.

*"We want to look our past in the face, see it for what
it really was, and release it so we can live today."*

Basic Text, p. 29

❖

Many of us had trouble identifying our resentments when we
were new in recovery. There we sat with our Fourth Step in front
of us, thinking and thinking, finally deciding that we just didn't
have any resentments. Perhaps we talked ourselves into believing
that we weren't so sick after all.

Such unwitting denial of our resentments stems from the
conditioning of our addiction. Most of our feelings were buried,
and buried deep. After some time in recovery, a new sense of
understanding develops. Our most deeply buried feelings begin
to surface, and those resentments we thought we didn't have
suddenly emerge.

As we examine these resentments, we may feel tempted to
hold onto some of them, especially if we think they are "justified."
But what we need to remember is that "justified" resentments are
just as burdensome as any other resentment.

As our awareness of our liabilities grows, so does our
responsibility to let go. We no longer need to hang on to our
resentments. We want to rid ourselves of what's undesirable and
set ourselves free to recover.

❖

Just for today: When I discover a resentment, I'll see it for what
it is and let it go.

> *"We can also use the steps to improve our attitudes.*
> *Our best thinking got us into trouble. We recognize*
> *the need for change."*

Basic Text, p. 55

❖

When new in recovery, most of us had at least one person we just couldn't stand. We thought that person was the rudest, most obnoxious person in the program. We knew there was something we could do, some principle of recovery we could practice to get over the way we felt about this person—but what? We asked our sponsor for guidance. We were probably assured, with an amused smile, that if we just kept coming back, we'd see the person get better. That made sense to us. We believed that the steps of NA worked in the lives of everyone. If they could work for us, they could work for this horrible person, too.

Time passed, and at some point we noticed that the person didn't seem as rude or obnoxious as before. In fact, he or she had become downright tolerable, maybe even likeable. We got a pleasant jolt as we realized who had really gotten better. Because we had kept coming back, because we had kept working the steps, our perception of this person had changed. The person who'd plagued us had become "tolerable" because we'd developed some tolerance; he or she had become "likeable" because we'd developed the ability to love.

So who really gets better? *We do!* As we practice the program, we gain a whole new outlook on those around us by gaining a new outlook on ourselves.

❖

Just for today: As I get better, so will others. Today, I will practice tolerance and try to love those I meet.

> *"Living just for today relieves the burden of the past and the fear of the future. We learned to take whatever actions are necessary and to leave the results in the hands of our Higher Power."*

Basic Text, p. 94

❖

In our active addiction, fear of the future and what might happen was a reality for many of us. What if we got arrested? lost our job? our spouse died? we went bankrupt? and on, and on, and on. It was not unusual for us to spend hours, even whole days thinking about what *might* happen. We played out entire conversations and scenarios before they ever occurred, then charted our course on the basis of "what if..." By doing this, we set ourselves up for disappointment after disappointment.

From listening in meetings, we learn that living in the present, not the world of "what if," is the only way to short-circuit our self-fulfilling prophecies of doom and gloom. We can only deal with what is real today, not our fearful fantasies of the future.

Coming to believe that our Higher Power has only the best in store for us is one way we can combat that fear. We hear in meetings that our Higher Power won't give us more than we can handle in one day. And we know from experience that, if we ask, the God we've come to understand will surely care for us. We stay clean through adverse situations by practicing our faith in the care of a Power greater than ourselves. Each time we do, we become less fearful of "what if" and more comfortable with what *is*.

❖

Just for today: I will look forward to the future with faith in my Higher Power.

*"Ongoing recovery is dependent on our relationship
with a loving God who cares for us and will do for us
what we find impossible to do for ourselves."*

Basic Text, p. 99

❖

How often have we heard it said in meetings that "God does for us what we cannot do for ourselves"? At times we may get stuck in our recovery, unable, afraid, or unwilling to make the decisions we know we must make to move forward. Perhaps we are unable to end a relationship that just isn't working. Maybe our job has become a source of too much conflict. Or perhaps we feel we need to find a new sponsor but are afraid to begin the search. Through the grace of our Higher Power, unexpected change may occur in precisely the area we felt unable to alter.

We sometimes allow ourselves to become stuck in the problem instead of moving forward toward the solution. At these times, we often find that our Higher Power does for us what we cannot do for ourselves. Perhaps our partner decides to end our relationship. We may get fired or laid off. Or our sponsor tells us that he or she can no longer work with us, forcing us to look for a new one.

Sometimes what occurs in our lives can be frightening, as change often seems. But we also hear that "God never closes a door without opening another one." As we move forward with faith, the strength of our Higher Power is never far from us. Our recovery is strengthened by these changes.

❖

Just for today: I trust that the God of my understanding will do for me what I cannot do for myself.

❖ ❖ ❖

May

❖ ❖ ❖

"Being involved in service makes me feel worthwhile."

❖

When most of us arrived in Narcotics Anonymous, we had very little self-worth left to salvage. Many members say that they began to develop self-esteem through being of service early in their recovery. Something just short of a miracle occurs when we begin to have a positive impact on others' lives through our service efforts.

Most of us don't have a lot of experience, strength, or hope to share at thirty days clean. In fact, some members will tell us in no uncertain terms that what we can do best is listen. But at thirty days, we do offer something to that addict just coming into the rooms of NA, struggling to get twenty-four hours clean. The very newest NA member, the one with only the desire to stop using and none of the tools, can hardly imagine anyone staying clean for a year, or two years, or ten. But he or she can relate to those people with thirty days clean, picking up a keytag with a look of pride and disbelief emblazoned on their faces.

Service is something that is our unique gift—something that no one can take away from us. We give, and we get. Through service, many of us start on the sometimes long road back to becoming productive members of society.

❖

Just for today: I will be grateful for the opportunity to be of service.

> *"There is one thing more than anything else that*
> *will defeat us in our recovery; this is an attitude of*
> *indifference or intolerance toward spiritual principles."*

Basic Text, p. 18

❖

When we first came to NA, many of us had great difficulty accepting the spiritual principles underlying this program—and for good reason. No matter how we'd tried to control our addiction, we'd found ourselves powerless. We grew angry and frustrated with anyone who suggested there was hope for us, because we knew better. Spiritual ideas may have had some bearing on other peoples' lives, but not on ours.

Despite our indifference or intolerance toward spiritual principles, we were drawn to Narcotics Anonymous. There, we met other addicts. They'd been where we'd been, powerless and hopeless, yet they'd found a way not only to stop using but to live and enjoy life clean. They spoke of the spiritual principles that had pointed the way for them to this new life of recovery. For them, these principles were not just theories but a part of their practical experience. Yes, we had good reason to be skeptical, but these spiritual principles spoken of by other NA members really seemed to work.

Once we admitted this, we didn't necessarily accept every single spiritual idea we heard. But we did start to think that, if these principles had worked for others, just maybe they'd work for us, too. For a beginning, that willingness was enough.

❖

Just for today: Just maybe the spiritual principles I hear spoken of in NA might work for me. I am willing, at least, to open my mind to the possibility.

*"My gratitude speaks when I care
and when I share with others the NA way."*

Gratitude Prayer

❖

The longer we stay clean, the more we experience feelings of gratitude for our recovery. These feelings of gratitude aren't limited to particular gifts like new friends or the ability to be employed. More frequently, they arise from the overall sense of joy we feel in our new lives. These feelings are enhanced by our certainty of the course our lives would have taken if it weren't for the miracle we've experienced in Narcotics Anonymous.

These feelings are so all-encompassing, so wondrous, and sometimes so overwhelming that we often can't find words for them. We sometimes openly weep with happiness while sharing in a meeting, yet we grope for words to express what we are feeling. We want so badly to convey to newcomers the gratitude we feel, but it seems that our language lacks the superlatives to describe it.

When we share with tears in our eyes, when we choke up and can't talk at all—these are the times when our gratitude speaks most clearly. We share our gratitude directly from our hearts; with their hearts, others hear and understand. Our gratitude speaks eloquently, though our words may not.

❖

Just for today: My gratitude has a voice of its own; when it speaks, the heart understands. Today, I will share my gratitude with others, whether I can find the words or not.

---

*"Each group has but one primary purpose—to carry
the message to the addict who still suffers."*

Tradition Five

❖

Our home group means a lot to us. After all, where would
we be without our favorite NA meeting? Our group sometimes
sponsors picnics or other activities. Often, home group members
get together to see a movie or go bowling. We have all made good
friendships through our home group, and we wouldn't trade that
warmth for the world.

But sometimes we must take inventory of what our group is
doing to fulfill its primary purpose—to carry the message to the
still-suffering addict. Sometimes when we go to our meetings,
we know almost everyone and get caught up in the laughter and
fun. But what about the newcomer? Have we remembered to
reach out to the new people who may be sitting by themselves,
lonely and frightened? Do we remember to welcome those visiting
our group?

The love found in the rooms of Narcotics Anonymous helps
us recover from addiction. But once we have gotten clean, we
must remember to give to others what was so freely given to us.
We need to reach out to the addict who still suffers. After all, "the
newcomer is the most important person at *any* meeting."

❖

Just for today: I'm grateful for the warm fellowship I've found
in my home group. I will reach out my hand to the still-suffering
addict, offering that same fellowship to others.

"... I was ready to go to any lengths to stay clean."

Basic Text, p. 132

❖

"Any lengths?" newcomers ask. "What do you mean, *any lengths?*" Looking back at our active addiction and the lengths we were willing to go to in order to stay high can help to explain. Were we willing to drive many miles to get drugs? Yes, we usually were. Then it makes sense that, if we are as concerned about staying clean as we were about using, we will try anything to find a ride to a meeting.

In our addiction, didn't we often do crazy, insane things or use unknown substances at the direction of others? Then why do we often find it so hard to take direction in recovery, especially when the direction is designed to help us grow? And when we used, didn't we often, in desperation, turn to our Higher Power, saying, "Please, just get me out of this one!" Then why do we find it so hard to ask for God's help in our recovery?

When we used, we usually had an open mind when it came to finding ways and means to get more drugs. If we can apply this same principle of open-mindedness to our recovery, we may surprise ourselves by how easily we begin to grasp the NA program. Our best thinking, it is often said, got us into the rooms of Narcotics Anonymous. If we are willing to go to any lengths, follow directions, and stay open-minded, we can stay clean.

❖

Just for today: I am willing to go to any lengths to stay clean. I will become as open-minded and ready to take direction as I need to be.

> *"In time, we can relax and enjoy
> the atmosphere of recovery."*

Basic Text, p. 56

❖

Imagine what would happen if a newcomer walked into one of our meetings and was met by a group of grim-faced people gripping the arms of their chairs with white knuckles. That newcomer would probably bolt, perhaps muttering, "I thought I could get off drugs and be happy."

Thankfully, our newcomers are usually met by a group of friendly, smiling folks who are obviously fairly content with the lives they've found in Narcotics Anonymous. What an enormous amount of hope this provides! A newcomer, whose life has been deadly serious, is strongly attracted by an atmosphere of laughter and relaxation. Coming from a place where everything is taken seriously, where disaster always waits around the next corner, it's a welcome relief to enter a room and find people who generally don't take themselves too seriously, who are ready for something wonderful.

We learn to lighten up in recovery. We laugh at the absurdity of our addiction. Our meetings—those rooms filled with the lively, happy sounds of percolating coffee, clattering chairs, and laughing addicts—are the gathering places where we first welcome our newcomers and let them know that, yes, we're having fun now.

❖

Just for today: I can laugh at myself. I can take a joke. I will lighten up and have some fun today.

*"With the world in such a turmoil, I feel
I have been blessed to be where I am."*

Basic Text, p. 145

❖

Some days it doesn't pay to turn on the news, we hear so many stories about violence and mayhem. When we used, many of us grew accustomed to violence. Through the fog of our addiction, we rarely got too disturbed by the state of the world. When we are clean, however, many of us find we are particularly sensitive to the world around us. As recovering people, what can we do to make it a better place?

When we find ourselves disturbed by the turmoil of our world, we can find comfort in prayer and meditation. When it seems like everything is turned upside down, our contact with our Higher Power can be our calm in the midst of any storm. When we are centered on our spiritual path, we can respond to our fears with peace. And by living peaceably ourselves, we invite a spirit of peace to enter our world. As recovering people, we can affect positive change by doing our best to practice the principles of our program.

❖

Just for today: I will enhance peace in the world by living, speaking, and acting peacefully in my own life.

*"We have learned that it is okay to not know all
the answers, for then we are teachable and can learn
to live our new life successfully."*

Basic Text, p. 96

❖

In a way, addiction is a great teacher. And if addiction teaches us nothing else, it will teach us humility. We hear it said that it took our very best thinking to get to NA. Now that we're here, we're here to learn.

The NA Fellowship is a wonderful learning environment for the recovering addict. We aren't made to feel stupid at meetings. Instead, we find others who've been exactly where we've been and who've found a way out. All we have to do is admit that we don't have all the answers, then listen as others share what's worked for them.

As recovering addicts and as human beings, we have much to learn. Other addicts—and other humans—have much to teach us about what works and what doesn't. As long as we remain teachable, we can take advantage of the experience of others.

❖

Just for today: I will admit that I don't have all the answers. I will look and listen to the experience of others for the answers I need.

"We sit down with a notebook, ask for guidance, pick up our pen, and start writing."

Basic Text, p. 30

❖

When we're confused or in pain, our sponsor sometimes tells us to "write about it." Though we may groan as we drag out the notebook, we know that it will help. By laying it all out on paper, we give ourselves the chance to sort through what's bothering us. We know we can get to the bottom of our confusion and find out what's really causing our pain when we put the pen to the paper.

Writing can be rewarding, especially when working through the steps. Many members maintain a daily journal. Simply thinking about the steps, pondering their meaning, and analyzing their effect is not sufficient for most of us. There's something about the physical action of writing that helps to fix the principles of recovery in our minds and hearts.

The rewards we find through the simple action of writing are many. Clarity of thought, keys to locked places inside of us, and the voice of conscience are but a few. Writing helps us be more honest with ourselves. We sit down, quiet our thoughts, and listen to our hearts. What we hear in the stillness are the truths that we put down on paper.

❖

Just for today: One of the ways I can search for truth in recovery is to write. I will write about my recovery today.

> *"We... get a good look at what these defects*
> *are doing to our lives. We begin to long*
> *for freedom from these defects."*

Basic Text, p. 34

❖

Becoming entirely ready to have our defects of character removed can be a long process, often taking place over the course of a lifetime. Our state of readiness grows in direct proportion to our awareness of these defects and the destruction they cause.

We may have trouble seeing the devastation our defects are inflicting on our lives and the lives of those around us. If this is the case, we would do well to ask our Higher Power to reveal those flaws which stand in the way of our progress.

As we let go of our shortcomings and find their influence waning, we'll notice that a loving God replaces those defects with quality attributes. Where we were fearful, we find courage. Where we were selfish, we find generosity. Our delusions about ourselves will disappear to be replaced by self-honesty and self-acceptance.

Yes, becoming entirely ready means we will change. Each new level of readiness brings new gifts. Our basic nature changes, and we soon find our readiness is no longer sparked only by pain but by a desire to grow spiritually.

❖

Just for today: I will increase my state of readiness by becoming more aware of my shortcomings.

*"A lot of our chief concerns and major difficulties
come from our inexperience with living without drugs.
Often when we ask an oldtimer what to do,
we are amazed at the simplicity of the answer."*

Basic Text, p. 43

❖

Finding balance in recovery is quite a bit like sitting down with a set of scales and a pile of sand. The goal is to have an equal amount of sand on each side of the scales, achieving a balance of weight.

We do the same thing in recovery. We sit down with the foundation of our clean time and the Twelve Steps, then attempt to add employment, household responsibilities, friends, sponsees, relationships, meetings, and service in equal weights so that the scales balance. Our first try may throw our personal scales out of kilter. We may find that, because of our over-involvement in service, we have upset our employer or our family. But when we try to correct this problem by resigning from NA service altogether, the other side of the scales go out of balance.

We can ask for help from members who have stabilized their scales. These people are easy to recognize. They appear serene, composed, and self-assured. They'll smile in recognition at our dilemma and share how they slowed down, added only a few grains of sand at a time to either side of the scales, and were rewarded with balance in recovery.

❖

Just for today: I seek balance in my life. Today, I will ask others to share their experience in finding that balance.

*"For meditation to be of value, the results
must show in our daily lives."*

Basic Text, p. 47

❖

In working our program, we are given many indirect indications of a Higher Power's presence in our lives: the clean feeling that comes to so many of us in taking our Fifth Step; the sense that we are finally on the right track when we make amends; the satisfaction we get from helping another addict. Meditation, however, occasionally brings us *extraordinary* indications of God's presence in our lives. These experiences do not mean we have become perfect or that we are "cured." They are tastes given us of the source of our recovery itself, reminding us of the true nature of the thing we are pursuing in Narcotics Anonymous and encouraging us to continue walking our spiritual path.

Such experiences demonstrate, in no uncertain terms, that we have tapped a Power far greater than our own. But how do we incorporate that extraordinary Power into our ordinary lives? Our NA friends, our sponsor, and others in our communities may be more seasoned in spiritual matters than we are. If we ask, they can help us fit our spiritual experiences into the natural pattern of recovery and spiritual growth.

❖

Just for today: I will seek whatever answers I may need to understand my spiritual experiences and incorporate them into my daily life.

> *"The progression of recovery is
> a continuous uphill journey."*

Basic Text, p. 83

❖

The longer we stay clean, the steeper and narrower our path seems to become. But God doesn't give us more than we can handle. No matter how difficult the road becomes, no matter how narrow, how winding the turns, there is hope. That hope lies in our spiritual progression.

If we keep showing up at meetings and staying clean, life gets... well, *different.* The continual search for answers to life's ups and downs can lead us to question all aspects of our lives. Life isn't always pleasant. This is when we must turn to our Higher Power with even more faith. Sometimes all we can do is hold on tight, believing that things will get better.

In time, our faith will produce understanding. We will begin to see the "bigger picture" of our lives. As our relationship with our Higher Power unfolds and deepens, acceptance becomes almost second-nature. No matter what happens as we walk through recovery, we rely on our faith in a loving Higher Power and continue onward.

❖

Just for today: I accept that I don't have all the answers to life's questions. Nonetheless, I will have faith in the God of my understanding and continue on the journey of recovery.

*"Insanity is repeating the same mistakes
and expecting different results."*

Basic Text, p. 23

❖

Mistakes! We all know how it feels to make them. Many of us feel that our entire *lives* have been a mistake. We often regard our mistakes with shame or guilt—at the very least, with frustration and impatience. We tend to see mistakes as evidence that we are still sick, crazy, stupid, or too damaged to recover.

In truth, mistakes are a very vital and important part of being human. For particularly stubborn people (such as addicts), mistakes are often our best teachers. There is no shame in making mistakes. In fact, making new mistakes often shows our willingness to take risks and grow.

It's helpful, though, if we learn from our mistakes; repeating the same ones may be a sign that we're stuck. And expecting different results from the same old mistakes—well, that's what we call "insanity." It just doesn't work.

❖

Just for today: Mistakes aren't tragedies. But please, Higher Power, help me learn from them!

*"As we approach this step, most of us are afraid
that there is a monster inside of us that, if released,
will destroy us."*

Basic Text, p. 27

❖

Most of us are terrified to look at ourselves, to probe our insides. We're afraid that if we examine our actions and motives, we'll find a bottomless black pit of selfishness and hatred. But as we take the Fourth Step, we'll find that those fears were unwarranted. We're human, just like everyone else—no more, no less.

We all have personality traits that we're not especially proud of. On a bad day, we may think that our faults are worse than anyone else's. We'll have moments of self-doubt. We'll question our motives. We may even question our very existence. But if we could read the minds of our fellow members, we'd find the same struggles. We're no better or worse than anyone else.

We can only change what we acknowledge and understand. Rather than continuing to fear what's buried inside us, we can bring it out into the open. We'll no longer be frightened, and our recovery will flourish in the full light of self-awareness.

❖

Just for today: I fear what I don't know. I will expose my fears and allow them to vanish.

*"God's will for us becomes
our own true will for ourselves."*

Basic Text, p. 48

❖

The Twelve Steps are a path to spiritual awakening. This awakening takes the form of a developing relationship with a loving Higher Power. Each succeeding step strengthens that relationship. As we continue to work the steps, the relationship grows, becoming ever more important in our lives.

In the course of working the steps, we make a personal decision to allow a loving Higher Power to direct us. That guidance is always available; we need only the patience to seek it. Often, that guidance manifests itself in the inner wisdom we call our conscience.

When we open our hearts wide enough to sense our Higher Power's guidance, we feel a calm serenity. This peace is the beacon that guides us through our troubled feelings, providing clear direction when our minds are busy and confused. When we seek and follow God's will in our lives, we find the contentment and joy that often elude us when we strike out on our own. Fear or doubt may plague us when we attempt to carry out our Higher Power's will, but we've learned to trust the moment of clarity. Our greatest happiness lies in following the will of our loving God.

❖

Just for today: I will seek to strengthen my relationship with my Higher Power. I know from experience that knowledge of my Higher Power's will provides a sense of clarity, direction, and peace.

> *"We were entirely ready to have God remove
> all these defects of character."*

Step Six

❖

After taking the Fifth Step, many of us spend some time considering "the exact nature of our wrongs" and the part they'd played in making us who we were. What would our lives be like without, say, our arrogance?

Sure, arrogance had kept us apart from our fellows, preventing us from enjoying and learning from them. But arrogance had also served us well, propping up our ego in the face of critically low self-esteem. What advantage would be gained if our arrogance were removed, and what support would we be left with?

With arrogance gone, we would be one step closer to being restored to our proper place among others. We would become capable of appreciating their company and their wisdom and their challenges as their equals. Our support and guidance would come, if we chose, from the care offered us by our Higher Power; "low self-esteem" would cease to be an issue.

One by one, we examined our character defects this way, and found them all defective—after all, that's why they're *called* defects. And were we entirely ready to have God remove all of them? *Yes.*

❖

Just for today: I will thoroughly consider all my defects of character to discover whether I am ready to have the God of my understanding remove them.

> *"We made direct amends to such people*
> *wherever possible, except when to do so*
> *would injure them or others."*

Step Nine

❖

In every relationship, we don't always handle things the way we would have hoped. But friendships don't have to end when we make mistakes; instead, we can make amends. If we are sincerely willing to accept the responsibilities involved in friendship and make the amends we owe, those friendships can become stronger and richer than ever.

Making amends is simple. We approach the person we have harmed and say, "I was wrong." Sometimes we avoid getting to the point, evading an admission of our own part in the affair. But that frustrates the intent of the Ninth Step. To make effective amends, we have to keep it simple: we admit our part, and leave it at that.

There will be times when our friends won't accept our amends. Perhaps they need time to process what has happened. If that is the case, we must give them that time. After all, we were the ones in the wrong, not them. We have done our part; the rest is out of our hands.

❖

Just for today: I want to be a responsible friend. I will strive to keep it simple when making amends.

> *"We review our past performance and*
> *our present behavior to see what we want to keep*
> *and what we want to discard."*

Basic Text, p. 29

❖

As each day winds to a close, many of us reflect on the past twenty-four hours and consider how we can live differently in the future. It's easy for our thoughts to remain trapped in the mundane: change the oil in the car, keep the living room clean, or empty the litter box. Sometimes it takes a special effort to jog our thinking out of the daily rut and onto a higher track.

One simple question can put us on the high road: What do we think our Higher Power wants for us tomorrow? Maybe we need to improve our flagging conscious contact with the God of our understanding. Perhaps we've been uncomfortable in our job or our relationship, holding on only out of fear. We might be hiding some troubling defect of character, afraid to share it with our sponsor. The question is, in what parts of our lives do we really want to grow?

As each day ends, we find it beneficial to take some moments to spend time with our Higher Power. We can begin to reflect on what will benefit our program of spiritual growth most in the coming day. We think about the areas in which we have grown recently, and target areas that still require work. What more fitting way to end the day?

❖

Just for today: I will set aside some time at the end of the day to commune with my Higher Power. I will review the past day, meditating on what stands between me and my Higher Power's will for my life.

> *"We find ourselves doing and enjoying things
> that we never thought we would be doing."*

Basic Text, p. 102

❖

Active addiction kept us isolated for many reasons. In the beginning, we avoided family and friends so they wouldn't find out we were using. Some of us avoided *all* nonaddicts, fearing moral backlash and legal repercussions. We belittled people who had "normal" lives with families and hobbies; we called them "uncool," believing we could never enjoy the simple pleasures of life. Eventually, we even avoided other addicts because we didn't want to share our drugs. Our lives narrowed, and our concerns were confined to the daily maintenance of our disease.

Today, our lives are much fuller. We enjoy activities with other recovering addicts. We have time for our families. And we've discovered many other pursuits that give us pleasure. What a change from the past! We can live life just as fully as the "normal" people we once scorned. Enjoyment has returned to our lives, a gift of recovery.

❖

Just for today: I can find pleasure in the simple routines of daily living.

> *"Meetings keep us in touch with where we've been,
> but more importantly, with where we could go
> in our recovery."*

Basic Text, p. 56

❖

In many ways, addicts are different. When we came to Narcotics Anonymous we found others like ourselves, people who understood us and whom we could understand. No longer did we feel like aliens, strangers wherever we went. We were at home in NA meetings, among friends.

We don't stop being addicts after we've been clean awhile. We still need to identify with other addicts. We continue coming to NA meetings to keep in touch with who we are, where we've come from, and where we're going. Every meeting reminds us that we can never use drugs successfully. Every meeting reminds us that we'll never be cured, but that by practicing the principles of the program we can recover. And every meeting offers us the experience and example of other addicts in ongoing recovery.

At meetings, we see how different people work their program, and the results are apparent in their lives. If we want the lives we see others living, we can find out what they've done to get where they are. Narcotics Anonymous meetings offer us identification with where we've been and where we can go—identification we can't do without and can't get anywhere else. That keeps us coming back.

❖

Just for today: I will attend an NA meeting to remind myself of who I am, where I've come from, and where I can go in my recovery.

*"The steps lead to an awakening of a spiritual nature.
This awakening is evidenced by changes in our lives."*

Basic Text, p. 49

❖

We know how to recognize the disease of addiction. Its symptoms are indisputable. Besides an uncontrollable appetite for drugs, those suffering exhibit self-centered, self-seeking behavior. When our addiction was at its peak of activity, we were obviously in a great deal of pain. We relentlessly judged ourselves and others, and spent most of our time worrying or trying to control outcomes.

Just as the disease of addiction is evidenced by definite symptoms, so is a spiritual awakening made manifest by certain obvious signs in a recovering addict. We may observe a tendency to think and act spontaneously, a loss of interest in judging or interpreting the actions of anyone else, an unmistakable ability to enjoy each moment, and frequent attacks of smiling.

If we see someone exhibiting symptoms of a spiritual awakening, we should be aware that such awakenings are contagious. Our best course of action is to get close to these people. As we begin having frequent, overwhelming episodes of gratitude, an increased receptiveness to the love extended by our fellow members, and an uncontrollable urge to return this love, we'll realize that we, too, have had a spiritual awakening.

❖

Just for today: My strongest desire is to have a spiritual awakening. I will watch for its symptoms and rejoice when I discover them.

*"We want to be free of our guilt, but we don't wish
to do so at the expense of anyone else."*

Basic Text, p. 40

❖

Let's face it: Most of us left trails of destruction in our wakes and harmed anyone who got in our way. Some of the people we hurt most in our addiction were the people we loved most. In an effort to purge ourselves of the guilt we feel for what we've done, we may be tempted to share with our loved ones, in gruesome detail, things that are better left unsaid. Such disclosures could do much harm and may do little good.

The Ninth Step is not about easing our guilty consciences; it's about taking responsibility for the wrongs we've done. In working our Eighth and Ninth Steps, we should seek the guidance of our sponsor and amend our wrongs in a manner that won't cause us to owe more amends. We are not just seeking freedom from remorse—we are seeking freedom from our defects. We never again want to inflict harm on our loved ones. One way to insure that we do not is by working the Ninth Step responsibly, checking our motives, and discussing with our sponsor the particular amends we plan to make before we make them.

❖

Just for today: I wish to accept responsibility for my actions. Before making any amends, I will talk with my sponsor.

"As we grow, we learn to overcome the tendency to run and hide from ourselves and our feelings."

Basic Text, p. 85

❖

Rather than risk vulnerability, many of us have developed habits that keep others at a safe distance. These patterns of emotional isolation can give us the feeling we are hopelessly locked behind our masks. We used to take risks with our lives; now we can take risks with our feelings. Through sharing with other addicts, we learn that we are not unique; we do not make ourselves unduly vulnerable simply by letting others know who we are, for we are in good company. And by working the Twelve Steps of the NA program, we grow and change. We no longer want or need to hide our emerging selves. We are offered the opportunity to shed the emotional camouflage we developed to survive our active addiction.

By opening ourselves to others, we risk becoming vulnerable, but that risk is well worth the rewards. With the help of our sponsor and other recovering addicts, we learn how to express our feelings honestly and openly. In turn, we become nourished and encouraged by the unconditional love of our companions. As we practice spiritual principles, we find strength and freedom, both in ourselves and in those around us. We are set free to be ourselves and to enjoy the company of our fellow addicts.

❖

Just for today: I will openly and honestly share with another recovering addict. I will risk becoming vulnerable and celebrate my self and my friendship with other NA members. I will grow.

*"A lot happens in one day, both negative and positive.
If we do not take time to appreciate both, perhaps
we will miss something that will help us grow."*

IP No. 8, *Just for Today*

❖

Most of us seem to unconsciously judge what happens in our lives each day as good or bad, success or failure. We tend to feel happy about the "good" and angry, frustrated, or guilty about the "bad." Good and bad feelings, though, often have little to do with what's truly good or bad for us. We may learn more from our failures than our successes, especially if failure has come from taking a risk.

Attaching value judgments to our emotional reactions ties us to our old ways of thinking. We can change the way we think about the incidents of everyday life, viewing them as opportunities for growth, not as good or bad. We can search for lessons rather than assigning value. When we do this, we learn something from each day. Our daily Tenth Step is an excellent tool for evaluating the day's events and learning from both success and failure.

❖

Just for today: I am offered an opportunity to apply the principles of recovery so that I will learn and grow. When I learn from life's events, I succeed.

*"Our understanding of a Higher Power is up to us....
We can call it the group, the program,
or we can call it God."*

Basic Text, p. 24

❖

Many of us have a hard time with the idea of a Higher Power until we fully accept the depth of our own powerlessness over addiction. Once we do, most of us are at least willing to consider seeking the help of some Power greater than our disease. The first practical exposure many of us have to that kind of Power is in the NA group. Perhaps that's where we should start in developing our own understanding of God.

One evidence of the Power in the group is the unconditional love shown when NA members help one another without expectation of reward. The group's collective experience in recovery is itself a Power greater than our own, for the group has practical knowledge of what works and what doesn't. And the fact that addicts keep coming to NA meetings, day after day, is a demonstration of the presence of a Higher Power, some attractive, caring force at work that helps addicts stay clean and grow.

All these things are evidence of a Power that can be found in NA groups. When we look around with an open mind, each of us will be able to identify other signs of that Power. It doesn't matter if we call it God, a Higher Power, or anything else—just as long as we find a way to incorporate that Power into our daily lives.

❖

Just for today: I will open my eyes and my mind to signs of a Power that exists in my NA group. I will call upon that Power to help me stay clean.

*"...the decision to ask for God's help is our greatest
source of strength and courage."*

Basic Text, p. 26

❖

A challenge is anything that dares us to succeed. Things new and unfamiliar serve as challenges, whether those things appear good or bad to us. We are challenged by obstacles and opposition from within ourselves and from without. New and difficult things, obstacles and opposition, all are a part of "life on life's terms." Living clean means learning to meet challenges.

Many of us, consciously or unconsciously, took drugs to avoid meeting challenges. Many of us were equally afraid of failure and success. Each time we declined the day's challenge, we suffered a loss of self-esteem. Some of us used drugs to mask the shame we felt. Each time we did that, we became even less able to meet our challenges and more likely to use.

By working the NA program, we've found the tools we need to successfully meet any challenge. We've come to believe in a Power greater than ourselves, a Power that cares for our will and our lives. We've asked that Power to remove our character defects, those things that made our lives unmanageable. We've taken action to improve our conscious contact with that Higher Power. Through the steps, we've been given the ability to stop using drugs and start living.

Each day, we are faced with new challenges. And each day, through working our program of recovery, we are given the grace to meet those challenges.

❖

Just for today: I will ask my Higher Power to help me squarely meet today's challenge.

*"We examined our lives and discovered who
we really are. To be truly humble is to accept and
honestly try to be ourselves."*

Basic Text, p. 36

❖

As using addicts, the demands of our disease determined our personality. We could be whoever or whatever we needed to be in order to get our "fix." We were survival machines, adapting easily to every circumstance of the using life.

Once we began our recovery, we entered a new and different life. Many of us had no idea what behavior was appropriate for us in any given situation. Some of us didn't know how to talk to people, how to dress, or how to behave in public. We couldn't be ourselves because we didn't know who we were anymore.

The Twelve Steps give us a simple method for finding out who we really are. We uncover our assets and our defects, the things we like about ourselves and the things we're not so thrilled about. Through the healing power of the Twelve Steps, we begin to understand that we are individuals, created to be who we are by the Higher Power of our understanding. The real healing begins when we understand that if our Higher Power created us this way, it must be okay to be who we really are.

❖

Just for today: By working the steps I can experience the freedom to be myself, the person my Higher Power intended me to be.

"We believe that our Higher Power will take care of us."
Basic Text, p. 58

❖

We all have times when it seems as though our lives are falling apart. There are days, or even weeks, when it seems that everything that *can* go wrong *is* going wrong. Whether it's the loss of a job, the death of a loved one, or the end of a relationship, we doubt that we'll survive the changes taking place in our lives.

It's during the times when the world is crashing down around our ears that we find our greatest faith in a loving Higher Power. No human being could relieve our suffering; we know that only God's care can provide the comfort we seek. We feel broken but we go on, knowing that our lives will be repaired.

As we progress in our recovery and our faith in our Higher Power grows, we are sure to greet the difficult times with a sense of hope, despite the pain we may be in. We need not despair, for we know that our Higher Power's care will carry us through when we can't walk on our own.

❖

Just for today: I will rely on God's care through the painful times, knowing that my Higher Power will always be there.

*"Sharing with others keeps us
from feeling isolated and alone."*

Basic Text, p. 85

❖

There is a difference between being alone and being lonely. Being lonely is a state of the heart, an emptiness that makes us feel sad and sometimes hopeless. Loneliness is not always alleviated when we enter into relationships or surround ourselves with others. Some of us are lonely even in a room full of people.

Many of us came to Narcotics Anonymous out of the desperate loneliness of our addiction. After coming to meetings, we begin to make new friends, and often our feelings of loneliness ease. But many of us must contend with loneliness throughout our recovery.

What is the cure for loneliness? The best cure is to begin a relationship with a Higher Power that can help fill the emptiness of our heart. We find that when we have a belief in a Higher Power, we never have to feel lonely. We can be alone more comfortably when we have a conscious contact with a God of our understanding.

We often find deep fulfillment in our interactions with others as we progress in our recovery. Yet we also find that, the closer we draw to our Higher Power, the less we need to surround ourselves with others. We begin to find a spirit within us that is our constant companion as we continue to explore and deepen our connection with a Power greater than ourselves. We realize we are spiritually connected with something bigger than we are.

❖

Just for today: I will take comfort in my conscious contact with a Higher Power. I am never alone.

"We live a day at a time but also from moment to moment. When we stop living in the here and now, our problems become magnified unreasonably."

Basic Text, p. 99

❖

Life often seems too complicated to understand, especially for those of us who've dodged it for so long. When we stopped using drugs, many of us came face to face with a world that was confusing, even terrifying. Looking at life and all its details, all at once, may be overwhelming. We think that maybe we can't handle life after all and that it's useless to try. These thoughts feed themselves, and pretty soon we're paralyzed by the imagined complexity of life.

Happily, we don't have to fix everything at once. Solving a single problem seems possible, so we take them one at a time. We take care of each moment as it comes, and then take care of the next moment as it comes. We learn to stay clean just for today, and we approach our problems the same way. When we live life in each moment, it's not such a terrifying prospect. One breath at a time, we can stay clean and learn to live.

❖

Just for today: I will keep it simple by living in this moment only. Today, I will tackle only today's problems; I will leave tomorrow's problems to tomorrow.

❖ ❖ ❖
June
❖ ❖ ❖

*"We don't have to be clean when we get here but,
after the first meeting, we suggest that newcomers keep
coming back and come back clean. We don't have
to wait for an overdose or a jail sentence
to get help from Narcotics Anonymous."*

Basic Text, pp. 10–11

❖

Very few of us arrive in NA brimming with willingness. Some of us are here because we are court-ordered to attend. Some have come to save our families. Some come in an effort to salvage a career teetering on the brink of ruin. It doesn't matter why we are here. It only matters that we are.

We have heard it said that "if we bring the body, the mind will follow." We may come to meetings with a chip on our shoulders. We may be one of those who sits in the back of the rooms with our arms folded across our chest, glaring threateningly at anyone who approaches us. Perhaps we leave before the final prayer.

But if we keep coming back, we find that our minds begin to open up. We start to drop our guard, and begin to really listen when others share. We may even hear someone talking with whom we can relate. We begin the process of change.

After some time in NA, we find that more than our minds have arrived in our meeting rooms. More importantly, our hearts have arrived, too. After that happens, the miracles really begin!

❖

Just for today: I will strive to listen with an open mind to what I hear shared.

"We wanted an easy way out.... When we did seek help, we were only looking for the absence of pain."

Basic Text, p. 5

❖

Something's not working. In fact, something's been wrong for a long time, causing us pain and complicating our lives. The problem is that, at any given moment, it always appears easier to continue bearing the pain of our defects than to submit to the total upheaval involved in changing the way we live. We may long to be free of pain, but only rarely are we willing to do what's truly necessary to remove the source of pain from our lives.

Most of us didn't begin seeking recovery from addiction until we were "sick and tired of being tired and sick." The same is true of the lingering character defects we've carried through our lives. Only when we can't bear our shortcomings one moment longer, only when we know that the pain of change *can't* be as bad as the pain we're in today, are most of us willing to try something different.

Thankfully, the steps are always there, no matter what we're sick and tired of. The irony is that, as soon as we make the decision to begin the Twelve Step process, we realize our fears of change were groundless. The steps offer a gentle program of change, one step at a time. No single step is so frightening that we can't work it, by itself. As we apply the steps to our lives, we experience a change that frees us.

❖

Just for today: No matter what prevents me from living a full, happy life, I know the program can help me change, a step at a time. I need not be afraid of the Twelve Steps.

"We make our amends to the best of our ability."

Basic Text, p. 40

❖

The Ninth Step tells us to make direct amends wherever possible. Our experience tells us to follow up those direct amends with long-lasting changes in our attitudes and our behavior—that is, with *indirect* amends.

For example, say we've broken someone's window because we were angry. Looking soulfully into the eyes of the person whose window we've broken and apologizing would not be sufficient. We directly amend the wrong we've done by admitting it and replacing the window—we mend what we have damaged.

Then, we follow up our direct amends with *indirect* amends. If we've acted out on our anger, breaking someone's window, we examine the patterns of our behavior and our attitudes. After we repair the broken window, we seek to repair our broken attitudes as well—we try to "mend our ways." We modify our behavior, and make a daily effort not to act out on our anger.

We make direct amends by repairing the damage we do. We make indirect amends by repairing the attitudes that cause us to do damage in the first place, helping insure we won't cause further damage in the future.

❖

Just for today: I will make direct amends, wherever possible. I will also make indirect amends, "mending my ways," changing my attitudes, and altering my behavior.

"Our negative sense of self has been replaced by a positive concern for others."

Basic Text, p. 16

❖

Spreading gossip feeds a dark hunger in us. Sometimes we think the only way we can feel good about ourselves is to make someone else look bad by comparison. But the kind of self-esteem that can be purchased at another's expense is hollow and not worth the price.

How, then, do we deal with our negative sense of self? Simple. We replace it with a positive concern for others. Rather than dwell on our low self-esteem, we turn to those around us and seek to be of service to them.

This may seem to be a way of avoiding the issue, but it's not. There's nothing we can do by dwelling on our low sense of self except work ourselves into a stew of self-pity. But by replacing our self-pity with active, loving concern for others, we become the kind of people we *can* respect.

The way to build our self-esteem is not to tear others down, but to build them up through love and positive concern. To help us with this, we can ask ourselves if we are contributing to the problem or to the solution. Today, we can choose to build instead of destroy.

❖

Just for today: Though I may be feeling low, I don't need to tear someone down to build myself up. Today, I will replace my negative sense of self with a positive concern for others. I will build, not destroy.

> *"Although honesty is difficult to practice,*
> *it is most rewarding."*

Basic Text, p. 96

❖

How difficult we find it to be honest! Many of us come to NA so confused about what really happened in our lives that it sometimes takes months and years to sort it all out. The truth of our history is not always as we have told it. How can we begin to be more truthful?

Many of us find it the easiest to be honest in prayer. With our fellow addicts, we sometimes find that we have a hard time telling the whole truth. We feel certain that we won't be accepted if we let others know us as we really are. It's hard to live up to the "terminally hip and fatally cool" image so many of us portrayed! In prayer, we find an acceptance from our Higher Power that allows us to open our hearts with honesty.

As we practice this honesty with the God of our understanding, we often find that it has a ripple effect in our communications with others. We get in the habit of being honest. We begin to practice honesty when we share at meetings and work with others. In return, we find our lives enriched by deepening friendships. We even find that we can be more honest with ourselves, the most important person to be truthful with!

Honesty is a quality that is developed through practice. It isn't always easy to be totally truthful, but when we begin with our Higher Power, we find it easier to extend our honesty to others.

❖

Just for today: I will be honest with God, myself, and others.

> *"The Twelve Steps of Narcotics Anonymous*
> *are a progressive recovery process established*
> *in our daily living."*

Basic Text, p. 99

❖

After some time in recovery, we may find we are faced with what seem like overwhelming personal problems, angry feelings, and despair. When we realize what's going on, we may wail, "But I've been working so hard. I thought I was..." Recovered, maybe? Not hardly. Over and over, we hear that recovery is an ongoing process and that we are never cured. Yet we sometimes believe that if we just work our steps enough, pray enough, or go to enough meetings, we'll eventually... well, maybe not be *cured*, but be *something*!

And we are "something." We're recovering—recovering from active addiction. No matter what we've dealt with through the process of the steps, there will always be more. What we didn't remember or didn't think was important in our first inventory will surely present itself later on. Again and again, we'll turn to the process of the steps to deal with what's bothering us. The more we use this process, the more we'll trust it, for we can see the results. We go from anger and resentment to forgiveness, from denial to honesty and acceptance, and from pain to serenity.

Recovery doesn't happen overnight, and ours will never be complete. But each day brings new healing and the hope for more tomorrow.

❖

Just for today: I will do what I can for my recovery today and maintain hope in the ongoing process of recovery.

"Just for today I will have faith in someone in NA who believes in me and wants to help me in my recovery."

Basic Text, p. 100

❖

Not all of us arrive in NA and automatically stay clean. But if we keep coming back, we find in Narcotics Anonymous the support we need for our recovery. Staying clean is easier when we have someone who believes in us even when we don't believe in ourselves.

Even the most frequent relapser in NA usually has one staunch supporter who is always there, no matter what. It is imperative that we find that one person or group of people who believes in us. When we ask them if we will ever get clean, they will always reply, "Yes, you can and you will. Just keep coming back!"

We all need someone who believes in us, especially when we can't believe in ourselves. When we relapse, we undermine our already shattered self-confidence, sometimes so badly that we begin to feel utterly hopeless. At such times, we need the support of our loyal NA friends. They tell us that this can be our last relapse. They know from experience that if we keep coming to meetings, we will eventually get clean and stay clean.

It's hard for many of us to believe in ourselves. But when someone loves us unconditionally, offering support no matter how many times we've relapsed, recovery in NA becomes a little more real for us.

❖

Just for today: I will find someone who believes in me. I will believe in them.

*"This program offers hope. All you have to bring
with you is the desire to stop using and the willingness
to try this new way of life."*

IP No. 16, *For the Newcomer*

❖

From time to time we wonder if we're "doing it right" in Narcotics Anonymous. Are we attending enough meetings? Are we using our sponsor, or working the steps, or speaking, or reading, or living the "right" way? We value the fellowship of recovering addicts—we don't know what we'd do without it. What if the way we're practicing our program is "wrong"? Does that make us "bad" NA members?

We can settle our insecurities by reviewing our Third Tradition, which assures us that "the *only* requirement for membership is a desire to stop using." There aren't any rules that say we've got to attend *this* many meetings or these *particular* meetings, or work the steps *this* way at *this* pace, or live our lives to suit *these* people in order to remain NA members in good standing.

It's true that, if we want the kind of recovery we see in members we respect, we'll want to practice the kind of program that's made their recovery possible. But NA is a fellowship of freedom; we work the program the best way for *us,* not for someone else. The only requirement for membership is a desire to stop using.

❖

Just for today: I will look at the program I'm working in light of my own recovery. I will practice that program to the best of my ability.

"Lost dreams awaken and new possibilities arise."

Basic Text, p. 91

❖

Most of us had dreams when we were young. Whether we dreamed of a dynamic career, a large and loving family, or travels abroad, our dreams died when our addiction took hold. Anything we ever wanted for ourselves was cast away in our pursuit of drugs. Our dreams didn't go beyond the next drug and the euphoria we hoped it would bring.

Now in recovery, we find a reason to hope that our lost dreams could still come true. No matter how old we are, how much our addiction has taken from us, or how unlikely it may seem, our freedom from active addiction gives us the freedom to pursue our ambitions. We may discover that we're very talented at something, or find a hobby we love, or learn that continuing our education can bring remarkable rewards.

We used to put most of our energy into spinning excuses and rationalizations for our failures. Today, we go forward and make use of the many opportunities life presents to us. We may be amazed at what we're capable of. With our foundation of recovery, success, fulfillment, and satisfaction are within our reach at last.

❖

Just for today: Starting today, I'll do whatever I can to realize my dreams.

> *"When we finally get our own selfish motives*
> *out of the way, we begin to find a peace that*
> *we never imagined possible."*

Basic Text, p. 45

❖

As we examine our beliefs, our actions, and our motives in recovery, we'll find that sometimes we do things for the wrong reasons. In our early recovery, we may have spent a great deal of money and time on people, wanting only for them to like us. Later on, we may find that we still spend money on people, but our motives have changed. We do it because *we* like *them*. Or perhaps we used to get romantically involved because we felt hollow inside and were seeking fulfillment through another person. Now our reasons for romantic involvement are based in a desire to share our already rewarding lives with an equal partner. Maybe we used to work the steps because we were afraid we'd relapse if we didn't. Today we work the steps because we want to grow spiritually.

We have a new purpose in life today, and our changing motives reflect that. We have so much more to offer than our neediness and insecurities. We have developed a wholesomeness of spirit and a peace of mind that moves our recovery into a new realm. We extend our love and share our recovery with complete generosity, and the difference we make is the legacy we leave to those who have yet to join us.

❖

Just for today: In recovery, my motives have changed. I want to do things for the right reason, not just for my personal benefit. Today, I will examine my motives.

"As we recover, we gain a new outlook on being clean.... Life can become a new adventure for us."

Basic Text, p. 91

❖

The using life is not a clean one—no one knows this better than we do. Some of us lived in physical squalor, caring neither for our surroundings nor ourselves. Worse, though, than any external filth was the way most of us felt inside. The things we did to get our drugs, the way we treated other people, and the way we treated ourselves had us feeling dirty. Many of us recall waking too many mornings just wishing that, for once, we could feel clean about ourselves and our lives.

Today, we have a chance to feel clean by living clean. For us addicts, living clean starts with not using—after all, that's our primary use for the word "clean" in Narcotics Anonymous. But as we stay "clean" and work the Twelve Steps, we discover another kind of clean. It's the clean that comes from admitting the truth about our addiction rather than hiding or denying our disease. It's the freshness that comes from owning up to our wrongs and making amends for them. It's the vitality that comes from the new set of values we develop as we seek a Higher Power's will for us. When we practice the principles of our program in all our affairs, we have no reason to feel dirty about our lives or our lifestyles—we're living clean, and are grateful to be doing so at last.

"Clean living" used to be just for the "squares." Today, living clean is the only way we'd have it.

❖

Just for today: I feel clean because I'm living clean—and that's the way I want to keep it.

"Yes, we are a vision of hope..."

Basic Text, p. 53

❖

By the time we reached the end of our road, many of us had lost all hope for a life without the use of drugs. We believed we were destined to die from our disease. What an inspiration it was, then, coming to our first meeting and seeing a room full of addicts who were staying clean! A clean addict is, indeed, a vision of hope.

Today, we give that same hope to others. The newcomers see the joyful light in our eyes, notice how we carry ourselves, listen to us speak in meetings, and often want what we have found. They believe in us until they learn to believe in themselves.

Newcomers hear us carry a message of hope to them. They tend to see us through "rose-colored glasses." They don't always recognize our struggle with a particular character defect or our difficulties with improving our conscious contact with our Higher Power. It takes them time to realize that we, the "oldtimers" with three or six or ten years clean, often place personalities before principles or suffer from some other unsightly character defects.

Yes, the newcomer sometimes places us on a pedestal. It is good, though, to openly admit the nature of our struggles in recovery for, in time, the newcomer will be walking through those same trials. And that newcomer will remember that others walked through that difficulty and stayed clean.

❖

Just for today: I will remember that I am a beacon to all who follow in my path, a vision of hope.

*"The program works a miracle in our lives....
We become free to live."*

Basic Text, p. 11

❖

Most of us—if we've been in recovery for any length of time at all—have heard some member complaining in a meeting about being terribly overworked, too busy for meetings or sponsorship or other activities. In fact, *we* may have been the complaining member. The days seem so full: job, family and friends, meetings, activities, sponsorship, step work. "There just aren't enough hours in the day," the member complains, "to get everything done and meet everyone's demands on my time!"

When this happens, usually there's soft laughter from some of the other members—probably members who had planned to grumble about the same sort of thing. The laughter stems from our recognition that we are complaining about the miracle of the life that is ours today. Not so long ago, few of us were capable of having *any* of these "problems" in our life. We devoted all of our energy to maintaining our active addiction. Today we have full lives, complete with all the feelings and problems that go with living in reality.

❖

Just for today: I will remember that my life is a miracle. Instead of resenting how busy I am, I will be thankful my life is so full.

*"If we maintain our spiritual condition daily,
we find it easier to deal with the pain and confusion."*

Basic Text, p. 95

❖

When we first began searching for a Power greater than ourselves, many of us got stuck in old beliefs or ideas. These ranged from the fear of a punishing or vengeful God to no belief at all. Some of us felt we had done such terrible things that a loving Power would never have anything to do with us. Others were convinced that the "bad" things that happened to us would not have occurred if a loving Power had actually existed. It took time, effort, open-mindedness, and faith to acquire a working belief in a loving Higher Power that would guide us through life's challenges.

Even after we come to believe in a Power greater than ourselves, our old ideas can come back to haunt us. Major setbacks in our lives and the insecurity such events can trigger may give rise to the return of our old, inadequate ideas about God. When this happens, we need to assure ourselves that our Higher Power has not abandoned us but is waiting to help us make it through the hard times in our recovery. No matter how painful our loss may be, we will survive our setback and continue to grow if we maintain the faith our program has given us.

❖

Just for today: I have worked hard to build my faith in a loving, caring Higher Power that will guide me through life's challenges. Today, I will trust that Power.

> *"Many of us cling to our fears, doubts, self-loathing,*
> *or hatred because there is a certain distorted security*
> *in familiar pain. It seems safer to embrace what*
> *we know than to let go of it for the unknown."*

Basic Text, p. 34

❖

We have often heard it said that "when the pain of remaining the same becomes greater than the pain of changing, we will change." Our fear can keep us from growing, afraid to end relationships, change careers, attend new meetings, begin new friendships, or attempt anything out of the ordinary. We stay in situations that are no longer working far longer than we have to simply because what is familiar feels safer than the unknown.

Any change involves overcoming fear. "What if I'm alone forever?" we might think if we consider leaving our lover. "What if I find out I'm incompetent?" we may wonder when we contemplate changing careers. We may balk at attending new meetings because we will have to reach out. Our minds manufacture a hundred excuses for remaining right where we are, afraid to try something new.

We find that most of our pain comes not from change but from *resistance* to change. In NA, we learn that change is how we move forward in our lives. New friends, new relationships, new interests and challenges will replace the old. With these new things in our lives, we find new joys and loves.

❖

Just for today: I will release the old, embrace the new, and grow.

*"Some things we must accept, others we can change.
The wisdom to know the difference comes with growth
in our spiritual program."*

Basic Text, p. 95

❖

It's relatively easy to accept the things we like—it's the things we *don't* like that are hard to accept. But remaking the world and everyone in it to suit our tastes would solve nothing. After all, the idea that the world was to blame for all our problems was the attitude that kept us using—and that attitude nearly killed us.

In the course of working the steps, we begin to ask ourselves hard questions about the roles we ourselves have played in creating the unacceptable lives we've lived. In most cases, we've found that what needed changing was our own attitude and our own actions, not the people, places, and things around us.

In recovery, we pray for wisdom to know the difference between what can and can't be changed. Then, once we see the truth of our situation, we pray for the willingness to change ourselves.

❖

Just for today: Higher Power, grant me the wisdom to know the difference between what can be changed and what I must accept. Please help me gratefully accept the life I've been given.

> *"Reaching out is the beginning of the struggle*
> *that will set us free. It will break down the walls*
> *that imprison us."*

Basic Text, p. 83

❖

Many of us came to NA emotionally shattered. Years of using people and allowing them to use us had taken their toll on our ability to trust anyone, ourselves included. But the love and acceptance we found in Narcotics Anonymous encouraged us to reach out and get close to others.

The longer we stayed clean, the more we began to long for greater intimacy with our loved ones. We began reaching out in deeper, more meaningful ways, even though we might get hurt. Despite our fears of rejection, we decided to risk revealing ourselves, our beliefs, and our needs. We decided to let down our defensive walls.

The freedom we've found has been worth the risk involved. We know there is still work to do before we will be completely free of the barriers built by years of active addiction. But by reaching out to other addicts and allowing them to reach out to us, despite our human failings, we have come to know that we have a great capacity for love and intimacy. When set free of their restraining walls, our hearts hold great power.

❖

Just for today: I will let down my personal walls and reach out to others. I will allow my heart the freedom to love and be loved.

*"Indirect amends may be necessary where direct ones
would be unsafe or endanger other people."*

Basic Text, p. 41

❖

When we used, we allowed nothing to stand in the way of that next high. As a result, many of us didn't always know precisely whom we had injured, either financially or emotionally. When it came time to make amends through our Ninth Step, we found that there were so many people we had victimized that we might never remember them all.

With the help of our sponsor and other recovering members of NA, we found a solution to this obstacle. We vowed to complete these nameless amends by making restitution to our communities. We focused our service efforts on helping the still-suffering addict. In this manner, we found a way to give back to society.

Today, with the love and guidance of members in NA, we are giving back to the world around us rather than taking. We are making our communities better places to live by carrying the message of recovery to those we encounter in our daily lives.

❖

Just for today: I will make indirect amends by reaching out to an addict who may need help. I will strive in some small way to make my community a better place in which to live.

> *"We find that when we lose self-obsession,*
> *we are able to understand what it means*
> *to be happy, joyous, and free."*

Basic Text, p. 107

❖

The laughter in our meetings often surprises the newcomer. As a group, we appreciate the healing that healthy laughter brings. Even if we are deeply troubled, the joy that often fills the meeting rooms allows us, for a time, to have some fun with our recovery. Through humor, we can be temporarily relieved of our obsession with self.

Life on life's terms is often anything but funny. But if we can keep a sense of humor about us, things that might overwhelm us can be made bearable. How often have we allowed ourselves to be upset by incidents that, taken with a bit of humor, are not all that intolerable? When we become annoyed with people and events, a search for the humor in the situation can put things in a brighter perspective. An ability to find humor in a difficult situation is a gift to develop.

❖

Just for today: I will look to find the humor in adversity. When I make mistakes, I will find a way to laugh at the humor of my imperfections.

"For some, prayer is asking for God's help; meditation is listening for God's answer.... Quieting the mind through meditation brings an inner peace that brings us into contact with the God within us."

Basic Text, pp. 46–47

❖

"Be patient when you're learning to meditate," many of us were told. "It takes practice to know what to 'listen' for."

We're glad someone told us that, or many of us would have quit after a week or two of meditating. For the first few weeks, we may have sat each morning, stilled our thoughts, and "listened," just as the Basic Text said—but "heard" nothing. It may have taken a few more weeks before anything really happened. Even then, what happened was often barely noticeable. We were rising from our morning meditations feeling just a little better about our lives, a little more empathy for those we encountered during the day, and a little more in touch with our Higher Power.

For most of us, there was nothing dramatic in that awareness— no bolts of lightning or claps of thunder. Instead, it was something quietly powerful. We were taking time to get our egos and our ideas out of the way. In that clear space, we were improving our conscious contact with the source of our daily recovery, the God of our understanding. Meditation was new, and it took time and practice. But, like all the steps, it worked—when we worked it.

❖

Just for today: I will practice "listening" for knowledge of God's will for me, even if I don't know what to "listen" for yet.

> *"We have been experts at*
> *self-deception and rationalization."*

Basic Text, p. 28

❖

When we come to our first meeting and hear that we must be honest, we may think, "Well now, that shouldn't be too difficult. All I have to do is stop lying." To some of us, this comes easily. We no longer have to lie to our employers about our absence from work. We no longer have to lie to our families about where we were the night before. By not using drugs anymore, we find we have less to lie about. Some of us may have difficulty even with this kind of honesty, but at least learning not to lie is simple—you just don't do it, no matter what. With courage, determined practice, the support of our fellow NA members, and the help of our Higher Power, most of us eventually succeed at this kind of honesty.

Honesty, though, means more than just not lying. The kind of honesty that is truly indispensable in recovery is self-honesty, which is neither easy nor simple to achieve. In our addiction, we created a storm of self-deception and rationalization, a whirlwind of lies in which the small, quiet voice of self-honesty could not be heard. To become honest with ourselves, we first must stop lying to ourselves. In our Eleventh Step meditations, we must become quiet. Then, in the resulting stillness, we must listen for truth. When we become silent, self-honesty will be there for us to find.

❖

Just for today: I will be quiet and still, listening for the voice of truth within myself. I will honor the truth I find.

*"In our recovery, we find it essential to accept reality.
Once we can do this, we do not find it necessary to use
drugs in an attempt to change our perceptions."*

Basic Text, p. 90

❖

Drugs used to buffer us from the full force of life. When we
stop using drugs and enter recovery, we find ourselves confronted
directly with life. We may experience disappointment, frustration,
or anger. Events may not happen the way we want them to. The
self-centeredness we cultivated in our addiction has distorted our
perceptions of life; it is difficult to let go of our expectations and
accept life as it is.

We learn to accept our lives by working the Twelve Steps of
Narcotics Anonymous. We discover how to change our attitudes
and let go of character defects. We no longer need to distort the
truth or to run from situations. The more we practice the spiritual
principles contained in the steps, the easier it becomes to accept
life exactly as it comes to us.

❖

Just for today: I will practice self-acceptance by practicing the
Twelve Steps.

*"We didn't stumble into this fellowship brimming with love, honesty, open-mindedness, or willingness....
When we were beaten, we became willing."*

Basic Text, p. 20

❖

Surrender may be the necessary foundation for recovery, but sometimes we fight it. Most of us look back after some clean time and wonder why on earth we fought so hard to deny our powerlessness when surrender is what finally saved our lives.

As we recover, new opportunities to surrender present themselves. We can either struggle with everyone and everything we encounter or we can recall the benefits of our first surrender and stop fighting.

Most of the pain we experience comes from fighting, not surrendering. In fact, when we surrender, the pain ends and hope takes its place. We begin to believe that all will be well and, after some time, realize that our lives are much better as a result. We feel the same way we did when we gave up the illusion that we could control our using—relieved, free, and filled with fresh hope.

❖

Just for today: Is there a surrender I need to make today? I will remember my first surrender and remind myself that I don't need to fight anymore.

> *"...ever reminding us to place*
> *principles before personalities."*

Tradition Twelve

❖

Sometimes it's hard to accept others' character defects. As we recover together, we not only listen to others talk in meetings, we also watch how they walk through their recovery. The more we get to know other members, the more we become aware of how they live their lives. We may form opinions about how they "work their program." We may find that certain members upset us, or we may even hear ourselves say, "If I worked their program, I would surely use."

We have found tolerance to be a principle that strengthens not only our own recovery but also our relationships with individuals who are a source of irritation to us. It becomes easier to accept other members' frailties when we remember that we ourselves rarely turn over our own character defects until we become painfully aware of them.

❖

Just for today: I will strive to accept others as they are. I will try not to judge others. I will focus on the principles of love and acceptance.

*"The process of coming to believe restores us to sanity.
The strength to move into action comes
from this belief."*

Basic Text, p. 25

❖

Coming to believe is a process that stems from personal experience. Each of us has this experience; all addicts who find recovery in NA have solid evidence of a benevolent Power acting for good in their lives. Those of us who are recovering today, after all, are the fortunate ones. Many, many addicts die from our disease, never to experience what we have found in Narcotics Anonymous.

The process of coming to believe involves a willingness to recognize miracles for what they are. We share the miracle of being here clean, and each of us has other miracles that await only our acknowledgment. How many car accidents or overdoses or other near-catastrophes have we survived? Can we look back at our lives and see that we were not just "lucky"? Our experience in recovery, too, gives us examples of a Higher Power working for our good.

When we can look back at the evidence of a loving Higher Power acting on our behalf, it becomes possible to trust that this Higher Power will continue to help us in the future. And trust offers us the strength to move forward.

❖

Just for today: My recovery is more than coincidence. My strength comes from the knowledge that my Higher Power has never let me down and will continue to guide me.

"Our fears are lessened and faith begins to grow as we learn the true meaning of surrender. We are no longer fighting fear, anger, guilt, self-pity, or depression."

Basic Text, p. 27

❖

Surrender is the beginning of a new way of life. When driven primarily by self-will, we constantly wondered whether we'd covered all the bases, whether we'd manipulated that person in just the right way to achieve our ends, whether we'd missed a critical detail in our efforts to control and manage the world. We either felt afraid, fearing our schemes would fail; angry or self-pitying when they fell through; or guilty when we pulled them off. It was hard, living on self-will, but we didn't know any other way.

Not that surrender is always easy. On the contrary, surrender can be difficult, especially in the beginning. Still, it's easier to trust God, a Power capable of managing our lives, than to trust only ourselves, whose lives are unmanageable. And the more we surrender, the easier it gets.

When we turn our will and our lives over to the care of our Higher Power, all we have to do is our part, as responsibly and conscientiously as we can. Then we can leave the results up to our Higher Power. By surrendering, acting on faith, and living our lives according to the simple spiritual principles of this program, we can stop worrying and start living.

❖

Just for today: I will surrender self-will. I will seek knowledge of God's will for me and the power to carry it out. I will leave the results in my Higher Power's hands.

> *"When someone points out a shortcoming,
> our first reaction may be defensive. There will always
> be room for growth."*

Basic Text, p. 36

❖

Recovery is a process that brings about change in our lives. We need that change if we are to continue our growth toward freedom. It's important that we remain open-minded when others point out our shortcomings, for they are bringing to light opportunities for us to change and grow. Reacting defensively limits our ability to receive the help they are offering us; letting go of our defenses opens the door to change, growth, and new freedom.

Each day in the recovery process will bring an opportunity for further change and growth. The more we learn to greet change with an open mind and heart, the more we will grow and the more comfortable we will become with our recovery.

❖

Just for today: I will greet each opportunity for growth with an open mind.

> *"Working with others is only the beginning
> of service work."*

Basic Text, p. 59

❖

Service work calls for a selfless devotion to carrying the message to the still-suffering addict. But our attitude of service cannot stop there. Service also requires that we look at ourselves and our motives. Our efforts at service make us highly visible to the fellowship. In NA, it is easy to become a "big fish in a little pond." Our controlling attitude can easily drive away the newcomer.

Group conscience is one of the most important principles in service. It is vital to remember that the group conscience is what counts, not just our individual beliefs and desires. We lend our thoughts and beliefs to the development of a group conscience. Then when that conscience arises, we accept its guidance. The key is working with others, not against them. If we remember that we strive together to develop a collective conscience, we will see that all sides have equal merit. When all the discussions are over, all sides will come back together to carry a unified message.

It is often tempting to think that we know what is best for the group. If we remember that it doesn't matter if we get our way, then it is easier to allow service to be the vehicle it is intended to be—a way to carry the message to the addict who still suffers.

❖

Just for today: I will take part in the development of group conscience. I will remember that the world won't end just because I don't get my way. I will think about our primary purpose in all my service efforts. I will reach out to a newcomer.

*"Complacency is the enemy of members
with substantial clean time. If we remain complacent
for long, the recovery process ceases."*

Basic Text, p. 84

❖

After the first couple of years in recovery, most of us start to feel like there are no more big deals. If we've been diligent in working the steps, the past is largely resolved and we have a solid foundation on which to build our future. We've learned to take life pretty much as it comes. Familiarity with the steps allows us to resolve problems almost as quickly as they arise.

Once we discover this level of comfort, we may tend to treat it as a "rest stop" on the recovery path. Doing so, however, discounts the nature of our disease. Addiction is patient, subtle, progressive, and incurable. It's also fatal—we can *die* from this disease, unless we continue to treat it. And the treatment for addiction is a vital, ongoing program of recovery.

The Twelve Steps are a process, a path we take to stay a step ahead of our disease. Meetings, sponsorship, service, and the steps always remain essential to ongoing recovery. Though we may practice our program somewhat differently with five years clean than with five months, this doesn't mean the program has changed or become less important, only that our practical understanding has changed and grown. To keep our recovery fresh and vital, we need to stay alert for opportunities to practice our program.

❖

Just for today: As I keep growing in my recovery, I will search for new ways to practice my program.

*"Our newly found faith serves as a firm foundation
for courage in the future."*

Basic Text, p. 96

❖

The foundation of our lives is what the rest of our lives is built upon. When we were using, that foundation affected everything we did. When we decided that recovery was important, that's where we began to put our energy. As a result, our whole lives changed. In order to maintain those new lives, we must maintain the foundation of those lives: our recovery program.

As we stay clean and our lifestyles change, our priorities will also change. Work and school may become important because they improve the quality of our lives. And new relationships may bring excitement and mutual support. But we need to remember that our recovery program is the foundation upon which our new lives are built. Each day, we must renew our commitment to recovery, maintaining that as our top priority.

❖

Just for today: I want to continue enjoying the life I've found in recovery. Today, I will take steps to maintain my foundation.

July

❖ ❖ ❖

July

❖ ❖ ❖

*"The program is simply sharing,
working the Twelve Steps, attending meetings,
and practicing the principles of the program."*

❖

Our complicated lives can be made a lot less complicated if we concentrate on a few simple things—sharing our experience, strength, and hope with others, regular meeting attendance, and practicing the principles of the program in our daily lives.

By sharing our experience, strength, and hope with other addicts, we provide a powerful example for newcomers to follow. The effort we put into helping others also helps keep self-centeredness, the core of our disease, at bay.

Many of us pick one group, a "home group," whose meetings we attend faithfully. This regularity gives some routine to our lives, and lets others know where they can find us if they need us.

Practicing the Twelve Steps in our daily lives makes the difference between a balanced recovery and simply not using. The steps give us some much-needed guidance in managing our everyday affairs.

Yes, we are complex people. But the NA program simplifies our lives, enabling us to live a life free from active addiction. Our lives can be filled with serenity and hope when we live by the guidance of the simple principles of our program.

❖

Just for today: I will remember that, while I am a complex person, NA is the simplest way for me to make my life less complicated.

*"Our personal stories may vary in individual pattern,
but in the end we all have the same thing in common."*

Basic Text, p. 87

❖

We addicts are a varied bunch, coming from different backgrounds, having used different drugs, and recalling different experiences. Our differences don't disappear in recovery; for some, those differences become even more pronounced. Freedom from active addiction gives us the freedom to be ourselves, as we truly are. The fact that we are all recovering doesn't mean that we all necessarily have the same needs or goals. Each of us has our own lessons to learn in recovery.

With so many differences from one addict to the next, how do we help one another in recovery and how do we use each other's experience? We come together to share our lives in light of the principles of recovery. Though our lives are different, the spiritual principles we apply are the same. It is by the light of these principles, shining through our differences, that we illuminate one another's way on our individual paths.

We all have two things in common: addiction and recovery. When we listen carefully, we hear others tell of suffering from the same disease we have suffered from, regardless of their specific backgrounds. When we open our ears, we hear other addicts talk of applying spiritual principles that promise hope to us as well, regardless of our personal goals.

❖

Just for today: I have my own path to follow, yet I'm grateful for the fellowship of others who've suffered from addiction and who are learning to apply the principles of recovery, just like me.

> *"Many of us have found that setting aside quiet time
> for ourselves is helpful in making conscious contact
> with our Higher Power."*

Basic Text, p. 95

❖

Most of us pay lip-service to the value of conscious contact with a Higher Power. Yet how many of us consistently take time to improve that conscious contact? If we've not already established a regular regimen of prayer and meditation, today is the day to start one.

A "quiet time" need not be long. Many of us find that twenty to thirty minutes is enough time to quiet ourselves, focus our attention with a spiritual reading, share our thoughts and concerns in prayer, and take a few moments to listen for an answer in meditation. Our "quiet time" need not be lengthy to be effective, provided it is consistent. Twenty minutes taken once a month to pray will probably do little but frustrate us with the poor quality of our conscious contact. Twenty minutes taken regularly each day, however, renews and reinforces an already lively contact with our Higher Power.

In the hustle and bustle of the recovering addict's day, many of us end up going from morning to night without taking time out to improve our conscious contact with the God we've come to understand. However, if we set aside a particular time of the day, every day, as "quiet time," we can be sure that our conscious contact will improve.

❖

Just for today: I will set aside a few moments, once I finish reading today's entry, to pray and meditate. This will be the beginning of a new pattern for my recovery.

> *"We learn that conflicts are a part of reality,*
> *and we learn new ways to resolve them*
> *instead of running from them."*

Basic Text, p. 90

❖

From time to time, we all experience conflicts. It may be that we just can't get along with that new coworker. Maybe our friends are driving us crazy. Or perhaps our partner isn't living up to our expectations. Dealing with any conflict is difficult for recovering addicts.

When tempers rise, it is often a good idea to back away from the situation until cooler minds prevail. We can always return for further discussion when we have calmed down. We can't avoid troubling situations, but we can use time and distance to find perspective.

Conflict is a part of life. We can't go through our entire recovery without encountering disagreements and differences of opinion. Sometimes we can back away from these situations, taking time to reflect on them, but there always comes a time when conflict must be resolved. When that time comes, we take a deep breath, say a prayer, and apply the principles our program has given us: honesty, openness, responsibility, forgiveness, trust, and all the rest. We didn't get clean to keep running from life—and in recovery, we don't have to run anymore.

❖

Just for today: The principles my program has given me are sufficient to guide me through any situation. I will strive to confront conflict in a healthy way.

*"The nature of our belief will determine the manner
of our prayers and meditation."*

Basic Text, p. 44

❖

How do we pray? For each NA member, this is a deeply personal matter. Many of us find that, over time, we develop a manner of prayer and meditation based on what we learn from others and what we are comfortable with.

Some of us arrive in NA with a closed mind toward a Power greater than ourselves. But when we sit down with our sponsor and discuss our difficulty, looking at the Second Step in depth, we are pleased to find that we can choose any concept of a Higher Power that appeals to us.

Just as our definition of a Power greater than ourselves differs from addict to addict, so does our manner of achieving a "conscious contact." Some attend religious services; some chant; some sit quietly or talk with whatever is out there; some find a spiritual connection by communing with nature. The "right way" to pray and meditate is whatever way helps us improve our conscious contact with our own Higher Power.

Asking others how they found their spiritual guidance is always a good place to begin. Reading literature before we enter periods of meditation can also help us. Many have gone before us on this search. As we seek spiritual growth, we can greatly benefit from their experience.

❖

Just for today: I will explore my options for improving my conscious contact with the God of my understanding.

> *"The main thing [the Eighth Step] does for us is*
> *to help build awareness that, little by little,*
> *we are gaining new attitudes about ourselves*
> *and how we deal with other people."*

Basic Text, p. 39

❖

To say "I'm sorry" probably isn't such a foreign idea to most of us. In our active addiction, it may have been a very familiar phrase. We were always telling people how sorry we were, and were probably deeply surprised when someone, tired of our meaningless apologies, responded with, "You sure are. In fact, you're the sorriest excuse for..." That may have been our first clue that an "I'm sorry" didn't really make any difference to those we harmed, especially when we both knew that we'd just do the same thing again.

Many of us thought that making amends would be another "I'm sorry." However, the action we take in those steps is entirely different. Making amends means to make changes and, above all, to make the situation *right*. If we stole money, we don't just say, "I'm sorry. I'll never do it again now that I'm clean." We pay the money back. If we neglected or abused our families, we don't just apologize. We begin to treat them with respect.

Amending our behavior and the way we treat ourselves and others is the whole purpose of working the steps. We're no longer just "sorry"; we're responsible.

❖

Just for today: I accept responsibility for myself and my recovery. Today, I will amend some particular thing I'm sorry for.

"One aspect of our spiritual awakening comes through the new understanding of our Higher Power that we develop by sharing another addict's recovery."

Basic Text, p. 52

❖

We've heard it said that we often see God most clearly in one another. We see the truth of this when we practice our Twelfth Step. When we carry the recovery message to another addict, we sense the presence of a Power greater than ourselves. And as we watch the message take hold, we realize something else: It's the message that brings recovery, not the messenger. A Higher Power, not our own power, is the source of the change that begins when we carry the message to a still-suffering addict.

As the message does its work, transforming the life of another addict, we see a Higher Power in action. We watch as acceptance and hope replace denial and despair. Before our very eyes, the first traces of honesty, open-mindedness, and willingness begin to appear. Something's happening inside this person, something bigger and more powerful than either of us. We're watching the God we've come to understand at work in someone's life. We see the Higher Power in them. And we know with greater certainty than ever that this Higher Power is in us, too, as the force driving our recovery.

❖

Just for today: As I carry the message of recovery to other addicts, I will try to pay attention to the Power behind the message. Today, as I watch other addicts recover, I will try to recognize the God in them so I can better recognize the God in myself.

> *"It is important for you to know that you will hear
> God mentioned at NA meetings. What we are referring
> to is a Power greater than ourselves that makes possible
> what seems impossible."*

IP No. 22, *Welcome to NA*

❖

Most of us come to Narcotics Anonymous with a variety of preconceptions about what the word "God" means, many of them negative. Yet the "G" word is used very regularly in NA, if not constantly. It occurs 92 times in the first 107 pages of our Basic Text, and appears prominently in a third of our Twelve Steps. Rather than sidestep the sensitivity many of us feel toward the word, let's address it head on.

It's true that Narcotics Anonymous is a spiritual program. Our Twelve Steps offer a way to find freedom from addiction through the help of a spiritual Power greater than we are. The program, however, doesn't tell us anything about what we have to think about that Power. In fact, over and over again, in our literature and our steps and our meetings, we hear it said, "the God of our understanding"—*whatever* that understanding may be.

We use the word "God" because it's used in our Basic Text and because it communicates most effectively to most people a basic understanding of the Power underlying our recovery. The word, we use for the sake of convenience. The Power behind the word, however, we use for more than convenience. We use that Power to maintain our freedom from addiction and to ensure our ongoing recovery.

❖

Just for today: Whether I believe in "God" or not, I will use the Power that keeps me clean and free.

> *"...the time has come when that tired old lie, 'Once an addict, always an addict,' will no longer be tolerated by either society or the addict himself. We do recover."*

Basic Text, p. 89

❖

From time to time, we hear speakers share that they don't really understand spiritual principles yet. They tell us that if we knew what went on in their minds, we'd be amazed at how insane they still are. They tell us that the longer they're clean, the less they know about anything. In the next breath, these same speakers tell us about the profound changes recovery has made in their lives. They have moved from complete despair to unfailing hope, from uncontrollable drug use to total abstinence, from chronic unmanageability to responsibility through working the Twelve Steps of Narcotics Anonymous. Which story is true? Do we or don't we recover?

We may think we demonstrate humility or gratitude by underplaying the change that recovery has brought to our lives. True, we do injustice to the program when we take credit for this miracle ourselves. But we do an equal injustice—to ourselves and to those we share with—when we don't acknowledge this miracle's magnitude.

We do recover. If we have trouble seeing the miracle of recovery, we'd better look again. Recovery is alive and at work in Narcotics Anonymous—in our oldtimers, in the newcomers flooding our meetings, and most of all in ourselves. All we have to do is open our eyes.

❖

Just for today: I will acknowledge the miracle of my recovery and be grateful that I've found it.

*"That old nest of negativism followed me
everywhere I went."*

Basic Text, p. 137

❖

A negative attitude is the trademark of active addiction. Everything that occurred in our lives was someone or something else's fault. We had blaming others for our shortcomings down to a fine science. In recovery, one of the first things we strive to develop is a new attitude. We find that life goes a lot easier when we replace our negative thinking with positive principles.

While a negative attitude dogged us in our active addiction, all too often it can follow us into the rooms of Narcotics Anonymous. How can we begin to adjust our attitudes? By altering our actions. It isn't easy, but it can be done.

We can start by listening to the way we talk. Before we open our mouths, we ask ourselves some simple questions: Does what I'm going to say speak to the problem, or the solution? Is what I'm going to say framed in a kind manner? Is what I have to say important, or would everyone be just as well off if I kept my mouth shut? Am I talking just to hear myself talk, or is there some purpose to my "words of wisdom"?

Our attitudes are expressed in our actions. Often, it's not what we say, but the way we say it, that really matters. As we learn to speak in a more positive manner, we will notice our attitudes improving as well.

❖

Just for today: I want to be free of negativity. Today, I will speak and act positively.

"We share comfort and encouragement with others."

Basic Text, p. 99

❖

Many of us have watched as babies take their first steps. The mother holds the child on its feet. The father kneels nearby with outstretched arms, encouraging the little one, his face flooded with devotion. The baby takes a few small steps toward its father. An older brother and sister cheer the tyke on. Baby falls down. Its mother, murmuring words of comfort, picks the child up and starts over again. This time, baby stays up until it is close enough to fall into the safety of its father's arms.

As newcomers, we arrive in the rooms of NA much like this small child. Accustomed to living a life crippled by addiction, full of fear and uncertainty, we need help to stand. Just like a child beginning its march toward adulthood, we take our halting first steps toward recovery. We learn to live this new way of life because others who have gone before us encourage and comfort us by telling us what worked—and what didn't work—for them. Our sponsor is there for us when we need a push in the right direction.

Many times we feel like we can't take another step in recovery. Just like a child learning to walk, we sometimes stumble or fall. But our Higher Power always awaits us with outstretched arms. And like the child's brothers and sisters shouting their encouragement, we, too, are supported by other NA members as we walk toward a full life in recovery.

❖

Just for today: I will seek encouragement from others. I will encourage others who may need my strength.

---

*"We were trapped by our need for the instant
gratification that drugs gave us."*

Basic Text, p. 25

❖

"I want what I want, and I want it *now*!" That's about as patient as most of us ever got in our active addiction. The obsession and compulsion of our disease gave us a "one-track" way of thinking; when we wanted something, that's all we thought about. And the drugs we took taught us that instant gratification was never more than a dose away. It's no wonder that most of us came to Narcotics Anonymous with next to no patience.

The problem is, we can't always get what we want whenever we want it. Some of our wishes are pure fantasy; if we think about it, we'll realize we have no reason to believe those wishes will be fulfilled in our lifetimes. We probably can't even fulfill all our realistic desires; we certainly can't fulfill them all at once. In order to acquire or achieve some things, we will have to sacrifice others.

In our addiction we sought instant gratification, squandering our resources. In recovery we must learn to prioritize, sometimes denying the gratification of some desires in order to fulfill more important long-term goals. To do so requires patience. To find that patience, we practice our program of recovery, seeking the kind of full-bodied spiritual awakening that will allow us to live and enjoy life on life's terms.

❖

Just for today: Higher Power, help me discover what's most important in my life. Help me learn patience, that I can devote my resources to the important things.

"If we are hurting, and most of us do from time to time, we learn to ask for help."

Basic Text, p. 83

❖

Sometimes recovery gets downright difficult. It can be even more difficult to get humble enough to ask for help. We think, "I have all this time clean. I should be better than this!" But the reality of recovery is simple: Whether we have thirty days or thirty years clean, we must be willing to ask for help when we need it.

Humility is a common theme in our Twelve Steps. The program of Narcotics Anonymous is not about keeping up appearances. Instead, the program helps us get the most from our recovery. We must be willing to lay bare our difficulties if we expect to find solutions to problems that arise in our lives.

There's an old expression sometimes heard in Narcotics Anonymous: We can't save our face and our ass at the same time. It isn't easy to share in a meeting when we have a number of years clean only to dissolve into tears because life on life's terms has made us realize our powerlessness. But when the meeting ends and another member comes up and says, "You know, I really needed to hear what you had to say," we know that there is a God working in our lives.

The taste of humility is never bitter. The rewards of humbling ourselves by asking for help sweeten our recovery.

❖

Just for today: If I need help, I will ask for it. I will put humility into action in my life.

"Social acceptability does not equal recovery."
                                              Basic Text, p. 22

❖

One of the first things that happens to many of us in recovery is that we start to look better. We get healthier; we bathe; we dress more appropriately. And without the goading of active addiction, many of us finally stop stealing, lying, and hustling. We start to look *normal*—just by removing the drugs.

Looking normal is very different from being normal. Acceptability in the eyes of the world is a benefit of recovery; it is not the same thing as recovery. We can enjoy the benefits of recovery, but we must take care to nurture their true source. Lasting recovery isn't found in acceptance from others, but in the inner growth set in motion by the Twelve Steps.

❖

Just for today: I know that looking good isn't enough. Lasting recovery is an inside job.

"We made a list of all persons we had harmed and became willing to make amends to them all."

Step Eight

❖

All human beings struggle with self-centeredness. The chronic self-centeredness that lies at the very core of addiction makes that struggle doubly difficult for people like us. Many of us have lived as if we believed we were the last people on earth, utterly blind to the effect our behavior has had on those around us.

The Eighth Step is the process our program has given us to honestly examine our past relationships. We take a look at the writing we did on our Fourth Step to identify the effects our actions had on the people in our lives. When we recognize harm done to some of those people, we become willing to take responsibility for our actions by making amends to them.

The variety of people we encounter in our day and the quality of our relations with them determines, to a great extent, the quality of our very lives. Love, humor, excitement, caring—the things that make life worth living derive much of their meaning from being shared with others. Understanding this, we want to discover the true nature of our relationships with other people and mend whatever breaks we may find in those relations. We want to work the Eighth Step.

❖

Just for today: I want to fully enjoy the companionship of my fellows. I will examine my relationships with the people in my life. Where I find I've harmed others, I will seek the willingness to make amends to them.

*"Deep inside, I had feelings
of inadequacy and inferiority."*

❖

Somewhere along the way, many of us developed strong feelings of inadequacy and inferiority. Deep inside was a voice that continually cried out, "You're worthless!" Many of us learn to recognize this characteristic of low self-esteem very early in our recovery. Some of us may feel that our feelings of inferiority were where all our problems began.

Whether we learn this low self-esteem in our families or through our interactions with others, in NA we learn the tools for reclaiming ourselves. Building up our fractured self-esteem sometimes begins by simply accepting a service position. Or perhaps our phone begins to ring, and for the first time people are calling just to see how we are. They don't want anything from us but to reach out and help.

Next we get a sponsor, someone who teaches us that we are worthwhile and believes in us until we can believe in ourselves. Our sponsor guides us through the Twelve Steps where we learn who we really are, not who we have built ourselves up or down to be.

Low self-esteem doesn't go away overnight. Sometimes it takes years for us to really get in touch with ourselves. But with the help of other members of NA who share our same feelings, and by working the Twelve Steps, we blossom into individuals whom others and, most importantly, we ourselves respect.

❖

Just for today: I will remember that I am deserving of my Higher Power's love. I know that I am a worthy human being.

"Do we fully accept the fact that our every attempt to stop using or to control our using failed?"

Basic Text, p. 19

❖

The room is dark. Your forehead is bathed in cold sweat. Your heart is racing. You open your eyes, sure that you've just blown your clean time. You've had a "using dream," and it was just like being there—the people, the places, the routine, the sick feeling in your stomach, everything. It takes a few moments to realize it was just a nightmare, that it didn't actually happen. Slowly, you settle down and return to sleep.

The next morning is the time to examine what really happened the night before. You didn't use last night—but how close are you to using today? Do you have any illusions about your ability to control your using? Do you know, without a doubt, what would happen once you took the first drug? What stands between you and a real, live relapse? How strong is your program? Your relationships with your sponsor, your home group, and your Higher Power?

Using dreams don't necessarily indicate a hole in our program; for a drug addict, there's nothing more natural than to dream of using drugs. Some of us think of using dreams as gifts from our Higher Power, vividly reminding us of the insanity of active addiction and encouraging us to strengthen our recovery. Seen in that light, we can be grateful for using dreams. Frightening as they are, they can prove to be great blessings—if we use them to reinforce our recovery.

❖

Just for today: I will examine my personal program. I will talk with my sponsor about what I find, and seek ways to strengthen my recovery.

*"Our disease always resurfaced or continued to progress
until in desperation, we sought help from each
other in Narcotics Anonymous."*

Basic Text, p. 13

❖

When we think of being desperate, we envision an undesirable
state: a poor, bedraggled soul frantically clawing at something
sorely needed, a desperate look in the eyes. We think of hunted
animals, hungry children, and of ourselves before we found NA.

Yet it was the desperation we felt before coming to NA that
compelled us to accept the First Step. We were fresh out of ideas,
and so became open to new ones. Our insanity had finally risen
higher than our wall of denial, forcing us to get honest about
our disease. Our best efforts at control had only worn us out;
hence, we became willing to surrender. We had received the gift
of desperation and, as a result, were able to accept the spiritual
principles that make it possible for us to recover.

Desperation is what finally drives many of us to ask for help.
Once we've reached this state, we can turn around and start anew.
Just as the desperate, hunted animal seeks a safe haven, so do
we: in Narcotics Anonymous.

❖

Just for today: The gift of desperation has helped me become
honest, open-minded, and willing. I am grateful for this gift because it has made my recovery possible.

*"Dreams that we gave up long ago can
now become realities."*

Basic Text, p. 71

❖

All things begin with a dream. But how many of us fulfilled our dreams while using? Even if we managed to complete something we had started, our addiction usually robbed us of any pride in our accomplishment. Perhaps when we used, we dreamed of the day when we would be clean. That day has come. We can use this day to make our dreams come true.

To fulfill our dreams we must take action, but our lack of self-confidence may keep us from trying. We can begin by setting realistic goals. The success we experience when we attain our initial goals allows us to dream bigger dreams the next time around.

Some of our members share that when they compare the ambitions they had when they first got clean with what they have actually achieved in recovery, they are astounded. In recovery, we often find more dreams come true than we could ever have imagined.

❖

Just for today: I will remember that all things begin with a dream. Today, I will allow myself to make my dreams come true.

*"We admitted that we were powerless over our
addiction, that our lives had become unmanageable."*

Step One

❖

The First Step begins with "we," and there's a reason for that. There is great strength in making a verbal admission of our powerlessness. And when we go to meetings and make this admission, we gain more than personal strength. We become members, part of a collective "we" that allows us, together, to recover from our addiction. With membership in NA comes a wealth of experience: the experience of other addicts who have found a way to recover from their disease.

No longer must we try to solve the puzzle of our addiction on our own. When we honestly admit our powerlessness over our addiction, we can begin the search for a better way to live. We won't be searching alone—we're in good company.

❖

Just for today: I will start the day with an admission of my powerlessness over addiction. I will remind myself that the First Step starts with "we," and know that I never have to be alone with my disease again.

> *"If, after a period of time, we find ourselves in trouble
> with our recovery, we have probably stopped
> doing one or more of the things that helped us
> in the earlier stages of our recovery."*

Basic Text, p. 95

❖

Surrender is just for newcomers, right? Wrong!

After we've been around awhile, some of us succumb to a condition particular to oldtimers. We think we know something about recovery, about God, about NA, about ourselves—and we do. The problem is, we think we know *enough,* and we think that merely *knowing* is enough. But it's what we learn and what we do *after* we think we know it all that really makes the difference.

Conceit and complacency can land us in deep trouble. When we find that "applying the principles" on our own power just isn't working, we can practice what worked for us in the beginning: surrender. When we find we are still powerless, our lives again unmanageable, we need to seek the care of a Power greater than ourselves. And when we discover that self-therapy isn't so therapeutic after all, we need to take advantage of "the therapeutic value of one addict helping another."

❖

Just for today: I need guidance, support, and a Power beyond my own. I will go to a meeting, reach out to a newcomer, call my sponsor, pray to my Higher Power—I will do something that says, "I surrender."

"For us, to use is to die, often in more ways than one."

Basic Text, p. 82

❖

As newcomers, many of us came to our first meeting with only a small spark of life remaining. That spark, our spirit, wants to survive. Narcotics Anonymous nurtures that spirit. The love of the fellowship quickly fans that spark into a flame. With the Twelve Steps and the love of other recovering addicts, we begin to blossom into that whole, vital human being our Higher Power intended us to be. We begin to enjoy life, finding purpose in our existence. Each day we choose to stay clean, our spirit is revitalized and our relationship with our God grows. Our spirit becomes stronger each day we choose life by staying clean.

Despite the fact that our new life in recovery is rewarding, the urge to use can sometimes be overwhelming. When everything in our lives seems to go wrong, a return to using can seem like the only way out. But we know what the consequence will be if we use—the loss of our carefully nurtured spirituality. We have traveled too far along the spiritual path to dishonor our spirit by using. Snuffing the spiritual flame we have worked so hard to restore in our recovery is too dear a price to pay for getting high.

❖

Just for today: I am grateful that my spirit is strong and vital. Today, I will honor that spirit by staying clean.

> *"We want and demand that things always go our way.*
> *We should know from our past experience that*
> *our way of doing things did not work."*

Basic Text, p. 93

❖

All of us have ideas, plans, goals for our lives. There's nothing in the NA program that says we shouldn't think for ourselves, take initiative, and put responsible plans into action. It's when our lives are driven by self-will that we run into problems.

When we are living willfully, we go beyond thinking *for* ourselves—we think only *of* ourselves. We forget that we are but a part of the world and that whatever personal strength we have is drawn from a Higher Power. We might even go so far as to imagine that other people exist solely to do our bidding. Quickly, we find ourselves at odds with everyone and everything around us.

At this point, we have two choices. We can continue in our slavery to self-will, making unreasonable demands and becoming frustrated because the planet doesn't spin our way. Or we can surrender, relax, seek knowledge of God's will and the power to carry that out, and find our way back to a condition of peace with the world. Thinking, taking initiative, making responsible plans—there's nothing wrong with these things, so long as they serve God's will, not merely our own.

❖

Just for today: I will plan to do God's will, not mine. If I find myself at odds with everything around me, I will surrender self-will.

*"...we covered low self-esteem by hiding behind phony
images that we hoped would fool people.
The masks have to go."*

Basic Text, p. 33

❖

Over-sensitivity, insecurity, and lack of identity are often associated with active addiction. Many of us carry these with us into recovery; our fears of inadequacy, rejection, and lack of direction do not disappear overnight. Many of us have images, false personalities we have constructed either to protect ourselves or please others. Some of us use masks because we're not sure who we really are. Sometimes we think that these images, built to protect us while using, might also protect us in recovery.

We use false fronts to hide our true personality, to disguise our lack of self-esteem. These masks hide us from others and also from our own true selves. By living a lie, we are saying that we cannot live with the truth about ourselves. The more we hide our real selves, the more we damage our self-esteem.

One of the miracles of recovery is the recognition of ourselves, complete with assets and liabilities. Self-esteem begins with this recognition. Despite our fear of becoming vulnerable, we need to be willing to let go of our disguises. We need to be free of our masks and free to trust ourselves.

❖

Just for today: I will let go of my masks and allow my self-esteem to grow.

214

"Having had a spiritual awakening as a result of these steps, we tried to carry this message to addicts, and to practice these principles in all our affairs."

Step Twelve

❖

There is no such thing as a "failed" Twelfth Step call. Even if our prospect doesn't get clean, we have accomplished two purposes. We have planted the seed of recovery in the mind of the addict with whom we have shared our experience, strength, and hope. And we ourselves have stayed clean another day. Rarely does a recovering addict leave a Twelve Step call with anything but a deep dose of gratitude.

Sometimes we are practicing the Twelfth Step without realizing it. When our co-workers or other acquaintances know some of our history and see what kind of person we are today, they know where to go when they have a friend or loved one in need of our help. We are often the best attraction that NA has to offer!

For many addicts, the Twelfth Step is the cornerstone of recovery. We truly believe that "we can only keep what we have by giving it away." The paradox of the Twelfth Step is evident, for in giving, we receive.

❖

Just for today: I will remember that I am a living example of the Twelfth Step. I cannot "fail" when I try to carry the message to another addict.

"Help for addicts begins only when we are able to admit complete defeat. This can be frightening, but it is the foundation on which we have built our lives."

Basic Text, p. 22

❖

Most of us have tried everything we can think of, exerted every ounce of force possible, to fill the spiritual hole inside us. Nothing—not drugs, not control and management, not sex, money, property, power, or prestige—has filled it. We *are* powerless; our lives *are* unmanageable, at least by ourselves alone. Our denial will not change that fact.

So we surrender; we ask a Higher Power to care for our will and our lives. Sometimes in surrendering, we don't *know* that a Power greater than ourselves exists which can restore us to wholeness. Sometimes we're not *sure* that the God of our understanding will care for our unmanageable lives. Our lack of certainty, though, does not affect the essential truth: We are powerless. Our lives are unmanageable. We must surrender. Only by doing so can we open ourselves wide—wide enough for our old ideas and past wreckage to be cleared, wide enough for a Higher Power to enter.

❖

Just for today: I will surrender unconditionally. I can make it as easy or as hard as I choose. Either way, I will do it.

*"After coming to NA, we found ourselves among
a very special group of people who have suffered like us
and found recovery. In their experiences, freely shared,
we found hope for ourselves. If the program
worked for them, it would work for us."*

Basic Text, p. 10

❖

A newcomer walks into his or her first meeting, shaking and confused. People are milling about. Refreshments and literature are set out. The meeting starts after everyone has drifted over to their chairs and settled themselves in. After taking a bewildered glance at the odd assortment of folks in the room, the newcomer asks, "Why should I bet my life on this group? After all, they're just a bunch of addicts like me."

Though it may be true that not many of our members had much going for us when we got here, the newcomer soon learns that the way we are living today is what counts. Our meetings are filled with addicts whose lives have turned completely around. Against all odds, we are recovering. The newcomer can relate to where we've been and draw hope from where we are now. Today, every one of us has the opportunity to recover.

Yes, we can safely entrust our lives to our Higher Power and to Narcotics Anonymous. So long as we work the program, the payoff is certain: freedom from active addiction and a better way of life.

❖

Just for today: The recovery I've found in Narcotics Anonymous is a sure thing. By basing my life on it, I know I will grow.

*"We feared that if we ever revealed ourselves
as we were, we would surely be rejected."*

Basic Text, p. 32

❖

Having relationships without barriers, ones in which we can be entirely open with our feelings, is something many of us desire. At the same time, the possibility of such intimacy causes us more fear than almost any other situation in life.

If we examine what frightens us, we'll usually find that we are attempting to hide an aspect of our personalities that we are ashamed of, an aspect we sometimes haven't even admitted to ourselves. We don't want others to know of our insecurities, our pain, or our neediness, so we simply refuse to expose them. We may imagine that if no one knows about our imperfections, those imperfections will cease to exist.

This is the point where our relationships stop. Anyone who enters our lives will not get past the point at which our secrets begin. To maintain intimacy in a relationship, it is essential that we acknowledge our defects and accept them. When we do, the fortress of denial, erected to keep these things hidden, will come crashing down, enabling us to build up our relationships with others.

❖

Just for today: I have opportunities to share my inner self. I will take advantage of those opportunities and draw closer to those I love.

> *"As we realize our need to be forgiven,*
> *we tend to be more forgiving."*

Basic Text, p. 39

❖

Our behavior toward other people in our life is a mirror of our behavior toward ourselves. When we demand perfection of ourselves, we come to demand it from others around us, too. As we strive to repair and heal our lives in recovery, we may also expect others to work just as hard and to recover at the same pace as we do. And just as we are often unforgiving of our own mistakes, we may shut out friends and family members when they don't meet our expectations.

Working the steps helps us understand our own limitations and our humanity. We come to see our failures as human mistakes. We realize that we will never be perfect, that we will, at times, disappoint ourselves and others. We hope for forgiveness.

As we learn to gently accept ourselves, we can start to view others with the same accepting and tolerant heart. These people, too, are only human, trying to do their best and sometimes falling short.

❖

Just for today: I will treat others with the tolerance and forgiveness I seek for myself.

*"Continuing to take a personal inventory means that
we form a habit of looking at ourselves, our actions,
attitudes, and relationships on a regular basis."*

Basic Text, p. 42

❖

Taking a regular inventory is a key element in our new pattern of living. In our addiction, we examined ourselves as little as possible. We weren't happy with how we were living our lives, but we didn't feel that we could change the way we lived. Self-examination, we felt, would have been a painful exercise in futility.

Today, all that is changing. Where we were powerless over our addiction, we've found a Power greater than ourselves that has helped us stop using. Where we once felt lost in life's maze, we've found guidance in the experience of our fellow recovering addicts and our ever-improving contact with our Higher Power. We need not feel trapped by our old, destructive patterns. We can live differently if we choose.

By establishing a regular pattern of taking our own inventory, we give ourselves the opportunity to change anything in our lives that doesn't work. If we've started doing something that causes problems, we can start changing our behavior before it gets completely out of hand. And if we're doing something that prevents problems from occurring, we can take note of that, too, and encourage ourselves to keep doing what works.

❖

Just for today: I will make a commitment to include a regular inventory in my new pattern of living.

*"Narcotics Anonymous offers only one promise
and that is freedom from active addiction, the solution
that eluded us for so long."*

Basic Text, p. 106

❖

NA offers no promises other than freedom from active addiction. It is true that some of our members meet with financial success in recovery. They buy nice houses, drive new cars, wear fine clothes, and form beautiful families. These outward signs of prosperity are not the lot of all of our members, however. A great many of us never achieve financial success. This does not necessarily reflect on the quality of our recovery.

When we are tempted to compare ourselves to these other, seemingly more affluent members, it is good to remember why we came to the rooms of Narcotics Anonymous. We came because our lives had fallen down around us. We were emotionally, physically, and spiritually defeated. Our Basic Text reminds us that "in *desperation* we sought help from each other in Narcotics Anonymous." We came because we were beaten.

For addicts, even one day clean is a miracle. When we remember why we came to Narcotics Anonymous and in what condition we arrived, we realize that material wealth pales in comparison to the spiritual riches we have gained in recovery.

❖

Just for today: I have been given a spiritual gift greater than material wealth: my recovery. I will thank the God of my understanding for my freedom from active addiction.

❖ ❖ ❖
August
❖ ❖ ❖

*"Our addiction enslaved us. We were prisoners of
our own mind and were condemned by our own guilt."*

Basic Text, p. 7

❖

Guilt is one of the most commonly encountered stumbling blocks in recovery. One of the more notorious forms of guilt is the self-loathing that results when we try to forgive ourselves but don't feel forgiven.

How can we forgive ourselves so we *feel* it? First, we remember that guilt and failure are not links in an unbreakable chain. Honestly sharing with a sponsor and with other addicts shows this to be true. Often the result of such sharing is a more sensible awareness of the part we ourselves have played in our affairs. Sometimes we realize that our expectations have been too high. We increase our willingness to participate in the solutions rather than dwelling on the problems.

Somewhere along the way, we discover who we really are. We usually find that we are neither the totally perfect nor the totally imperfect beings we have imagined ourselves to be. We need not live up to or down to our illusions; we need only live in reality.

❖

Just for today: I am grateful for my assets and accept my liabilities. Through willingness and humility, I am freed to progress in my recovery and achieve freedom from guilt.

*"When we feel trapped or pressured, it takes great
spiritual and emotional strength to be honest."*

Basic Text, p. 85

❖

Many of us try to wiggle out of a difficult spot by being dishonest, only to have to humble ourselves later and tell the truth. Some of us twist our stories as a matter of course, even when we could just as easily tell the plain truth. Every time we try to avoid being honest, it backfires on us. Honesty may be uncomfortable, but the trouble we have to endure when we are dishonest is usually far worse than the discomfort of telling the truth.

Honesty is one of the fundamental principles of recovery. We apply this principle right from the beginning of our recovery, when we finally admit our powerlessness and unmanageability. We continue to apply the principle of honesty each time we are faced with the option of either living in fantasy or living life on its own terms. Learning to be honest isn't always easy, especially after the covering up and deception so many of us practiced in our addiction. Our voices may shake as we test our newfound honesty. But before long, the sound of the truth coming from our own mouths settles any doubts: Honesty feels good! It's easier living the truth than living a lie.

❖

Just for today: I will honestly embrace life, with all its pressures and demands. I will practice honesty, even when it is awkward to do so. Honesty will help, not hurt, my efforts to live clean and recover.

"Many of us would have had nowhere else to go if we could not have trusted NA groups and members."

Basic Text, p. 84

❖

Trusting people is a risk. Human beings are notoriously forgetful, unreliable, and imperfect. Most of us come from backgrounds where betrayal and insensitivity among friends were common occurrences. Even our most reliable friends weren't very reliable. By the time we arrive at the doors of NA, most of us have hundreds of experiences bearing out our conviction that people are untrustworthy. Yet our recovery demands that we trust people. We are faced with this dilemma: People are not always trustworthy, yet we must trust them. How do we do that, given the evidence of our pasts?

First, we remind ourselves that the rules of active addiction don't apply in recovery. Most of our fellow members are doing their level best to live by the spiritual principles we learn in the program. Second, we remind ourselves that we aren't 100% reliable, either. We will surely disappoint someone in our lives, no matter how hard we try not to. Third, and most importantly, we realize that we *need* to trust our fellow members of NA. Our lives are at stake, and the only way we can stay clean is to trust these well-intentioned folks who, admittedly, aren't perfect.

❖

Just for today: I will trust my fellow members. Though certainly not perfect, they are my best hope.

*"Addicts tend to live secret lives.... It is a great relief
to get rid of all our secrets and to share
the burden of our past."*

Basic Text, p. 33

❖

We've heard it said that "we're as sick as our secrets." What do we keep secret, and why?

We keep secret those things that cause us shame. We may hold onto such things because we don't want to surrender them. Yet if they're causing us shame, wouldn't we live more easily with ourselves if we were rid of them?

Some of us hold onto the things that cause us shame for another reason. It's not that we don't *want* to be rid of them; we just don't believe we *can* be rid of them. They've plagued us for so long, and we've tried so many times to rid ourselves of them, that we've stopped hoping for relief. Yet still they shame us, and still we keep them secret.

We need to remember who we are: recovering addicts. We who tried so long to keep our drug use a secret have found freedom from the obsession and compulsion to use. Though many of us enjoyed using right to the end, we sought recovery anyway. We just couldn't stand the toll our using was taking on us. When we admitted our powerlessness and sought help from others, the burden of our secret was lifted from us.

The same principle applies to whatever secrets may burden us. Yes, we're as sick as our secrets. Only when our secrets stop being secret can we begin to find relief from those things that cause us shame.

❖

Just for today: My secrets can make me sick only as long as they stay secret. Today, I will talk with my sponsor about my secrets.

*"By shaping our thoughts with spiritual ideals,
we are freed to become who we want to be."*

Basic Text, p. 105

❖

Addiction shaped our thoughts in its own way. Whatever their shape may once have been, they became misshapen once our disease took full sway over our lives. Our obsession with drugs and self molded our moods, our actions, and the very shape of our lives.

Each of the spiritual ideals of our program serves to straighten out one or another of the kinks in our thinking that developed in our active addiction. Denial is counteracted by admission, secretiveness by honesty, isolation by fellowship, and despair by faith in a loving Higher Power. The spiritual ideals we find in recovery are restoring the shape of our thoughts and our lives to their natural condition.

And what is that "natural condition"? It is the condition we truly seek for ourselves, a reflection of our highest dreams. How do we know this? Because our thoughts are being shaped in recovery by the spiritual ideals we find in our developing relationship with the God we've come to understand in NA.

No longer does addiction shape our thoughts. Today, our lives are being shaped by our recovery and our Higher Power.

❖

Just for today: I will allow spiritual ideals to shape my thoughts. In that design, I will find the shape of my own Higher Power.

*"Since the beginning of our recovery, we have found
that joy doesn't come from material things,
but from within ourselves."*

Basic Text, p. 107

❖

Some of us came to Narcotics Anonymous impoverished by our disease. Everything we'd owned had been lost to our addiction. Once we got clean, we put all our energy into recovering our material possessions, only to feel even more dissatisfied with our lives than before.

Other members have sought to ease their emotional pain with material things. A potential date has rejected us? Let's buy something. The dog has died? Let's go to the mall. Problem is, emotional fulfillment can't be bought, not even on an easy installment plan.

There's nothing inherently wrong with material things. They can make life more convenient or more luxurious, but they can't fix us. Where, then, can true joy be found? We know; the answer is within ourselves.

When have we found joy? When we've offered ourselves in service to others, without expectation of reward. We've found true warmth in the fellowship of others—not only in NA, but in our families, our relationships, and our communities. And we've found the surest source of satisfaction in our conscious contact with our God. Inner peace, a sure sense of direction, and emotional security do not come from material things, but from within.

❖

Just for today: True joy can't be bought. I will seek my joy in service, in fellowship, in my Higher Power—I will seek within.

*"We focus on anything that isn't going our way
and ignore all the beauty in our lives."*

Basic Text, p. 80

❖

It's easy to be grateful when everything runs smoothly. If we get a raise at work, we're grateful. If we get married, we're grateful. If someone surprises us with a nice present or an unasked favor, we're grateful. But if we get fired, divorced, or disappointed, gratitude flies out the window. We find ourselves becoming obsessed with the things that are wrong, even though everything else may be wonderful.

This is where we can use a gratitude list. We sit down with a pen and paper and list the people for whom we are grateful. We all have people who've supported us through life's upheavals. We list the spiritual assets we have attained, for we know we could never make it through our present circumstances without them. Last, but not least, we list our recovery itself. Whatever we have that we are grateful for goes on the list.

We're sure to find that we have literally hundreds of things in our lives that inspire our gratitude. Even those of us who are suffering from an illness or who have lost all material wealth will find blessings of a spiritual nature for which we can be thankful. An awakening of the spirit is the most valuable gift an addict can receive.

❖

Just for today: I will write a list of things, both material and spiritual, for which I am grateful.

*"...we accept responsibility for our problems and
see that we're equally responsible for our solutions."*

Basic Text, p. 97

❖

Some of us, well accustomed to leaving our personal responsibilities to others, may attempt the same behavior in recovery. We quickly find out it doesn't work.

For instance, we are considering making a change in our lives, so we call our sponsor and ask what we should do. Under the guise of seeking direction, we are actually asking our sponsor to assume responsibility for making decisions about our life. Or maybe we've been short with someone at a meeting, so we ask that person's best friend to make our apologies for us. Perhaps we've imposed on a friend several times in the last month to cover our service commitment. Could it be that we've asked a friend to analyze our behavior and identify our shortcomings, rather than taking our own personal inventory?

Recovery is something that has to be worked for. It isn't going to be handed to us on a silver platter, nor can we expect our friends or our sponsor to be responsible for the work we must do ourselves. We recover by making our own decisions, doing our own service, and working our own steps. By doing it for ourselves, we receive the rewards.

❖

Just for today: I accept responsibility for my life and my recovery.

> *"We begin to see that God's love has been present
> all the time, just waiting for us to accept it."*

Basic Text, p. 47

❖

God's love is the transforming power that drives our recovery. With that love, we find freedom from the hopeless, desperate cycle of using, self-hatred, and more using. With that love, we gain a sense of reason and purpose in our once purposeless lives. With that love, we are given the inner direction and strength we need to begin a new way of life: the NA way. With that love, we begin to see things differently, as if with new eyes.

As we examine our lives through the eyes of love, we make what may be a startling discovery: The loving God we've so recently come to understand has always been with us and has always loved us. We recall the times when we asked for the aid of a Higher Power and were given it. We even recall times when we didn't ask for such help, yet were given it anyway. We realize that a loving Higher Power has cared for us all along, preserving our lives till the day when we could accept that love for ourselves.

The Power of love has been with us all along. Today, we are grateful to have survived long enough to become consciously aware of that love's presence in our world and our lives. Its vitality floods our very being, guiding our recovery and showing us how to live.

❖

Just for today: I accept the love of a Higher Power in my life. I am conscious of that Power's guidance and strength within me. Today, I claim it for my own.

*"Most of us pray when we are hurting.
We learn that if we pray regularly, we won't be
hurting as often or as intensely."*

Basic Text, p. 45

❖

Regular prayer and meditation are two more key elements in our new pattern of living. Our active addiction was more than just a bad habit waiting to be broken by force of will. Our addiction was a negative, draining dependence that stole all our positive energy. That dependence was so total, it prevented us from developing any kind of reliance on a Higher Power.

From the very beginning of our recovery, our Higher Power has been the force that's brought us freedom. First, it relieved us of our compulsion to keep taking drugs, even when we knew they were killing us. Then, it gave us freedom from the more deeply ingrained aspects of our disease. Our Higher Power gave us the direction, the strength, and the courage to inventory ourselves; to admit out loud to another person what our lives had been like, perhaps for the first time; to begin seeking release from the chronic defects of character underlying our troubles; and, at last, to make amends for the wrongs we'd done.

That first contact with a Higher Power, and that first freedom, has grown into a life full of freedom. We maintain that freedom by maintaining and improving our conscious contact with our Higher Power through regular prayer and meditation.

❖

Just for today: I will make a commitment to include regular prayer and meditation in my new pattern of living.

"Through active listening, we hear things that work for us."

Basic Text, pp. 106–107

❖

Most of us arrived in Narcotics Anonymous with a very poor ability to listen. But to take full advantage of "the therapeutic value of one addict helping another," we must learn to listen actively.

What is active listening for us? In meetings, it means we concentrate on what the speaker is sharing, *while* the speaker is sharing. We set aside our own thoughts and opinions until the meeting is over. That's when we sort through what we've heard to decide which ideas we want to use and which we want to explore further.

We can apply our active listening skills in sponsorship, too. Newcomers often talk with us about some "major event" in their lives. While such events may not seem significant to us, they are to the newcomer who has little experience living life on life's terms. Our active listening helps us empathize with the feelings such events trigger in our sponsee's life. With that understanding, we have a better idea of what to share with them.

The ability to listen actively was unknown to us in the isolation of our addiction. Today, this ability helps us actively engage with our recovery. Through active listening, we receive everything being offered us in NA, and we share fully with others the love and care we've been given.

❖

Just for today: I will strive to be an active listener. I will practice active listening when others share and when I share with others.

"Something inside cries out, 'Enough, enough, I've had enough,' and then they are ready to take that first and often most difficult step toward dealing with their disease."

❖

Have we really had enough? This is the crucial question we must ask ourselves as we prepare to work the First Step in Narcotics Anonymous. It doesn't matter whether or not we arrived in NA with our families intact, our careers still working for us, and all the outward appearances of wholeness. All that matters is that we have reached an emotional and spiritual bottom that precludes our return to active addiction. If we have, we will be truly ready to go to any lengths to quit using.

When we inventory our powerlessness, we ask ourselves some simple questions. Can I control my use of drugs in any form? What incidents have occurred as a result of my drug use that I didn't want to happen? How is my life unmanageable? Do I believe in my heart that I am an addict?

If the answers to these questions lead us to the doors of Narcotics Anonymous, then we are ready to move on to the next step toward a life free from active addiction. If we have truly had enough, then we will be willing to go to any lengths to find recovery.

❖

Just for today: I admit that I have had enough. I am ready to work my First Step.

*"By giving unconditional love ... we become
more loving, and by sharing spiritual growth
we become more spiritual."*

Basic Text, p. 103

❖

Most of us have one or two exceptionally difficult people in our lives. How do we deal with such a person in our recovery?

First, we take our own inventory. Have we wronged this person? Has some action or attitude of ours served as an invitation for the kind of treatment they have given us? If so, we will want to clear the air, admit we have been wrong, and ask our Higher Power to remove whatever defects may prevent us from being helpful and constructive.

Next, as people seeking to live spiritually oriented lives, we approach the problem from the other person's point of view. They may be faced with any number of challenges we either fail to consider or know nothing about, challenges that cause them to be unpleasant. As it's said, we seek in recovery "to forgive rather than be forgiven; to understand rather than be understood."

Finally, if it is within our power, we seek ways to help others overcome their challenges without injuring their dignity. We pray for their well-being and spiritual growth and for the ability to offer them the unconditional love that has meant so much to us in our recovery.

We cannot change the difficult people in our lives, nor can we please everyone. But by applying the spiritual principles we've learned in NA, we can learn to love them.

❖

Just for today: Higher Power, help me serve other people, not demand that they serve me.

*"We don't have to settle for the limitations of the past.
We can examine and reexamine our old ideas."*

Basic Text, p. 11

❖

Most of us come to the program with a multitude of self-imposed limitations that prevent us from realizing our full potential, limitations that impede our attempts to find the values that lie at the core of our being. We place limitations on our ability to be true to ourselves, limitations on our ability to function at work, limitations on the risks we're willing to take—the list seems endless. If our parents or teachers told us we would never succeed, and we believed them, chances are we didn't achieve much. If our socialization taught us not to stand up for ourselves, we didn't, even if everything inside us was screaming to do so.

In Narcotics Anonymous, we are given a process by which we can recognize these false limitations for what they are. Through our Fourth Step, we'll discover that we don't want to keep all the rules we've been taught. We don't have to be the lifelong victims of past experiences. We are free to discard the ideas that inhibit our growth. We are capable of stretching our boundaries to encompass new ideas and new experiences. We are free to laugh, to cry, and, above all, to enjoy our recovery.

❖

Just for today: I will let go of my self-imposed limitations and open my mind to new ideas.

*"We found that we do not recover physically,
mentally, or spiritually overnight."*

Basic Text, p. 28

❖

Have you ever approached a recovery celebration with the feeling that you should be further along in your recovery than you are? Maybe you have listened to newcomers sharing in meetings, members with much less clean time, and thought, "But I'm just barely beginning to understand what they're talking about!"

It's odd that we should come into recovery thinking that we will feel wonderful right away or no longer have any difficulty handling life's twists and turns. We expect our physical problems to correct themselves, our thinking to become rational, and a fully developed spiritual life to manifest itself overnight. We forget that we spent years abusing our bodies, numbing our minds, and suppressing our awareness of a Higher Power. We cannot undo the damage in a day. We can, however, apply the next step, go to the next meeting, help the next newcomer. We heal and recover bit by bit—not overnight, but over time.

❖

Just for today: My body will heal a little, my mind will become a little clearer, and my relationship with my Higher Power will strengthen.

> *"This is our road to spiritual growth. We change*
> *every day.... This growth is not the result of wishing*
> *but of action and prayer."*

Basic Text, p. 37

❖

Our spiritual condition is never static; if it's not growing, it's decaying. If we stand still, our spiritual progress will lose its upward momentum. Gradually, our growth will slow, then halt, then reverse itself. Our tolerance will wear thin; our willingness to serve others will wane; our minds will narrow and close. Before long, we'll be right back where we started: in conflict with everyone and everything around us, unable to bear even ourselves.

Our only option is to actively participate in our program of spiritual growth. We pray, seeking knowledge greater than our own from a Power greater than ourselves. We open our minds and keep them open, becoming teachable and taking advantage of what others have to share with us. We demonstrate our willingness to try new ideas and new ways of doing things, experiencing life in a whole new way. Our spiritual progress picks up speed and momentum, driven by the Higher Power we are coming to understand better each day.

Up or down—it's one or the other, with very little in between, where spiritual growth is concerned. Recovery is not fueled by wishing and dreaming, we've discovered, but by prayer and action.

❖

Just for today: The only constant in my spiritual condition is change. I cannot rely on yesterday's program. Today, I seek new spiritual growth through prayer and action.

> *"A symptom of our disease is alienation,*
> *and honest sharing will free us to recover."*

Basic Text, p. 83

Truth connects us to life while fear, isolation, and dishonesty alienate us from it. As using addicts, we hid as much of the truth about ourselves from as much of the world as we possibly could. Our fear kept us from opening ourselves up to those around us, providing protection against what others might do if we appeared vulnerable. But our fear also kept us from connecting with our world. We lived like alien beings on our own planet, always alone and getting lonelier by the minute.

The Twelve Steps and the fellowship of recovering addicts give people like us a place where we can feel safe telling the truth about ourselves. We are able to honestly admit our frustrating, humbling powerlessness over addiction because we meet many others who've been in the same situation—we're safe among them. And we keep on telling more of the truth about ourselves as we continue to work the steps. The more we do, the more truly connected we feel to the world around us.

Today, we need not hide from the reality of our relations with the people, places, and things in our lives. We accept those relationships just as they are, and we own our part in them. We take time every day to ask, "Am I telling the truth about myself?" Each time we do this, we draw that much further away from the alienation that characterizes our addiction, and that much closer to the freedom recovery can bring us.

❖

Just for today: Truth is my connection to reality. Today, I will take time to ask myself, "Am I telling the truth?"

*"The way to remain a productive, responsible member
of society is to put our recovery first."*

Basic Text, p. 106

❖

The meetings have been great! Each night we've attended, we've gathered with other addicts to share experience, strength, and hope. And each day, we've used what we've learned in the meetings to continue in our recovery.

Meanwhile, life goes on. Work, family, friends, school, sport, entertainment, community activities, civic obligations—all call out for our time. The demands of everyday living sometimes make us ask ourselves, "How long do I have to go to these meetings?"

Let's think about this. Before coming to Narcotics Anonymous, could we stay clean on our own? What makes us think we can now? Then there's the disease itself to consider—the chronic self-centeredness, the obsessiveness, the compulsive behavior patterns that express themselves in so many areas of our lives. Can we live and enjoy life without effective treatment for our disease? No.

"Ordinary" people may not have to worry about such things, but we're not "ordinary" people—we're addicts. We can't pretend we don't have a fatal, progressive illness, because we do. Without our program, we may not survive to worry about the demands of work, school, family, or anything else. NA meetings give us the support and direction we need to recover from our addiction, allowing us to live the fullest lives possible.

❖

Just for today: I want to live and enjoy life. To do that, I will put my recovery first.

> *"We apply effort to our most obvious problems
> and let go of the rest. We do the job at hand and,
> as we progress, new opportunities for improvement
> present themselves."*

Basic Text, p. 56

❖

It's been said that recovery is simple—all we've got to change is *everything*! That can seem a pretty tall order, especially when we first arrive in Narcotics Anonymous. After all, not many of us showed up at our first meeting because our lives were in great shape. On the contrary, a great many of us came to NA in the midst of the worst crises of our lives. We needed recovery, and quick!

The enormity of the change required in our lives can be paralyzing. We know we can't take care of all that needs to be done, not all at once. How do we start? Chances are, we've already started. We've done the first, most obvious things that needed to be done: We've stopped using drugs, and we've started going to meetings.

What do we do next? Pretty much the same thing, just more of it: From where we are, we do what we can. We walk the path of recovery by picking up our feet and taking the step that's right in front of us. Only when that's been accomplished must we concern ourselves with what comes next. Slowly but surely, we'll find ourselves making progress down the path, visibly drawing closer each day to becoming the kind of person we'd like to be.

❖

Just for today: I will walk the path of my recovery by taking the step right in front of me.

"Often we have to face some type of crisis during our recovery, such as the death of a loved one..."

Basic Text, p. 102

❖

Every life has a beginning and an end. However, when someone we love a great deal reaches the end of their life, we may have a very hard time accepting their sudden, final absence. Our grief may be so powerful that we fear it will completely overwhelm us—but it will not. Our sorrow may hurt more than anything we can remember, but it will pass.

We need not run from the emotions that may arise from the death of a loved one. Death and grieving are parts of the fullness of living "life on life's terms." By allowing ourselves the freedom to experience these feelings, we partake more deeply of both our recovery and our human nature.

Sometimes the reality of another's death makes our own mortality that much more pronounced. We reevaluate our priorities, appreciating the loved ones still with us all the more. Our life, and our life with them, will not go on forever. We want to make the most of what's most important while it lasts.

We might find that the death of someone we love helps strengthen our conscious contact with our Higher Power. If we remember that we can always turn to that source of strength when we are troubled, we will be able to stay focused on it no matter what may be going on around us.

❖

Just for today: I will accept the loss of one I love and turn to my Higher Power for the strength to accept my feelings. I will make the most of my love for those in my life today.

*"Our friendships become deep, and we experience
the warmth and caring which results from addicts
sharing recovery and a new life."*

IP No. 19, *Self-Acceptance*

❖

Most of us come to Narcotics Anonymous with few genuine friends. And most of us arrive without the slightest understanding of what it takes to build lasting friendships. Over time, though, we learn that friendships require work. At one time or another, all friendships are challenging. Like any relationship, friendship is a learning process.

Our friends love us enough to tell us the truth about ourselves. The old saying, "The truth will set you free, but first it will make you furious," seems especially true in friendship. This can make friendships awkward. We may find ourselves avoiding certain meetings rather than facing our friends. We have found, though, that friends speak out of concern for us. They want the best for us. Our friends accept us despite our shortcomings. They understand that we are still a work in progress.

Friends are there for us when we're not there for ourselves. Friends help us gain valuable perspective on the events in our lives and our recovery. It is important that we actively cultivate friendships, for we have learned that we cannot recover alone.

❖

Just for today: I will be grateful for the friends I have. I will take an active part in my friendships.

*"We recognize our spiritual growth when we are able
to reach out and help others."*

Basic Text, p. 58

❖

To make a difference in the world, to contribute something special, is perhaps the highest aspiration of the human heart. Each one of us, no matter what our personal makeup, has a unique quality to offer.

Chances are that at some time in our recovery we met someone who reached us when no one else could. Whether it was someone who made us laugh at our first meeting, a warm and compassionate sponsor, or an understanding friend who supported us through an emotional storm, that person made all the difference in the world.

All of us have had the gift of recovery shared with us by another recovering addict. For that, we are grateful. We express our gratitude by sharing freely with others what was given to us. The individual message we carry may help a newcomer only we can reach.

There are many ways to serve our fellowship. Each of us will find that we do some things better than others, but all service work is equally important. If we are willing to serve, we're sure to find that particular way to contribute that's right for us.

❖

Just for today: My contribution makes a difference. I will offer a helping hand today.

"Before we got clean, most of our actions were guided by impulse. Today, we are not locked into this type of thinking."

Basic Text, p. 90

❖

Life is a series of decisions, actions, and consequences. When we were using, our decisions were usually driven by our disease, resulting in self-destructive actions and dire consequences. We came to see decision-making as a rigged game, one we should play as little as possible.

Given that, many of us have great difficulty learning to make decisions in recovery. Slowly, by working the Twelve Steps, we gain practice in making healthy decisions, ones that give positive results. Where our disease once affected our will and our lives, we ask our Higher Power to care for us. We inventory our values and our actions, check our findings with someone we trust, and ask the God of our understanding to remove our shortcomings. In working the steps we gain freedom from the influence of our disease, and we learn principles of decision-making that can guide us in all our affairs.

Today, our decisions and their consequences need not be influenced by our disease. Our faith gives us the courage and direction to make good decisions and the strength to act on them. The result of that kind of decision-making is a life worth living.

❖

Just for today: I will use the principles of the Twelve Steps to make healthy decisions. I will ask my Higher Power for the strength to act on those decisions.

"We learn to be careful of praying for specific things."

Basic Text, p. 46

❖

In our active addiction, we usually did not pray for knowledge of God's will for us and the power to carry it out. On the contrary, most of our prayers were for God to get us out of the mess we had made for ourselves. We expected miracles on demand. That kind of thinking and praying changes when we begin practicing the Eleventh Step. The only way out of the trouble we have made for ourselves is through surrender to a Power greater than ourselves.

In recovery, we learn acceptance. We seek knowledge in our prayers and meditation of how we are to greet the circumstances that come our way. We stop fighting, surrender our own ideas of how things should be, ask for knowledge, and listen for the answers. The answers usually won't come in a flash of white light accompanied by a drum roll. Usually, the answers will come merely with a quiet sense of assurance that our lives are on course, that a Power greater than ourselves is guiding us on our paths.

We have a choice. We can spend all our time fighting to make things come out our way, or we can surrender to God's will. Peace can be found in accepting the ebb and flow of life.

❖

Just for today: I will surrender my expectations, look to my Higher Power for guidance, and accept life.

"We are achieving freedom from the wreckage of our past."

Basic Text, p. 42

❖

When we start the Ninth Step, we've reached an exciting stage in our recovery. The damage done in our lives is what led many of us to seek help in the first place. Now, we have a chance to clean up that wreckage, amend our past, and reclaim our lives.

We've spent a long time and much effort preparing for this step. When we came to NA, facing the debris of our past was probably the last thing we wanted to do. We started doing it privately with a personal inventory. Then, we opened our past up to the scrutiny of a select, trusted few: ourselves, our Higher Power, and one other person. We took a look at our shortcomings, the source of much of the chaos in our lives, and asked that all those defects of character be removed. Finally, we listed the amends needed to set our wrongs right—*all* of them—and became willing to make them.

Now, we have the opportunity to make amends—to acquire freedom from the wreckage of our past. Everything we've done so far in NA has led us here. At this point in the process of our recovery, the Ninth Step is exactly what we want to do. With the Twelve Steps and the help of a Higher Power, we are clearing away the rubble that for so long has stood in the way of our progress; we are gaining the freedom to live.

❖

Just for today: I will take advantage of the opportunity to re-claim my life. I will experience freedom from the wreckage of my past.

*"We continued to take personal inventory
and when we were wrong promptly admitted it."*

Step Ten

❖

A daily Tenth Step keeps us on a sound spiritual footing. While each member asks different questions, some questions have been found to be helpful to almost everyone. Two key Tenth Step questions are, "Am I honestly in touch with myself, my actions, and my motives? And have I prayed for God's will for me and the power to carry it out?" These two questions, answered honestly, will lead us into a more thorough look at our day.

When focusing on our relationships with others, we may ask, "Have I harmed anyone today, either directly or indirectly? Do I need to make amends to anyone as a result of my actions today?" We keep it simple in our inventory if we remember to ask, "Where was I wrong? How can I do it better next time?"

NA members often find that their inventories include other important questions. "Was I good to myself today? Did I do something for someone else and expect nothing in return? Have I reaffirmed my faith in a loving Higher Power?"

Step Ten is a maintenance step of the NA program. The Tenth Step helps us to continue living comfortably in recovery.

❖

Just for today: I will remember to review my day. If I have harmed another, I will make amends. I will think about how I can act differently.

> *"Change from self-destructive patterns*
> *of life became necessary."*

Basic Text, p. 15

❖

Active addiction is a smoldering death-wish. Each of us courted death every time we used. Our lifestyles, too, put us at risk. The life of an addict is sold cheaply with every day and every dose.

In recovery, the first pattern we change is the pattern of using. Staying clean is the start of our journey into life. But our self-destructive behavior usually went far deeper than just our using. Even in recovery, we may still treat ourselves as if we are worthless. When we treat ourselves badly, we feel badly. And when we feel badly, we seek relief—maybe even in our old solution, drugs.

Choosing recovery means choosing life. We decide each day that we want to live and be free. Each time we avoid self-destructive behavior, we choose recovery.

❖

Just for today: I will choose life by choosing recovery. I will take care of myself.

*"These defects grow in the dark and die in
the light of exposure."*

Basic Text, p. 32

❖

The Fifth Step asks us to share our true nature with God, with ourselves, and with another human being. It doesn't encourage us to tell everyone every little secret about ourselves. It doesn't ask us to disclose to the whole world every shameful or frightening thought we've ever had. Step Five simply suggests that our secrets cause us more harm than good when we keep them completely to ourselves.

If we give in to our reluctance to reveal our true nature to even one human being, the secret side of our lives becomes more powerful. And when the secrets are in control, they drive a wedge between ourselves, our Higher Power, and the things we value most about our recovery.

When we share our secret selves in confidence with at least one human being—our sponsor, perhaps, or a close friend—this person usually doesn't reject us. We disclose ourselves to someone else and are rewarded with their acceptance. When this happens, we realize that honest sharing is not life-threatening; the secrets have lost their power over us.

❖

Just for today: I can disarm the secrets in my life by sharing them with one human being.

*The steps offer "a big change from a life dominated
by guilt and remorse. Our futures are changed because
we don't have to avoid those who we have harmed.
As a result ... we receive a new freedom
that can end isolation."*

Basic Text, p. 39

❖

Many of us come to Narcotics Anonymous full of regrets about our past. Our steps help us begin to resolve those regrets. We examine our lives, admit our wrongs, make amends for them, and sincerely try to change our behavior. In doing so, we find a joyous sense of freedom.

No longer must we deny or regret our past. Once we've made our amends, what's done is truly over and gone. From that point on, where we come from ceases to be the most important thing about us. It's where we are going that counts.

In NA, we begin to look forward. True, we live and stay clean just for today. But we find that we can begin to set goals, dream dreams, and look ahead to the joys a life in recovery has to offer. Looking forward keeps us centered in where we are going, not remorseful or regretful about our past. After all, it is hard to move forward if we are looking back.

❖

Just for today: The steps have freed me from regrets over my past. Today, I look forward to my new life in recovery.

*"We examine our actions, reactions, and motives.
We often find that we've been doing better than
we've been feeling."*

Basic Text, p. 43

❖

The way we treat others often reveals our own state of being. When we are at peace, we're most likely to treat others with respect and compassion. However, when we're feeling off center, we're likely to respond to others with intolerance and impatience. When we take regular inventory, we'll probably notice a pattern: We treat others badly when we feel bad about ourselves.

What might not be revealed in an inventory, however, is the other side of the coin: When we treat others well, we feel good about ourselves. When we add this positive truth to the negative facts we find about ourselves in our inventory, we begin to behave differently.

When we feel badly, we can pause to pray for guidance and strength. Then, we make a decision to treat those around us with kindness, gentleness, and the same concern we'd like to be shown. A decision to be kind may nurture and sustain the happiness and peace of mind we all wish for. And the joy we inspire may lift the spirits of those around us, in turn fostering our own spiritual well-being.

❖

Just for today: I will remember that if I change my actions, my thoughts will follow.

*"Hopeless living problems have become joyously
changed. Our disease has been arrested,
and now anything is possible."*

Basic Text, p. 106

❖

The NA program has given us more freedom than we ever dreamed possible. Sometimes, though, in the daily routine, we lose track of how much we've been given. How, exactly, have our lives changed in Narcotics Anonymous?

The bottom line of recovery, of course, is freedom from the compulsion to use. No longer must we devote all our resources to feeding our addiction. No longer must we endanger, humiliate, or abuse ourselves or others just to get the next "fix." Abstinence itself has brought great freedom to our lives.

Narcotics Anonymous has given us much more than simple abstinence—we've been given a whole new life. We've taken our inventory and have identified the defects of character that bound us for so long, keeping us from living and enjoying life. We've surrendered those shortcomings, taken responsibility for them, and sought the direction and power we need to live differently. Our home group has given us the personal warmth and support that helps us continue living in recovery. And topping all this off, we have the love, care, and guidance of the God we've come to understand in NA.

In the course of day-to-day recovery, we sometimes forget how much our lives have changed in Narcotics Anonymous. Do we fully appreciate what our program has given us?

❖

Just for today: Recovery has given me freedom. I will greet the day with hope, grateful that anything is possible today.

253

❖ ❖ ❖

September

❖ ❖ ❖

> *"We become able to make wise and loving decisions*
> *based on principles and ideals that have*
> *real value in our lives."*

Basic Text, p. 105

❖

Addiction gave us a certain set of values, principles we applied in our lives. "You pushed me," one of those values told us, "so I pushed back, *hard.*" "It's *mine*" was another value generated by our disease. "Well, okay, maybe it wasn't mine to start with, but I liked it, so I *made* it mine." Those values were hardly values at all—more like rationalizations—and they certainly didn't help us make wise and loving decisions. In fact, they served primarily to dig us deeper and deeper into the grave we'd already dug for ourselves.

The Twelve Steps give us a strong dose of real values, the kind that help us live in harmony with ourselves and those around us. We place our faith not in ourselves, our families, or our communities, but in a Higher Power—and in doing so, we grow secure enough to be able to trust our communities, our families, and even ourselves. We learn to be honest, no matter what—and we learn to refrain from doing things we might want to hide. We learn to accept responsibility for our actions. "It's *mine*" is replaced with a spirit of selflessness. These are the kind of values that help us become a responsible, productive part of the life around us. Rather than digging us deeper into a grave, these values restore us to the world of the living.

❖

Just for today: I am grateful for the values I've developed. I am thankful for the ability they give me to make wise, loving decisions as a responsible, productive member of my community.

*"Daily practice of our Twelve Step program
enables us to change from what we were to people
guided by a Higher Power."*

Basic Text, p. 86

❖

Who have we been, and who have we become? There are a couple of ways to answer this question. One is very simple: We came to Narcotics Anonymous as addicts, our addiction killing us. In NA, we've been freed from our obsession with drugs and our compulsion to use. And our lives have changed.

But that's only the tip of the iceberg. Who have we *really* been? In the past, we were people without power or direction. We felt like we had no purpose, no reason for living. Our lives didn't make any more sense to us than they did to our families, our friends, or our neighbors.

Who are we *really* becoming? Today, we are not merely clean addicts, but people with a sense of direction, a purpose, and a Power greater than ourselves. Through daily practice of the Twelve Steps, we've begun to understand how our addiction warped our feelings, motivations, and behavior. Gradually, the destructive force of our disease has been replaced by the life-giving force of our Higher Power.

Recovery means more than cleaning up—it means *powering* up. We have done more than shed some bad habits; we are becoming new people, guided by a Higher Power.

❖

Just for today: The guidance I need to become a new person is ready at hand. Today, I will draw further away from my old lack of direction and closer to my Higher Power.

*"Humility is a by-product that allows us to grow
and develop in an atmosphere of freedom and removes
the fear of becoming known by our employers,
families, or friends as addicts."*

Basic Text, pp. 75–76

❖

Many of us may not have understood the idea that "anonymity is the spiritual foundation of all our traditions." We wondered how this could be. What does anonymity have to do with our spiritual life?

The answer is, plenty! By guarding and cherishing our anonymity, we earn spiritual rewards beyond comprehension. There is great virtue in doing something nice for someone and not telling anyone about it. By the same token, resisting the impulse to proudly announce our membership in NA to the world—in effect, asking everyone to acknowledge how wonderful we are—makes us value our recovery all the more.

Recovery is a gift that we've received from a Power greater than ourselves. Boasting about our recovery, as if it were our own doing, leads to prideful feelings and grandiosity. But keeping our anonymity leads to humility and feelings of gratitude. Recovery is its own reward; public acclaim can't make it any more valuable than it already is.

❖

Just for today: Recovery is its own reward; I don't need to have mine approved of publicly. I will maintain and cherish my anonymity.

*"We try to remember that when we make amends
we are doing it for ourselves."*

Basic Text, p. 41

❖

As long as we still owe amends, our spirits are cluttered with things we don't need. We're carrying the extra load of an apology owed, a resentment held, or unexpressed remorse. It's like having a messy house. We could leave so we don't have to see the mess, or maybe just step over the piles of debris and pretend they aren't there. But ignoring the disorder won't make it disappear. In the end, the dirty dishes, the crumb-filled carpet, and the overflowing wastebaskets are still there, waiting to be cleaned up.

A cluttered spirit is just as hard to live with as a messy home. We always seem to be tripping over yesterday's leavings. Every time we turn around and try to go somewhere, there is something blocking our path. The more we neglect our responsibility to make amends, the more cluttered our spirits become. And we can't even hire someone to clean up. We have to do the work ourselves.

We gain a deep sense of satisfaction from making our own amends. Just as we would feel after we've cleaned our homes and have time to enjoy a bit of sunshine through sparkling windows, so will our spirits rejoice at our freedom to truly enjoy our recovery. And once the big mess is cleaned up, all we have to do is pick up after ourselves as we go along.

❖

Just for today: I will clear away what's cluttering my spirit by making the amends I owe.

> *"We find that we suffer from a disease, not a moral
> dilemma. We were critically ill, not hopelessly bad."*
>
> **Basic Text, p. 16**

❖

For many of us, Narcotics Anonymous was the answer to a personal puzzle of long standing. Why did we always feel alone, even in a crowd, we wondered? Why did we do so many crazy, self-destructive things? Why did we feel so badly about ourselves so much of the time? And how had our lives gotten so messed up? We thought we were hopelessly bad, or perhaps hopelessly insane.

Given that, it was a great relief to learn we suffered from a disease. Addiction—*that* was the source of our problems. A disease, we realized, could be treated. And when we treat our disease, we can begin to recover.

Today, when we see symptoms of our disease resurfacing in our lives, we need not despair. After all, it's a treatable disease we have, not a moral dilemma. We can be grateful we can recover from the disease of addiction through the application of the Twelve Steps of NA.

❖

Just for today: I am grateful that I have a treatable disease, not a moral dilemma. I will continue applying the treatment for the disease of addiction by practicing the NA program.

*"We have learned from our group experience
that those who keep coming to our meetings
regularly stay clean."*

Basic Text, p. 9

❖

The NA program gives us a new pattern of living. One of the basic elements of that new pattern is regular meeting attendance. For the newcomer, living clean is a brand-new experience. All that once was familiar is changed. The old people, places, and things that served as props on the stage of our lives are gone. New stresses appear, no longer masked or deadened by drugs. That's why we often suggest that newcomers attend a meeting every day. No matter what comes up, no matter how crazy the day gets, we know that our daily meeting awaits us. There, we can renew contact with other recovering addicts, people who know what we're going through because they've been through it themselves. No day needs to go by without the relief we get only from such fellowship.

As we mature in recovery, we get the same kinds of benefits from regular meeting attendance. Regardless of how long we've been clean, we never stop being addicts. True, we probably won't immediately start using mass quantities of drugs if we miss our meetings for a few days. But the more regularly we attend NA meetings, the more we reinforce our identity as *recovering* addicts. And each meeting helps put us that much further from becoming *using* addicts again.

❖

Just for today: I will make a commitment to include regular meeting attendance as a part of my new pattern of living.

"Where there has been wrong, the program teaches us the spirit of forgiveness."

Basic Text, p. 12

❖

In NA, we begin to interact with the world around us. We no longer live in isolation. But freedom from isolation has its price: The more we interact with people, the more often we'll find someone stepping on our toes. And such are the circumstances in which resentments are often born.

Resentments, justified or not, are dangerous to our ongoing recovery. The longer we harbor resentments, the more bitter they become, eventually poisoning us. To stay clean, we must find the capacity to let go of our resentments, the capacity to forgive. We first develop this capacity in working Steps Eight and Nine, and we keep it alive by regularly taking the Tenth Step.

Sometimes when we are unwilling to forgive, it helps to remember that we, too, may someday require another person's forgiveness. Haven't we all, at one time or another, done something that we deeply regretted? And aren't we healed in some measure when others accept our sincere amends?

An attitude of forgiveness is a little easier to develop when we remember that we are all doing the very best we can. And someday we, too, will need forgiveness.

❖

Just for today: I will let go of my resentments. Today, if I am wronged, I will practice forgiveness, knowing that I need forgiveness myself.

"We need not lose faith when we become rebellious."

Basic Text, p. 35

❖

Many of us have lived our entire lives in revolt. Our initial response to any type of direction is often negative. Automatic rejection of authority seems to be a troubling character defect for many addicts.

A thorough self-examination can show us how we react to the world around us. We can ask ourselves if our rebellion against people, places, and institutions is justified. If we keep writing long enough, we can usually get past what others did and uncover our own part in our affairs. We find that what others did to us was not as important as how we responded to the situations we found ourselves in.

Regular inventory allows us to examine the patterns in our reactions to life and see if we are prone to chronic rebelliousness. Sometimes we will find that, while we may usually go along with what is suggested to us rather than risk rejection, we secretly harbor resentments against authority. If left to themselves, these resentments can lead us away from our program of recovery.

The inventory process allows us to uncover, evaluate, and alter our rebellious patterns. We can't change the world by taking an inventory, but we can change the way we react to it.

❖

Just for today: I want freedom from the turmoil of rebelliousness. Before I act, I will inventory myself and think about my true values.

*"One of the biggest stumbling blocks to recovery seems
to be placing unrealistic expectations on ... others."*

Basic Text, p. 82

❖

Many of us come into Narcotics Anonymous feeling pretty poorly about ourselves. By comparison, the recovering addicts we meet at meetings may seem almost superhumanly serene. These wise, loving people have many months, even years of living in accordance with spiritual principles, giving of themselves to others without expecting anything back. We trust them, allowing them to love us until we can love ourselves. We expect them to make everything alright again.

Then the glow of early recovery begins to fade, and we start to see the human side of our NA friends and sponsor. Perhaps a fellow member of our home group stands us up for a coffee date, or we see two oldtimers bickering at a committee meeting, or we realize our sponsor has a defect of character or two. We're crushed, disillusioned—these recovering addicts aren't perfect after all! How can we possibly trust them anymore?

Somewhere between "the heroes of recovery" and "the lousy NA bums" lies the truth: Our fellow addicts are neither completely bad nor completely good. After all, if they were perfect, they wouldn't need this program. Our friends and sponsor are ordinary recovering addicts, just like we are. We can relate to their ordinary recovery experience and use it in our own program.

❖

Just for today: My friends and my sponsor are human, just like me—and I trust their experience all the more for that.

*"We learn that a simple, loving hug can make
all the difference in the world..."*

Basic Text, p. 91

❖

Perhaps there have been times in our recovery when we were close to someone who was in great pain. We struggled with the question, "What can I do to make them feel better?" We felt anxious and inadequate to relieve their suffering. We wished we had more experience to share. We didn't know what to say.

But sometimes life deals wounds that can't be eased by even the most heartfelt words. Words can never express all we mean when our deepest feelings of compassion are involved. Language is inadequate to reach a wounded soul, as only the touch of a loving Higher Power can heal an injury to the spirit.

When those we love are grieving, simply being present is perhaps the most compassionate contribution we can offer. We can rest assured that a loving Higher Power is working hard at healing the spirit; our only responsibility is to be there. Our presence, a loving hug, and a sympathetic ear will surely express the depth of our feelings, and do more to reach the heart of a human being in pain than mere words ever could.

❖

Just for today: I will offer my presence, a hug, and a sympathetic ear to someone I love.

*"We learn to become flexible... As new things
are revealed, we feel renewed."*

Basic Text, p. 102

❖

"Flexibility" was not a part of the vocabulary we used in our using days. We'd become obsessed with the raw pleasure of our drugs and hardened to all the softer, subtler, more infinitely varied pleasures of the world around us. Our disease had turned life itself into a constant threat of jails, institutions, and death, a threat against which we hardened ourselves all the more. In the end we became brittle. With the merest breath of life's wind we crumbled at last, broken, defeated, with no choice but to surrender.

But the beautiful irony of recovery is that, in our surrender, we found the flexibility we had lost in our addiction, the very lack of which had defeated us. We regained the ability to bend in life's breeze without breaking. When the wind blew, we felt its loving caress against our skin, where once we would have hardened ourselves as if against the onrush of a storm.

The winds of life blow new airs our way each moment, and with them new fragrances, new pleasures, varied, subtly different. As we bend with life's wind, we feel and hear and touch and smell and taste all it has to offer us. And as new winds blow, we feel renewed.

❖

Just for today: Higher Power, help me bend with life's wind and glory in its passing. Free me from rigidity.

"My life is well-rounded and I am becoming a more comfortable version of myself, not the neurotic, boring person that I thought I'd be without drugs."

❖

Is there *really* life without drugs? Newcomers are sure that they are destined to lead a humdrum existence once they quit using. That fear is far from reality.

Narcotics Anonymous opens the door to a new way of life for our members. The only thing we lose in NA is our slavery to drugs. We gain a host of new friends, time to pursue hobbies, the ability to be stably employed, even the capacity to pursue an education if we so desire. We are able to start projects and see them through to completion. We can go to a dance and feel comfortable, even if we have two left feet. We start to budget money to travel, even if it's only with a tent to a nearby campsite. In recovery, we find out what interests us and pursue new pastimes. We dare to dream.

Life is certainly different when we have the rooms of Narcotics Anonymous to return to. Through the love we find in NA, we begin to believe in ourselves. Equipped with this belief, we venture forth into the world to discover new horizons. Many times, the world is a better place because an NA member has been there.

❖

Just for today: I can live a well-rounded, comfortable life—a life I never dreamed existed. Recovery has opened new horizons to me and equipped me to explore them.

"We had to have something different, and we thought we had found it in drugs."

Basic Text, p. 13

❖

Many of us have always felt different from other people. We know we're not unique in feeling that way; we hear many addicts share the same thing. We searched all our lives for something to make us all right, to fix that "different" place inside us, to make us whole and acceptable. Drugs seemed to fill that need. When we were high, at least we no longer felt the emptiness or the need. There was one drawback: The drugs, which were our solution, quickly became our problem.

Once we gave up the drugs, the sense of emptiness returned. At first we felt despair because we didn't have any solution of our own to that miserable longing. But we were willing to take direction and began to work the steps. As we did, we found what we'd been looking for, that "something different." Today, we believe that our lifelong yearning was primarily for knowledge of a Higher Power; the "something different" we needed was a relationship with a loving God. The steps tell us how to begin that relationship.

❖

Just for today: My Higher Power is the "something different" that's always been missing in my life. I will use the steps to re-store that missing ingredient to my spirit.

*"Eventually we are shown that we must get honest,
or we will use again."*

Basic Text, p. 85

❖

Everyone has secrets, right? Some of us have little secrets, items that would cause only minor embarrassment if found out. Some of us have big secrets, whole areas of our lives cloaked in thick, murky darkness. Big secrets may represent a more obvious, immediate danger to our recovery. But the little secrets do their own kind of damage, the more insidious perhaps because we think they're "harmless."

Big or little, our secrets represent spiritual territory we are unwilling to surrender to the principles of recovery. The longer we reserve pieces of our lives to be ruled by self-will and the more vigorously we defend our "right" to hold onto them, the more damage we do. Gradually, the unsurrendered territories of our lives tend to expand, taking more and more ground.

Whether the secrets in our lives are big or little, sooner or later they bring us to the same place. We must choose—either we surrender *everything* to our program, or we will lose our recovery.

❖

Just for today: I want the kind of recovery that comes from total surrender to the program. *Today*, I will talk with my sponsor and disclose my secrets, big or small.

> *"... we think that if we can just get enough food,
> enough sex, or enough money, we'll be satisfied
> and everything will be alright."*

Basic Text, p. 80

❖

In our addiction, we could never get enough drugs, or money, or sex, or anything else. Even too much was never enough! There was a spiritual emptiness inside us. Though we tried as hard as we could to fill that emptiness ourselves, we never succeeded. In the end, we realized that we lacked the power to fill it; it would take a Power greater than ourselves to do that.

So we stopped using, and we stopped trying to fill the emptiness in our gut with *things*. We turned to our Higher Power, asking for its care, strength, and direction. We surrendered and made way for that Power to begin the process of filling our inner void. We stopped grabbing things and started receiving the free gift of love our Higher Power had for us. Slowly, our inner emptiness was being filled.

Now that we've been given our Higher Power's gift of love, what do we do with it? If we clasp that gift tightly to ourselves, we will smother it. We must remember that love grows only when it is shared. We can only keep this gift by freely giving it away. The world of addiction is a world of taking and being taken; the world of recovery is a world of giving and being given. In which world do we choose to live?

❖

Just for today: I choose to live in the fullness of recovery. I will celebrate my conscious contact with the God of my understanding by freely sharing with others that which has been freely shared with me.

> *"Emotional balance is one of the first results*
> *of meditation, and our experience bears this out."*

Basic Text, p. 47

❖

Though each of us defines "emotional balance" a little differently, all of us must find it. Emotional balance can mean finding and maintaining a positive outlook on life, regardless of what may be happening around us. To some, it might mean an understanding of our emotions that allows us to respond, not react, to our feelings. It can mean that we experience our feelings as intensely as we can while also moderating their excessive expression.

Emotional balance comes with practice in prayer and meditation. We get quiet and share our thoughts and hopes and concerns with the God of our understanding. Then we listen for guidance, awaiting the power to act on that direction.

Eventually, our skills in maintaining near-balance get better, and the wild up-and-down emotional swings we used to experience begin to settle. We develop an ability to let others feel their feelings; we have no need to judge them. And we fully embrace our own personal range of emotions.

❖

Just for today: Through regular prayer and meditation, I will discover what emotional balance means to me.

> *"We may think that we have done enough by writing about our past. We cannot afford this mistake."*

Basic Text, p. 32

❖

Some of us aren't too keen on writing out our Fourth Step; others take it to an obsessive extreme. To our sponsor's growing dismay, we inventory ourselves again and again. We discover everything there is to know about why we were the way we were. We have the idea that thinking, writing, and talking about our past is enough. We hear none of our sponsor's suggestions to become entirely ready to have our defects removed or make amends for the harm we've caused. We simply write more about those defects and delightedly share our fresh insights. Finally, our worn-out sponsor withdraws from us in self-defense.

Extreme as this scenario may seem, many of us have found ourselves in just such a situation. Thinking, writing, and talking about what was wrong with us made us feel like we had it all under control. Sooner or later, however, we realized we were stuck in our problems, the solutions nowhere in sight. We knew that, if we wanted to live differently, we would have to move on beyond Step Five in our program. We began to seek the willingness to have a Higher Power remove the character defects of which we'd become so intensely aware. We made amends for the destruction we had caused others in acting out on those defects. Only then did we begin to experience the freedom of an awakening spirit. Today, we're no longer victims; we are free to move on in our recovery.

❖

Just for today: Although necessary, Steps Four and Five alone will not bring about emotional and spiritual recovery. I will take them, and then I will act on them.

*"One of the most profound changes in our lives is
in the realm of personal relationships."*

Basic Text, p. 57

❖

Recovery gives many of us relationships that are closer and more intimate than any we've had before. As time passes, we find ourselves gravitating toward those who eventually become our friends, our sponsor, and our partners in life. Shared laughter, tears, and struggles bring shared respect and lasting empathy.

What, then, do we do when we find that we don't agree with our friends on everything? We may discover that we don't share the same taste in music as our dearest friend, or that we don't agree with our spouse about how the furniture should be arranged, or even find ourselves voting differently from our sponsor at a service committee meeting. Does conflict mean that the friendship, the marriage, or the sponsorship is over? No!

These types of conflict are not only to be expected in any long-lasting relationship but are actually an indication that both people are emotionally healthy and honest individuals. In any relationship where both people agree on absolutely everything, chances are that only one person is doing the thinking. If we sacrifice our honesty and integrity to avoid conflicts or disagreements, we give away the best of what we bring to our relationships. We experience the full measure of partnership with another human being when we are fully honest.

❖

Just for today: I will welcome the differences that make each one of us special. Today, I will work on being myself.

*"In NA, our joys are multiplied by sharing good days;
our sorrows are lessened by sharing the bad.
For the first time in our lives, we don't have
to experience anything alone."*

IP No. 16, *For the Newcomer*

❖

When we practice using the steps and the other tools of our program to work through our hardships, we become able to take pleasure in the joys of living clean. But our joys pass all too quickly if we don't share them with others, while hardships borne alone may be long in passing. In the Fellowship of Narcotics Anonymous, we often multiply our joys and divide our burdens by sharing them with one another.

We addicts experience pleasures in recovery that, sometimes, only another addict can appreciate. Fellow members understand when we tell them of the pride we take today in fulfilling commitments, the warmth we feel in mending damaged relationships, the relief we experience in not having to use drugs to make it through the day. When we share these experiences with recovering addicts and they respond with similar stories, our joy is multiplied. The same principle applies to the challenges we encounter as recovering addicts. By sharing our challenges and allowing other NA members to share their strength with us, our load is lightened.

The fellowship we have in Narcotics Anonymous is precious. Sharing together, we enhance the joys and diminish the burdens of life in recovery.

❖

Just for today: I will share my joys and my burdens with other recovering addicts. I will also share in theirs. I am grateful for the strong bonds of fellowship in Narcotics Anonymous.

*"God, grant me the serenity to accept the things
I cannot change, the courage to change the things I can,
and the wisdom to know the difference."*

Serenity Prayer

❖

Recovery involves change, and change means doing things differently. The problem is, many of us resist doing things differently; what we're doing may not be working, but at least we're familiar with it. It takes courage to step out into the unknown. How do we find that courage?

We can look around ourselves at NA meetings. There, we see others who've found they needed to change what they were doing and who've done so successfully. Not only does that help quiet our fear that change—any change—spells disaster, it also gives us the benefit of their experience with what *does* work, experience we can use in changing what *doesn't*.

We can also look at our own recovery experience. Even if that experience, so far, has been limited to stopping the use of drugs, still we *have* made many changes in our lives—changes for the good. Whatever aspects of our lives we have applied the steps to, we have always found surrender better than denial, recovery superior to addiction.

Our own experience and the experience of others in NA tells us that "changing the things I can" is a big part of what recovery is all about. The steps and the power to practice them give us the direction and courage we need to change. We have nothing to fear.

❖

Just for today: I welcome change. With the help of my Higher Power, I will find the courage to change the things I can.

*"Prayer takes practice, and we should remind ourselves
that skilled people were not born with their skills."*

Basic Text, p. 46

❖

Many of us came into recovery with no experience in prayer and worried about not knowing the "right words." Some of us remembered the words we'd learned in childhood but weren't sure we believed in those words anymore. Whatever our background, in recovery we struggled to find words that spoke truly from our hearts.

Often the first prayer we attempt is a simple request to our Higher Power asking for help in staying clean each day. We may ask for guidance and courage or simply pray for knowledge of God's will for us and the power to carry that out. If we find ourselves stumbling in our prayers, we may ask other members to share with us about how they learned to pray. No matter whether we pray in need or pray in joy, the important thing is to keep making the effort.

Our prayers will be shaped by our experience with the Twelve Steps and our personal understanding of a Higher Power. As our relationship with that Higher Power develops, we become more comfortable with prayer. In time, prayer becomes a source of strength and comfort. We seek that source often and willingly.

❖

Just for today: I know that prayer can be simple. I will start where I am and practice.

*"Life takes on a new meaning when
we open ourselves to this gift."*

Basic Text, p. 107

❖

Neglecting our recovery is like neglecting any other gift we've been given. Suppose someone gave you a new car. Would you let it sit in the driveway until the tires rotted? Would you just drive it, ignoring routine maintenance, until it expired on the road? Of course not! You would go to great lengths to maintain the condition of such a valuable gift.

Recovery is also a gift, and we have to care for it if we want to keep it. While our recovery doesn't come with an extended warranty, there is a routine maintenance schedule. This maintenance includes regular meeting attendance and various forms of service. We'll have to do some daily cleaning—our Tenth Step—and, once in a while, a major Fourth Step overhaul will be required. But if we maintain the gift of recovery, thanking the Giver each day, it will continue.

The gift of recovery is one that grows with the giving. Unless we give it away, we can't keep it. But in sharing our recovery with others, we come to value it all the more.

❖

Just for today: My recovery is a gift, and I want to keep it. I'll do the required maintenance, and I'll share my recovery with others.

"In accordance with the principles of recovery, we try not to judge, stereotype or moralize with each other."

Basic Text, p. 11

❖

Let's face it: In Narcotics Anonymous, we live in a glass house of sorts. Our fellow members know more about our personal lives than anyone has ever known before. They know who we spend our time with, where we work, what step we're on, how many children we have, and so forth. And what our fellow members don't know, they will probably imagine.

We may be unhappy when others gossip about us. But if we withdraw from the fellowship and isolate ourselves to avoid gossip, we also rob ourselves of the love, friendship, and unparalleled experience with recovery that our fellow members have to offer. A better way to deal with gossip is to simply accept the way things are and the way *we* are, and live our lives according to principles. The more secure we become with our personal program, the decisions we make, and the guidance we receive from a loving God, the less the opinions of others will concern us.

❖

Just for today: I am committed to being involved in the NA Fellowship. The opinions of others will not affect my commitment to recovery.

*"The only suggested guidelines are that this Power
be loving, caring, and greater than ourselves. We don't
have to be religious to accept this idea. The point is
that we open our minds to believe."*

Basic Text, p. 24

❖

In a lifelong process of coming to believe, our understanding
of God will change. The understanding we have when new in
recovery will not be the same when we have a few months clean,
nor will that understanding be the same when we have a few
years clean.

Our initial understanding of a Power greater than ourselves will
most likely be limited. That Power will keep us clean but, we may
think, nothing more. We may hesitate to pray because we have
placed conditions on what we will ask our Higher Power to do for
us. "Oh, this stuff is *so* awful, even God couldn't do anything," we
might say, or "God's got a lot of people to take care of. There's
no time for me."

But, as we grow in recovery, so will our understanding. We'll
begin to see that the only limits to God's love and grace are those
we impose by refusing to step out of the way. The loving God
we come to believe in is infinite, and the power and love we find
in our belief is shared by nearly every recovering addict around
the world.

❖

Just for today: The God I am coming to understand has a limitless capacity for love and care. I will trust that my God is bigger
than any problem I may have.

*"We may fear that being in touch with our feelings
will trigger an overwhelming chain reaction
of pain and panic."*

Basic Text, p. 30

❖

A common complaint about the Fourth Step is that it makes us painfully conscious of our defects of character. We may be tempted to falter in our program of recovery. Through surrender and acceptance, we can find the resources we need to keep working the steps.

It's not the awareness of our defects that causes the most agony—it's the defects themselves. When we were using, all we felt was the drugs; we could ignore the suffering our defects were causing us. Now that the drugs are gone, we feel that pain. Refusing to acknowledge the source of our anguish doesn't make it go away; denial *protects* the pain and makes it stronger. The Twelve Steps help us deal with the misery caused by our defects by dealing directly with the defects themselves.

If we hurt from the pain of our defects, we can remind ourselves of the nightmare of addiction, a nightmare from which we've now awakened. We can recall the hope for release the Second Step gave us. We can again turn our will and our lives over, through the Third Step, to the care of the God of our understanding. Our Higher Power cares for us by giving us the help we need to work the rest of the Twelve Steps. We don't have to fear our feelings. Just for today, we can continue in our recovery.

❖

Just for today: I won't be afraid of my feelings. With the help of my Higher Power, I'll continue in my recovery.

*"It will not make us better people to judge
the faults of another."*

Basic Text, p. 38

❖

How easy it is to point out the faults of others! There's a reason for this: The defects we identify most easily in others are often the defects we are most familiar with in our own characters. We may notice our best friend's tendency to spend too much money, but if we examine our own spending habits we'll probably find the same compulsiveness. We may decide our sponsor is much too involved in service, but find that we haven't spent a single weekend with our families in the past three months because of one service commitment or another.

What we dislike in our fellows are often those things we dislike most in ourselves. We can turn this observation to our spiritual advantage. When we are stricken with the impulse to judge someone else, we can redirect the impulse in such a way as to recognize our own defects more clearly. What we see will guide our actions toward recovery and help us become emotionally healthy and happy individuals.

❖

Just for today: I will look beyond the character defects of others and recognize my own.

*"There is something in our self-destructive personalities
that cries for failure."*

Basic Text, p. 80

❖

"Poor me; woe is me; look at me, my life is such a mess! I've fallen, and no matter how hard I try, I continue to fail." Many of us came to NA singing this sad refrain.

Life isn't like that anymore. True, sometimes we still stumble; at times we even fall. Sometimes we feel like we can't move forward in our lives, no matter how hard we try. But the truth of the matter is that, with the help of other recovering addicts in NA, we find a hand to pull us up, dust us off, and help us start all over again. That's the new refrain in our lives today.

No longer do we say, "I'm a failure and I'm going nowhere." Usually, it's more like, "Rats! I hit that same bump in the road of life again. Pretty soon I'll learn to slow down or avoid it entirely." Until then, we may continue to fall down occasionally, but we've learned that there's always a helping hand to set us on our feet again.

❖

Just for today: If I begin to cry failure, I'll remember there is a way to move forward. I will accept the encouragement and support of NA.

*"Gradually, as we become more God-centered than
self-centered, our despair turns to hope."*

Basic Text, p. 95

❖

As using addicts, despair was our relentless companion. It colored our every waking moment. Despair was born of our experience in active addiction: No matter what measures we tried to make our lives better, we slid ever deeper into misery. Attempts we made to control our lives frequently met with failure. In a sense, our First Step admission of powerlessness was an acknowledgment of despair.

Steps Two and Three lead us gradually out of that despair and into new hope, the companion of the recovering addict. Having accepted that so many of our efforts to change have failed, we come to believe that there is a Power greater than ourselves. We believe this Power can—and will—help us. We practice the Second and Third Steps as an affirmation of our hope for a better life, turning to this Power for guidance. As we come to rely more and more on a Higher Power for the management of our day-to-day life, the despair arising from our long experiment with self-sufficiency disappears.

❖

Just for today: I will reaffirm my Third Step decision. I know that, with a Higher Power in my life, there is hope.

*"When we stop living in the here and now,
our problems become magnified unreasonably."*

Basic Text, p. 99

❖

"Just for today"—it's a comforting thought. If we try to live in the past, we may find ourselves torn by painful, disquieting memories. The lessons of our using are not the teachers we seek for recovery. Living in tomorrow means moving in with fear. We cannot see the shape of the secret future, and uncertainty brings worry. Our lives look overwhelming when we lose the focus of today.

Living in the moment offers freedom. In this moment, we know that we are safe. We are not using, and we have everything we need. What's more, life is happening in the here and now. The past is gone and the future has yet to arrive; our worrying won't change any of it. Today, we can enjoy our recovery, this very minute.

❖

Just for today: I will stay in the here and now. Today—this moment—I am free.

"Our real value is in being ourselves."

Basic Text, p. 105

❖

Over and over, we have tried to live up to the expectations of those around us. We may have been raised believing that we were okay if we earned good grades in school, cleaned our rooms, or dressed a certain way. Always wanting to belong and be loved, many of us spent a lot of time trying to fit in—yet we never quite seemed to measure up.

Now, in recovery, we are accepted as we are. Our real value to others is in being ourselves. As we work the steps, we learn to accept ourselves just as we are. Once this happens, we gain the freedom to become who we want to be.

We each have many good qualities we can share with others. Our experiences, honestly shared, help others find the level of identification they need to begin their recovery. We discover that we all have special gifts to offer those around us.

❖

Just for today: My experience in recovery is the greatest gift I can give another addict. I will share myself honestly with others.

❖ ❖ ❖

October

❖ ❖ ❖

*"We learn that pain can be
a motivating factor in recovery."*

Basic Text, p. 30

❖

"Pain—who needs it!" we think whenever we're in it. We see no good purpose for pain. It seems to be a pointless exercise in suffering. If someone happens to mention spiritual growth to us while we're in pain, we most likely snort in disgust and walk away, thinking we've never encountered a more insensitive person.

But what if human beings didn't feel pain—either physical or emotional? Sound like an ideal world? Not really. If we weren't capable of feeling physical pain, we wouldn't know when to blink foreign particles out of our eyes; we wouldn't know when to stop exercising; we wouldn't even know when to roll over in our sleep. We would simply abuse ourselves for lack of a natural warning system.

The same holds true for emotional pain. How would we have known that our lives had become unmanageable if we hadn't been in pain? Just like physical pain, emotional pain lets us know when to stop doing something that hurts.

But pain is not only a motivating factor. Emotional pain provides a basis for comparison when we are joyful. We couldn't appreciate joy without knowing pain.

❖

Just for today: I will accept pain as a necessary part of life. I know that to whatever level I can feel pain, I can also feel joy.

> *"We grasp the limitless strength provided for us*
> *through our daily prayer and surrender as long as*
> *we keep faith and renew it."*

Basic Text, p. 46

❖

There are two parts to recovery: getting clean, and staying clean. Getting clean is comparatively easy because we only have to do it once. Staying clean is more difficult, requiring attention every day of our lives. Yet both draw their power from faith.

We got clean on faith. We admitted that addiction was more powerful than we were, and we stopped trying to fight it on our own. We turned the battle over to a Power greater than ourselves, and that Higher Power got us clean.

We stay clean each day the same way: on faith. Just for today, we surrender. Life may be too big for us to tackle on our own power. When it is, we seek a Power greater than ourselves. We pray, asking our Higher Power for direction and the strength to follow it. By exercising and renewing our faith on a daily basis, we tap the resources we need to live clean, full lives.

There is limitless strength available to us whenever we need it. To grasp it, all we need to do is keep faith in the Higher Power that got us clean and keeps us clean.

❖

Just for today: Faith got me clean, and faith will keep me clean. Today, I will keep faith with my Higher Power. I will renew my surrender and pray for knowledge and strength.

*"Our egos, once so large and dominant, now take
a back seat because we are in harmony with
a loving God. We find that we lead richer, happier,
and much fuller lives when we lose self-will."*

Basic Text, p. 105

❖

Addiction and self-will go hand in hand. The unmanageability that we admitted to in Step One was as much a product of our self-will as it was of our chronic drug abuse. And today, living on self-will can make our lives just as unmanageable as they were when we were using. When *our* ideas, *our* desires, *our* demands take first place in our lives, we find ourselves in constant conflict with everyone and everything around us.

Self-will reflects our reliance on ego. The only thing that will free us from self-will and the conflict it generates in our lives is to break our reliance on ego, coming to rely instead on the guidance and power offered us by a loving God.

We are taught to consult spiritual principles, not our selfish desires, in making our decisions. We are taught to seek guidance from a Higher Power, one with a larger vision of things than our own. In doing this, we find our lives meshing more and more easily with the order of things around us. No longer do we exclude ourselves from the flow of life; we become a part of it, and discover the fullness of what recovery has to offer.

❖

Just for today: I seek freedom from ego and the conflicts generated by self-will. I will try to improve my conscious contact with the God of my understanding, seeking the guidance and power I need to live in harmony with my world.

*"When we first begin to enjoy relief from our addiction,
we run the risk of assuming control of our lives again.
We forget the agony and pain that we have known."*

Basic Text, p. 50

❖

Many of us have been "thirty-day wonders." We were desperate and dying when we showed up at our first NA meeting. We identified with the addicts we met there and the message they shared. With their support, we were finally able to stop using and catch a free breath. For the first time in a long, long time, we felt at home. Overnight, our lives were transformed; we walked, talked, ate, drank, slept, and dreamed Narcotics Anonymous.

Then, Narcotics Anonymous lost its novelty. Meetings that had been a thrill became monotonous. Our wonderful NA friends became bores; their uplifting NA talk, drivel. When our former friends called, inviting us back for some of the old fun, we kissed our recovery goodbye.

Sooner or later, we made our way back to the rooms of Narcotics Anonymous. Nothing had changed out there, we'd discovered—not us, not our friends, not the drugs, not anything. If anything, it had gotten worse than ever.

True, NA meetings may not be a laugh riot, and our NA friends may not be spiritual giants. But there's a power in the meetings, a common bond among the members, a life to the program that we can't do without. Today, our recovery is more than just a fad—it's a way of life. We're going to practice living our program like our lives depend on it, because *they do.*

❖

Just for today: I'm no "thirty-day wonder." The NA way is my way of life, and I'm here for the duration.

*"Many of us have difficulty admitting that we caused
harm for others... We cut away our justifications
and our ideas of being a victim."*

Basic Text, p. 38

❖

Our lives are progressing nicely. Things are going good, and each year in recovery brings more material and spiritual gifts. We may have a little money in the bank, a new car, or a committed relationship. We have a little self-confidence, and our faith in a Higher Power is growing.

Then, something happens. Someone breaks into our new car and steals the stereo, or the person we're in the relationship with becomes unfaithful. Right away, we feel victimized. "Where's the justice?" we wail. But if we take a look back on our own behavior, we may find that we've been guilty of doing what's just been done to us. We realize we wouldn't really want justice—not for ourselves, and not for others. What we want is mercy.

We thank a loving God for the compassion we've been shown, and we take the time to appreciate all the precious gifts that recovery brings.

❖

Just for today: I will pray for mercy, not justice. I am grateful for the compassion I've been shown, and will offer mercy to others.

*"Projections about actually making amends can be
a major obstacle both in making the list
and in becoming willing."*

Basic Text, p. 39

❖

The Eighth Step asks us to become willing to make amends to all persons we have harmed. As we approach this step, we may wonder what the outcome of our amends will be. Will we be forgiven? Relieved of any lingering guilt? Or will we be tarred and feathered by the persons we've harmed?

Our tendency to seek forgiveness must be surrendered if we expect to receive the spiritual benefits of the Eighth and Ninth Steps. If we approach these steps expecting anything, we're likely to be very disappointed with the results. We want to ask ourselves if we are pinning our hopes on gaining the forgiveness of the person to whom we are making amends. Or maybe we're hoping we'll be excused from our debts by some sympathetic creditor moved to tears by our hard-luck story.

We need to be willing to make our amends regardless of the outcome. We can plan the amends, but we can't plan the results. Although we may not be granted a full pardon by everyone to whom we owe amends, we will learn to forgive ourselves. In the process, we will find that we no longer have to carry the burdens of the past.

❖

Just for today: I will let go of any expectations I have on the people to whom I owe amends.

*"As recovering addicts, we find that we are still
dependent, but our dependence has shifted from the
things around us to a loving God and the inner strength
we get in our relationship with Him."*

Basic Text, p. 71

❖

For many addicts, rebelliousness is second nature. We didn't want to depend on anyone or anything, and especially not on God. The beauty of using, we thought, was that it gave us the power to be and feel anything we wanted, all by ourselves. But the price we paid for this illusory freedom was a dependence beyond our worst nightmares. Rather than freeing us, using enslaved us.

When we came to Narcotics Anonymous, we learned that dependence on God didn't have to mean what we may have thought it meant. Yes, if we wanted to be restored to sanity, we would need to tap "a Power greater than ourselves." However, we could choose our own concept of this Higher Power—we could even make one up. Dependence on a Higher Power would not limit us, we discovered; it would free us.

The Power we find in recovery is the power we lacked on our own. It is the love we were afraid to depend on others for. It is the sense of personal direction we never had, the guidance we couldn't humble ourselves to ask for or trust others to give. It is all these things, and it is our own. Today, we are grateful to have a Higher Power to depend on.

❖

Just for today: I will depend on the love and inner strength I draw from the God of my own understanding.

*"We suspect that if we do not use what we have,
we will lose what we have."*

Basic Text, p. 78

❖

Addiction gave a pattern to our lives, and with it a meaning—a dark, diseased meaning, to be sure, but a meaning nonetheless. The Narcotics Anonymous recovery program gives us a new pattern of living to replace our old routines. And with that new pattern comes a new meaning to our lives, one of light and hope.

What is this new pattern of living? Instead of isolation, we find fellowship. Instead of living blindly, repeating the same mistakes again and again, we regularly examine ourselves, free to keep what helps us grow and discard what doesn't. Rather than constantly trying to get by on our own limited power, we develop a conscious contact with a loving Power greater than ourselves.

Our life must have a pattern. To maintain our recovery, we must maintain the new patterns our program has taught us. By giving regular attention to these patterns, we will maintain the freedom we've found from the deadly disease of addiction, and keep hold of the meaning recovery has brought to our lives.

❖

Just for today: I will begin a new pattern in my life: the regular maintenance of my recovery.

*"We emphasize setting our house in order
because it brings us relief."*

Basic Text, p. 97

❖

Focusing on what others are doing can provide momentary relief from having to take a look at ourselves. But one of the secrets of success in Narcotics Anonymous is making sure our own house is in order. So what does "setting our house in order" mean, anyway?

It means we work the steps, allowing us to look at our role in our relationships with others. When we have a problem with someone, we can take our own inventory to find out what our part in the problem has been. With the help of our sponsor, we strive to set it right. Then, each day, we continue taking our inventory to avoid repeating the same mistakes in the future.

It's pretty simple. We treat others as we would like others to treat us. We promptly make amends when we owe them. And when we turn our lives over to the care of our Higher Power on a daily basis, we can start to avoid running on the self-will so characteristic of our active addiction. Guided by a Power that seeks the best for everyone, our relationships with others will surely improve.

❖

Just for today: I will set my own house in order. Today, I will examine my part in the problems in my life. If I owe amends, I will make them.

*"Before we got clean, most of our actions
were guided by impulse. Today, we are not locked
into this type of thinking."*

Basic Text, p. 90

❖

Ever been tempted to do something even when you knew the results would be disastrous? Ever thought about how much it was going to hurt to do what you were tempted to do, then proceed to do it anyway?

It is said that there are consequences to every action. Before we got clean, many of us simply didn't believe this. But now we know exactly what it means. When we act, we know there will be consequences to pay. No longer can we decide to do something in ignorance when we know full well that we won't like the price we'll have to pay.

There's a prize and a price. It's okay to act despite the consequences if we're willing to pay the price, but there's always one to pay.

❖

Just for today: I will think about the consequences of my actions before I take them.

> *"Our best thinking got us into trouble.... Recovery is*
> *an active change in our ideas and attitudes."*

Basic Text, p. 55

❖

In active addiction, the world probably looked like a horrible place. Using helped us tolerate the world we saw. Today, however, we understand that the world's condition wasn't really the problem. It was our ideas and attitudes about the world that made it impossible for us to find a comfortable place in it.

Our attitudes and our ideas are the eyeglasses through which we see our lives. If our "glasses" are smudged or dirty, our lives look dim. If our attitudes aren't well focused, the whole world appears distorted. To see the world clearly, we need to keep our attitudes and ideas clean, free of things like resentment, denial, self-pity, and closed-mindedness. To insure our vision of life is in focus, we have to bring our ideas in line with reality.

In addiction, our best thinking kept us from clearly seeing either the world or our part in it. Recovery serves to correct the prescriptions in our attitudinal eyewear. By stripping away our denial and replacing it with faith, self-honesty, humility, and responsibility, the steps help us see our lives in a whole new way. Then the steps help us keep our spiritual lenses clean, encouraging us to regularly examine our ideas, our attitudes, and our actions.

Today, seen through the clean lenses of faith and recovery, the world looks like a warm, inviting place to live.

❖

Just for today: I will view the world and my life through the clean spiritual lenses of my program.

> *"When we admit that our lives have become unmanageable, we don't have to argue our point of view.... We no longer have to be right all the time."*

Basic Text, p. 58

❖

Nothing isolates us more quickly from the warmth and camaraderie of our fellow NA members than having to be "right." Insecure, we pretend to be some kind of authority figure. Suffering from low self-esteem, we try to build ourselves up by putting others down. At best, such tactics push others away from us; at worst, they draw attack. The more we try to impress others with how "right" we are, the more wrong we become.

We don't have to be "right" to be secure; we don't have to pretend to have all the answers for others to love or respect us. In fact, just the opposite is true. None of us have all the answers. We depend upon one another to help bridge the gaps in our understanding of things, and we depend upon a Power greater than our own to make up for our personal powerlessness. We live easily with others when we offer what we know, admit what we don't, and seek to learn from our peers. We live securely in ourselves when we cease relying on our own power and start relying on the God we've come to understand in recovery.

We don't have to be "right" all the time, just recovering.

❖

Just for today: God, I admit my powerlessness and the un-manageability of my life. Help me live with others as an equal, dependent upon you for direction and strength.

*"Words cannot describe the sense of spiritual awareness
that we receive when we have given something,
no matter how small, to another person."*

Basic Text, p. 104

❖

Sometimes it seems as though there is so much wrong with the world that we might as well forget trying to make a difference. "After all," we think, "what in the world can I do? I'm just one person." Whether our concerns are so broad that we desire global peace or so personal that we simply want recovery made available to every addict who wants it, the task seems overwhelming. "So much work to do, so little time," we sigh, sometimes wondering how we'll ever do any good.

Amazingly enough, the smallest contributions can make the biggest difference. To gain more from life than an ordinary, plodding existence requires very little effort on our parts. We ourselves are transformed by the deep satisfaction we experience when we lift the spirits of just one person. When we smile at someone who is frowning, when we let someone in front of us on the freeway, when we call a newcomer just to say we care, we enter the realm of the extraordinary.

Want to change the world? Start with the addict sitting next to you tonight, and then imagine your act of kindness multiplied. One person at a time, each one of us makes a difference.

❖

Just for today: An act of kindness costs me nothing, but is priceless to the recipient. I will be kind to someone today.

"With the love that I am shown in Narcotics Anonymous, I have no excuse for loneliness."

❖

Addiction is a lonely disease. We may be surrounded by people but, sooner or later, our addiction drives a wedge between us and even our closest loved ones. Many of us are driven to Narcotics Anonymous by a desperate loneliness.

Though we may approach the rooms of NA with caution and suspicion, we are welcomed with a hug, a smile, and a warm "keep coming back." This may be the first place where we have felt welcome in a long, long while. We watch other members talking and laughing, leaving the meeting in groups for more talk at the local coffee shop. We wonder if we, too, could become a part of this loving bunch.

Our pattern of isolation can make it difficult for us to join in. Over time, however, we begin to feel "a part of" rather than "apart from." Soon, when we walk into the rooms, we feel at home. We begin to make friends and our lives start to change.

NA teaches us how to overcome our isolation. Through our first tentative friendships formed in our home group, we start to find that making friends isn't hard. A sense of belonging comes when we share ourselves with others.

❖

Just for today: I am thankful for the friendships my Higher Power has given me in NA. Because of them, I am lonely no more.

"We did not choose to become addicts."

Basic Text, p. 3

❖

When we were growing up, all of us had dreams. Every child has heard a relative or neighbor ask, "What do *you* want to be when you grow up?" Even if some of us didn't have elaborate dreams of success, most of us dreamed of work, families, and a future of dignity and respect. But no one asked, "Do you want to be a drug addict when you grow up?"

We didn't choose to become addicts, and we cannot choose to stop being addicts. We have the disease of addiction. We are not responsible for having it, but we are responsible for our recovery. Having learned that we are sick people and that there is a way of recovery, we can move away from blaming circumstances—or ourselves—and into living the solution. We didn't choose addiction, but we can choose recovery.

❖

Just for today: I choose recovery.

> *"...praying only for knowledge of His will for us*
> *and the power to carry that out."*

Step Eleven

❖

How do we pray? With little experience, many of us don't even know how to begin. The process, however, is neither difficult nor complicated.

We came to Narcotics Anonymous because of our drug addiction. But underlying that, many of us felt a deep sense of bewilderment with life itself. We seemed to be lost, wandering a trackless waste with no one to guide us. Prayer is a way to gain direction in life and the power to follow that direction.

Because prayer plays such a central part in NA recovery, many of us set aside a particular time each day to pray, establishing a pattern. In this quiet time, we "talk" to our Higher Power, either silently or aloud. We share our thoughts, our feelings, our day. We ask, "What would you have me do?" At the same time we ask, "Please give me the power to carry out your will."

Learning to pray is simple. We ask for "knowledge of His will for us and the power to carry that out." By doing that, we find the direction we lacked and the strength we need to fulfill our God's will.

❖

Just for today: I will set aside some quiet time to "talk" with my Higher Power. I will ask for that Power's direction and the ability to act on it.

*"Everything we know is subject to revision,
especially what we know about the truth."*

Basic Text, p. 94

❖

Many of us thought we could recognize "The Truth." We believed the truth was one thing, certain and unchanging, which we could grasp easily and without question. The *real* truth, however, was that we often couldn't see the truth if it hit us square in the face. Our disease colored everything in our lives, especially our perception of the truth—in fact, what we "knew" about the truth nearly killed us. Before we could begin to recognize truth, we had to switch our allegiance from our addiction to a Higher Power, the source of all that is good and true.

The truth has changed as our faith in a Higher Power has grown. As we've worked the steps, our entire lives have begun to change through the healing power of the principles of recovery. In order to open the door for that change, we have had to surrender our attachment to an unchanging and rigid truth.

The truth becomes purer and simpler each time we encounter it. And just as the steps work in our lives every day—if we allow them—our understanding of the truth may change each day as we grow.

❖

Just for today: I will open my eyes and my heart to the changes brought about by the steps. With an open mind, I can understand the truth in my life today.

*"Although 'politics makes strange bedfellows,' as the old
saying goes, addiction makes us one of a kind."*

Basic Text, p. 87

❖

What a mixture of folks we have in Narcotics Anonymous! In any given meeting on any given night, we'll find a variety of people who probably never would have sat down in a room together if it weren't for the disease of addiction.

A member who is a physician described his unwillingness to identify at his first meeting by refusing to go into "that room full of junkies." Another member with an extensive background in jails and institutions shared a similar story, except that her shock and surprise stemmed from the realization that "there were nice people there—wearing suits, yet!" These two friends recently celebrated their seventh wedding anniversary.

The most unlikely people form friendships, sponsor each other, and do service work together. We meet in the rooms of recovery together, sharing the bonds of past suffering and hope for the future. We meet on mutual ground with our focus on the two things we all have in common—addiction and recovery.

❖

Just for today: No matter what my personal circumstances, I belong.

> *"... we could feel time, touch reality, and recognize
> spiritual values long lost to many of us."*

Basic Text, p. 88

❖

In our active addiction, we were prepared to compromise everything we believed in just to get our hands on more drugs. Whether we stole from our families and friends, sold ourselves, or lied to our employers, we were ignoring the values that mattered most to us. Each time we compromised another dearly held belief, another chunk of the mortar holding our characters together fell away. By the time many of us came to our first meeting, nothing was left but the ruin of our former selves.

We will locate our lost values as we carry out our first honest self-examination. But in order to rebuild our characters, we'll find it necessary to maintain those values, no matter how great the temptation to shove them aside. We will need to be honest, even when we think we could fool everyone by lying. If we ignore our values, we'll discover that the biggest fibs we've told have been the ones we've told ourselves.

We don't want to start the demolition of our spirits again after all the work we've put into their restoration. It's essential that we stand for something, or we risk falling for anything. Whatever we find important to us, we honor.

❖

Just for today: I stand for something. My strength is the result of living my values.

"Enforced morality lacks the power that comes to us when we choose to live a spiritual life."

Basic Text, p. 45

❖

In our active addiction, many of us lived our lives by default. We were unwilling or unable to make choices about how we wanted to act, what we preferred to do, or even where we would live. We allowed the drugs or other people to make our most basic decisions for us. Freedom from active addiction means, among other things, the freedom to make those choices for ourselves.

Freedom of choice is a wonderful gift, but it's also a great responsibility. Choice allows us to find out who we are and what we believe in. However, in exercising it, we're called on to weigh our own choices and accept the consequences. This leads some of us to seek out someone who will make our choices for us—our sponsor, our home group, our NA friends—just as our disease made our choices for us when we were using. *That's not recovery.*

Seeking others' experience is one thing; abdicating personal responsibility is something else. If we don't use the gift of freedom we've been given, if we refuse to accept the responsibilities that go along with it, we'll lose that gift and our lives will be diminished. We are responsible for our own recovery and our own choices. Difficult as it may seem, we must make those choices for ourselves and become willing to accept the consequences.

❖

Just for today: I am grateful for the freedom to live as I choose. Today, I will accept responsibility for my recovery, make my own choices, and accept the consequences.

"This decision demands continued acceptance, ever-increasing faith, and a daily commitment to recovery."

IP No. 14, *One Addict's Experience...*

❖

Sometimes, we really live the Third Step—and it's great! We don't regret the past, we aren't afraid of the future, and we're generally pleased with the present. Sometimes, though, we lose our vision of God's will in our life.

Many of us dream of erasing the mistakes of our past, but the past cannot be erased. Many of us are grateful this is so, for our past experiences have brought us to the recovery we enjoy today. By working the program, we can learn to accept the past and reconcile ourselves with it by amending our wrongs. Those same Twelve Steps can help eliminate our worries over the future. When we practice NA principles on a daily basis in all our affairs, we can leave the results up to our Higher Power.

It seems as though our members with the strongest faith are the ones who are best able to live in the present moment. Enjoyment, appreciation, and gratitude for the quality of our lives—these are the results of faith in life itself. When we practice the principles of our program, today is the only day we need.

❖

Just for today: I will make the most of today, and trust that yesterday and tomorrow are in God's care.

> *"Our disease is so cunning that it can get us*
> *into impossible situations."*

Basic Text, p. 83

❖

Some of us say, "My disease is talking to me." Others say, "My head won't turn off." Still others refer to "the committee in my mind" or "the monkey on my back." Let's face it. We suffer from an incurable malady that continues to affect us, even in recovery. Our disease gives us warped information about what's going on in our lives. It tells us not to look at ourselves because what we'll see is too scary. Sometimes it tells us we're not responsible for ourselves and our actions; other times, it tells us that everything wrong with the world is our fault. Our disease tricks us into trusting it.

The NA program provides us with many voices that counter our addiction, voices we can trust. We can call our sponsor for a reality check. We can listen to the voice of an addict trying to get clean. The ultimate solution is to work the steps and draw on the strength of a Higher Power. That will get us through those times when "our disease is talking."

❖

Just for today: I will ignore the "voice" of my addiction. I will listen to the voice of my program and a Power greater than myself.

"By surrendering control, we gain a far greater power."
Basic Text, p. 44

❖

When we were using, we did everything we could to run things our way. We used every scheme imaginable to bring our world under control. When we got what we wanted, we felt powerful, invincible; when we didn't, we felt vulnerable, defeated. But that didn't stop us—it only led to more efforts to control and manipulate our lives into a manageable state.

Scheming was our way of denying our powerlessness. As long as we could distract ourselves with our plans, we could put off accepting that we were out of control. Only gradually did we realize that our lives had become unmanageable and that all the conning and manipulating in the world was not going to put our lives back in order.

When we admit our powerlessness, we stop trying to control and manage our way to a better life—we surrender. Lacking sufficient power of our own, we seek a Power greater than ourselves; needing support and guidance, we ask that Power to care for our will and our lives. We ask others in recovery to share their experience with living the NA program instead of trying to program our own lives. The power and direction we seek is all around us; we need only turn away from self to find it.

❖

Just for today: I will not try to scheme and manipulate my way to a manageable life. Through the NA program, I will surrender myself to my Higher Power's care.

> *"We are not responsible for our disease, only for our recovery. As we begin to apply what we have learned, our lives begin to change for the better."*

Basic Text, p. 91

❖

The further we go in recovery, the less we avoid responsibility for ourselves and our actions. By applying the principles of the Narcotics Anonymous program, we are able to change our lives. Our existence takes on new meaning as we accept responsibility and the freedom of choice responsibility implies. We do not take recovery for granted.

We take responsibility for our recovery by working the Twelve Steps with a sponsor. We go to meetings regularly and share with the newcomer what was freely given to us: the gift of recovery. We become involved with our home group and accept responsibility for our part in sharing recovery with the still-suffering addict. As we learn how to effectively practice spiritual principles in all areas of our lives, the quality of our lives improves.

❖

Just for today: Using the spiritual tools I've gained in recovery, I am willing and able to make responsible choices.

> *"Anonymity is the spiritual foundation of all our
> traditions, ever reminding us to place
> principles before personalities."*

Tradition Twelve

❖

"Principles before personalities." Many of us chant these words along with the reader whenever the Twelve Traditions are read. The fact that these words have become a cliche of sorts doesn't make them any less important, either in service or in our lives. These words are an affirmation: "We listen to our conscience and do what's right, no matter who's involved." And that principle serves as one of the cornerstones of recovery as well as our traditions.

What does "principles before personalities" really mean? It means we practice honesty, humility, compassion, tolerance, and patience with everyone, whether we like them or not. Putting principles before personalities teaches us to treat everyone equally. The Twelfth Step asks us to apply principles in *all* our affairs; the Twelfth Tradition suggests we apply them to our relations with *everyone*.

Practicing principles doesn't stop with our friends or when we leave a meeting. It's for every day, for everyone... in all areas of our lives.

❖

Just for today: I will listen to my conscience and do what's right. My focus will be on principles, not on people's personalities.

> *"The most effective means of achieving self-acceptance*
> *is through applying the Twelve Steps of recovery."*
>
> **IP No. 19, *Self-Acceptance***

❖

Our addiction has been a source of shame to many of us. We have hidden ourselves from others, sure that if anyone got to know who we really were they would reject us. NA helps us learn self-acceptance.

Many of us find a great deal of relief just from attending meetings, hearing fellow addicts share their stories, and discovering that others have felt the same way we feel about ourselves. When others share honestly with us who they are, we feel free to do the same. As we learn to tell others the truth about ourselves, we learn to accept ourselves.

Self-disclosure, however, is only the beginning. Once we've shared the things that make us uncomfortable with our lives, we need to find a different way to live—and that's where the steps come in. We develop a concept of a Higher Power. We inventory our lives, in detail, and discuss our inventory with our sponsor. We ask the God of our understanding to remove our character defects, the shortcomings that are the source of our troubles. We take responsibility for the things we've done and make amends for them. And we incorporate all these disciplines into our daily lives, "practicing these principles in all our affairs."

By working the steps, we can become people we are proud to be. We can freely tell the truth about ourselves, for we have nothing to hide.

❖

Just for today: I will walk the path to self-acceptance. I will show up, tell the truth, and work the steps.

> *"We want to look our past in the face, see it for what it really was, and release it so we can live today."*

Basic Text, p. 29

❖

For many of us, the past is like a bad dream. Our lives aren't the same any more, but we still have fleeting, highly charged emotional memories of a really uncomfortable past. The guilt, fear, and anger that once dominated us may spill into our new life, complicating our efforts to change and grow.

The Twelve Steps are the formula that helps us learn to put the past in its place. Through the Fourth and Fifth Steps, we become aware that our old behavior didn't work. We ask a Higher Power to relieve us of our shortcomings in the Sixth and Seventh Steps, and we begin to be relieved of the guilt and fear that plagued us for so many years. In the Eighth and Ninth Steps, by making amends, we demonstrate to others that our lives are changing. We are no longer controlled by the past. Once the past loses its control over us, we are free to find new ways to live, ways that reflect who we truly are.

❖

Just for today: I don't have to be controlled by my past. I will live this new day as the new person I am becoming.

"We can also use the steps to improve our attitudes."

Basic Text, p. 55

❖

Ever have a day when everything seems to be working against you? Do you go through periods when you are so busy taking people's inventories you can barely stand yourself? What about when you find yourself snapping at your coworker or loved one for no reason? When we find ourselves in this bleak frame of mind, we need to take action.

At any point in the day, we can set aside a few moments and take a "spot inventory." We examine how we are reacting to outside situations and other people. When we do, we may find that we are suffering from a plain old "bad attitude." A negative outlook can hurt our relationship with our Higher Power and the people in our lives. When we are honest with ourselves, we frequently find that the problem lies with us and our attitude.

We have no control over the challenges life gives us. What we can control is how we react to those challenges. At any point in time, we can change our attitude. The only thing that *really* changes in Narcotics Anonymous is *us*. The Twelve Steps give us the tools to move out of the problem and into the solution.

❖

Just for today: Throughout the day, I will check my attitude. I will apply the steps to improve it.

*"Living just for today relieves the burden of the past
and the fear of the future."*

Basic Text, p. 94

❖

Thoughts of how bad it was—or could be—can consume our hopes for recovery. Fantasies of how wonderful it was—or could be—can divert us from taking action in the real world. That's why, in Narcotics Anonymous, we talk about living and recovering "just for today."

In NA, we know that we can change. We've come to believe that our Higher Power can restore the soundness of our minds and hearts. The wreckage of our past can be dealt with through the steps. By maintaining our recovery, just for today, we can avoid creating problems in the future.

Life in recovery is no fantasy. Daydreams of how great using was or how we can use successfully in the future, delusions of how great things *could* be, overblown expectations that set us up for disappointment and relapse—all are stripped of their power by the program. We seek God's will, not our own. We seek to serve others, not ourselves. Our self-centeredness and the importance of how great things could or should be for us disappears. In the light of recovery, we perceive the difference between fantasy and reality.

❖

Just for today: I am grateful for the principles of recovery and the new reality they've given me.

"Our newly found faith serves as a firm foundation for courage in the future."

Basic Text, p. 96

❖

Narcotics Anonymous is no place for the faint of heart! Facing life on life's terms without the use of drugs isn't always easy. Recovery requires more than hard work; it requires a liberal dose of courage.

What is courage, anyway? A quick look at a dictionary will tell us. We have courage when we face and deal with anything that we think of as difficult, dangerous, or painful, rather than withdrawing from it. Courage means being brave; having a purpose; having spirit. So what is courage, really? Courage is an *attitude,* one of perseverance.

That's what an addict in recovery really needs—perseverance. We make that commitment to stick with our program, to avoid using, no matter what happens. A courageous addict is one who doesn't use, one day at a time, no matter what.

And what gives us courage? A relationship with a Higher Power gives us the strength and the courage to stay clean. We know that, so long as we are in our God's care, we will have the power we need to face life on its own terms.

❖

Just for today: I have a Higher Power who cares for me, no matter what. Knowing that, I will strive to have an attitude of courage today.

"Ongoing recovery is dependent on our relationship with a loving God who cares for us and will do for us what we find impossible to do for ourselves."

Basic Text, p. 99

❖

Working the Twelve Steps of Narcotics Anonymous gives us a fresh start in life and some guidance for living in the world. But the steps are more than a fresh start. When we do our best to work the steps, we develop a relationship with our personal Higher Power.

In the Third Step, we decide to allow a loving God to influence our lives. Much of the courage, trust, and willingness we need to continue through the succeeding steps comes from this decision. In the Seventh Step, we go even further by *asking* this Higher Power to change our lives. The Eleventh Step is a way for us to improve the relationship.

Recovery is a process of growth and change in which our lives are renewed. The Twelve Steps are the roadmap, the specific directions we take in order to continue in recovery. But the support we need to proceed with each step comes from our faith in a Higher Power, the belief that all will be well. Faith gives us courage to act. Each step we work is supported by our relationship with a loving God.

❖

Just for today: I will remember that the source of my courage and willingness is my relationship with my Higher Power.

❖ ❖ ❖

November

❖ ❖ ❖

"God helps us as we help each other."

Basic Text, p. 52

❖

Our addiction caused us to think almost exclusively of ourselves. Even our prayers—if we prayed at all—were self-centered. We asked God to fix things for us or get us out of trouble. Why? Because we didn't want to live with the problems we'd created for ourselves. We were insecure. We thought life was about *getting,* and we always wanted more.

And in recovery we *get* more—more than just not using. The spiritual awakening we experience in working the Twelve Steps reveals to us a life we never dreamed possible. We no longer need to worry about whether there will be "enough," for we come to rely on a loving Higher Power who meets all our daily needs. Relieved of our incessant insecurity, we no longer see the world as a place in which to compete with others for the fulfillment of our desires. Instead, we see the world as a place in which to live out the love our Higher Power has shown us. Our prayers are not for instant gratification; they are for help in helping each other.

Recovery awakens us from the nightmare of self-centeredness, strife, and insecurity that lies at the core of our disease. We wake up to a new reality: All that is worth having can be kept only by giving it away.

❖

Just for today: My God helps me as I help others. Today, I will seek help in giving away the love my Higher Power has given me, knowing that is the way to keep it.

*"It makes a difference to have friends
who care if we hurt."*

Basic Text, p. 56

❖

For most of our problems, the solution is simple. We call our sponsor, pray, work the steps, or go to a meeting. But what about those situations where the burden is ongoing and there's no end in sight?

Most of us know what it's like to live with a painful situation—a problem that just isn't going to disappear. For some of us, the problem is an incurable, life-threatening illness. Some of us have incorrigible children. Some of us find that our earnings simply don't cover our living expenses. Some of us care for a chronically ill friend or family member.

Those of us who have ever had to live with an unresolved problem know the relief that comes from just talking about our problem with our recovering friends. We may get some comic relief. Our friends may commiserate or cry in sympathy. Whatever they do, they ease our burden. They may not be able to solve our problem for us or take away our painful feelings, but just knowing that we are loved and cared about makes our problems bearable. We never have to be alone with our pain again.

❖

Just for today: Those problems I can't resolve can be made bearable by talking to a friend. Today, I will call someone who cares.

*"We eventually have to stand on our own feet and face
life on its own terms, so why not from the start?"*

Basic Text, p. 88

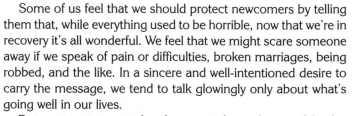

Some of us feel that we should protect newcomers by telling them that, while everything used to be horrible, now that we're in recovery it's all wonderful. We feel that we might scare someone away if we speak of pain or difficulties, broken marriages, being robbed, and the like. In a sincere and well-intentioned desire to carry the message, we tend to talk glowingly only about what's going well in our lives.

But most newcomers already suspect the truth, even if they've only been clean for a few days. Chances are that the "life on life's terms" the average newcomer is experiencing is quite a bit more stressful than what the average oldtimer deals with each day. If we do manage to convince a newcomer that everything becomes rosy in recovery, we had better make sure we are there to support that newcomer when something goes wrong in his or her life.

Perhaps we simply need to share realistically about how we use the resources of Narcotics Anonymous to accept "life on life's terms," whatever those terms may be on any given day. Recovery, and life itself, contain equal parts of pain and joy. It is important to share both so the newcomer can know that we stay clean no matter what.

❖

Just for today: I will be honest with the newcomers I share with and let them know that, no matter what life brings, we never have to use drugs again.

*"... we give love because it was given so freely to us.
New frontiers are open to us as we learn how to love.
Love can be the flow of life energy from
one person to another."*

Basic Text, p. 105

❖

Love given, and love received, is the essence of life itself. It is the universal common denominator, connecting us to those around us. Addiction deprived us of that connection, locking us within ourselves.

The love we find in the NA program reopens the world to us. It unlocks the cage of addiction which once imprisoned us. By receiving love from other NA members, we find out—perhaps for the first time—what love is and what it can do. We hear fellow members talk about the sharing of love, and we sense the substance it lends to their lives.

We begin to suspect that, if giving and receiving love means so much to others, maybe it can give meaning to our lives, too. We sense that we are on the verge of a great discovery, yet we also sense that we won't fully understand the meaning of love unless we give ours away. We try it, and discover the missing connection between ourselves and the world.

Today, we realize that what they said was true: "We keep what we have only by giving it away."

❖

Just for today: Life is a new frontier for me, and the vehicle I will use to explore it is love. I will give freely the love I have received.

*"Our Higher Power is accessible to us at all times.
We receive guidance when we ask for
knowledge of God's will for us."*

Basic Text, p. 95

❖

It's not always easy to make the right decision. This is especially true for addicts learning to live by spiritual principles for the first time. In addiction, we developed self-destructive, anti-social impulses. When conflict arose, we took our cues from those negative impulses. Our disease didn't prepare us to make sound decisions.

Today, to find the direction we need, we ask our Higher Power. We stop; we pray; and, quietly, we listen within for guidance. We've come to believe that we can rely on a Power greater than ourselves. That Power is accessible to us whenever we need it. All we need do is pray for knowledge of our God's will for us and the power to carry it out.

Each time we do this, each time we find direction amidst our confusion, our faith grows. The more we rely on our Higher Power, the easier it becomes to ask for direction. We've found the Power we were lacking in our addiction, a Power that is available to us at all times. To find the direction we need to live fully and grow spiritually, all we have to do is maintain contact with the God of our understanding.

❖

Just for today: My Higher Power is a source of spiritual guidance within me that I can always draw upon. When I lack direction today, I will ask for knowledge of my Higher Power's will.

"Humility is a result of getting honest with ourselves."
Basic Text, p. 36

❖

Humility was an idea so foreign to most of us that we ignored it as long as we could. When we first saw the word "humbly" ahead in Step Seven, we may have figured it meant we had quite a bit of humiliation in store. Perhaps we chose to look it up in the dictionary, only to become even more confused by the definition. We didn't understand how "lowliness and subservience" applied to recovery.

To be humble does not mean we are the lowest form of life. On the contrary, becoming humble means we attain a realistic view of ourselves and where we fit in the world. We grow into a state of awareness founded on our acceptance of all aspects of ourselves. We neither deny our good qualities nor overemphasize our defects. We honestly accept who we are.

No one of us will ever attain a state of perfect humility. But we can certainly strive to honestly admit our faults, accept our assets, and rely on our Higher Power as a source of strength. Humility doesn't mean we have to crawl life's path on our hands and knees; it just means we must admit we cannot recover on our own. We need each other and, above all, we need the power of a loving God.

❖

Just for today: To be humble, I will honestly accept all facets of myself, seeing my true place in the world. For the strength I need to fill that place, I will rely on the God of my understanding.

"I sincerely believed that a Higher Power could restore my sanity and that I would stop trying to figure out what God's will was, just accept things for what they were, and be grateful."

❖

The longer we stay clean, the less surely we "know" what our Higher Power's will for us is—and the less it matters. Knowledge of our Higher Power's will becomes less a "knowing" thing and more a "feeling" thing. We still practice the Eleventh Step faithfully. But rather than look for "signs" from our Higher Power, we begin to rely more on our intuition, trusting our feelings about what will make us comfortable.

After staying clean a few years, what we *do* seem to know is when we are acting *against* God's will for us. When we are going against God's will, we get that old uncomfortable feeling in our gut. That queasiness is a warning that, if we continue in this direction, ahead lie many sleepless nights. We need to pay attention to such feelings, for they are often signals that we are acting contrary to our Higher Power's will for us.

Our Eleventh Step clearly states the true goal of prayer and meditation: improvement of our conscious contact with the God of our understanding, bringing us clearer knowledge of our Higher Power's will for us and the power to carry it out. We know God's will most clearly by how it feels, not by "signs" or words—and it feels *right*.

❖

Just for today: I will pray for the knowledge of my Higher Power's will for me and the power to carry it out. I will pay attention to my feelings, and act when they feel right.

> *"Do I believe it would be insane to walk up to someone and say, 'May I please have a heart attack or a fatal accident?'"*

Basic Text, p. 24

❖

We've heard it said that unless we're in love, we can't remember what love feels like. The same could be said of insanity: Once we're freed of it, we may forget how truly bizarre our insane thinking can be. But to be grateful for the degree of sanity to which we've been restored in Narcotics Anonymous, we need to remember just how truly insane we've been.

Today, it may be hard to imagine saying something as ridiculous as, "May I please have a heart attack or a fatal accident?" No one in their right mind is going to ask for such things. And that's the point. In our active addiction, we were not in our right mind. Each day we practiced our addiction, we courted fatal disease, degradation, exploitation, impoverishment, imprisonment, death by violence, even death by sheer stupidity. In that context, the idea of asking for a heart attack or a fatal accident doesn't sound all that far out. That's how insane we've been.

The program, the fellowship, and our Higher Power—together, they've worked a miracle. The Second Step is not a vain hope—it is reality. Knowing the degree of the insanity we've experienced, we can appreciate all the more the miraculous Power that has restored us thus far to sanity. For that, we are truly grateful.

❖

Just for today: I will take some time to recall how insane I've been while practicing my addiction. Then, I will thank my Higher Power for the sanity that's been restored to my life.

> *"It is our actions that are important.*
> *We leave the results to our Higher Power."*
>
> **Basic Text, p. 91**

❖

There's an old saying we sometimes hear in our meetings: "If you want to make God laugh, make plans." When we hear this we usually laugh, too, but there's a nervous edge to our laughter. We wonder if all of our carefully laid plans are doomed to fail. If we're planning a big event—a wedding, a return to school, or perhaps a career change—we begin to wonder if our plans are the same as our Higher Power's plans. We are capable of working ourselves into such a frenzy of worry over this question that we refuse to make any plans at all.

But the simple fact is that we really don't know whether our Higher Power's plans for our lives are carved in stone or not. Most of us have opinions about fate and destiny but, whether we believe in such theories or not, we still have a responsibility to live our lives and make plans for the future. If we refuse to accept responsibility for our lives, we're still making plans—plans for a shallow, boring existence.

What we make in recovery are *plans,* not *results.* We'll never know whether the marriage, the education, or the new job is going to work out until we try it. We simply exercise our best judgment, check with our sponsor, pray, use all the information at hand, and make the most reasonable plans we can. For the rest, we trust in the loving care of the God of our understanding, knowing that we've acted responsibly.

❖

Just for today: I will make plans, but I will not plan the results. I will trust in my Higher Power's loving care.

"No matter how far we ran,
we always carried fear with us."

Basic Text, p. 14

❖

For many of us, fear was a constant factor in our lives before we came to Narcotics Anonymous. We used because we were afraid to feel emotional or physical pain. Our fear of people and situations gave us a convenient excuse to use drugs. A few of us were so afraid of everything that we were unable even to leave our homes without using first.

As we stay clean, we replace our fear with a belief in the fellowship, the steps, and a Higher Power. As this belief grows, our faith in the miracle of recovery begins to color all aspects of our lives. We start to see ourselves differently. We realize we are spiritual beings, and we strive to live by spiritual principles.

The application of spiritual principles helps eliminate fear from our lives. By refraining from treating other people in harmful or unlawful ways, we find we needn't fear how we will be treated in return. As we practice love, compassion, understanding, and patience in our relationships with others, we are treated in turn with respect and consideration. We realize these positive changes result from allowing our Higher Power to work through us. We come to believe—not to think, but to *believe*—that our Higher Power wants only the best for us. No matter what the circumstances, we find we can walk in faith instead of fear.

❖

Just for today: I no longer need to run in fear, but can walk in faith that my Higher Power has only the best in store for me.

*"We surrender quietly and let the
God of our understanding take care of us."*

Basic Text, p. 26

❖

Surrender and acceptance are like infatuation and love. Infatuation begins when we encounter someone special. Infatuation requires nothing but the acknowledgement of the object of our infatuation. For infatuation to become love, however, requires a great deal of effort. That initial connection must be slowly, patiently nurtured into a lasting, durable bond.

It's the same with surrender and acceptance. We *surrender* when we acknowledge our powerlessness. Slowly, we come to believe that a Power greater than ourselves can give us the care we need. Surrender turns to *acceptance* when we let this Power into our lives. We examine ourselves and let our God see us as we are. Having allowed the God of our understanding access to the depths of ourselves, we accept more of God's care. We ask this Power to relieve us of our shortcomings and help us amend the wrongs we've done. Then, we embark on a new way of life, improving our conscious contact and accepting our Higher Power's continuing care, guidance, and strength.

Surrender, like infatuation, can be the beginning of a lifelong relationship. To turn surrender into acceptance, however, we must let the God of our understanding take care of us each day.

❖

Just for today: My recovery is more than infatuation. I have surrendered. Today, I will nurture my conscious contact with my Higher Power and accept that Power's continuing care for me.

*"When we honestly tell our own story,
someone else may identify with us."*

Basic Text, p. 98

❖

Many of us have heard truly captivating speakers at Narcotics Anonymous conventions. We remember the audience alternating between tears of identification and joyous hilarity. "Someday," we may think, "I'm going to be a main speaker at a convention, too."

Well, for many of us, that day has yet to arrive. Once in awhile we may be asked to speak at a meeting near where we live. We might speak at a small convention workshop. But after all this time, we're still not "hot" convention speakers—and that's okay. We've learned that we, too, have a special message to share, even if it's only at a local meeting with fifteen or twenty addicts in attendance.

Each of us has only our own story to tell; that's it. We can't tell anyone else's story. Every time we get up to speak, many of us find all the clever lines and funny stories seem to disappear from our minds. But we *do* have something to offer. We carry the message of hope—we can and do recover from our addiction. And that's enough.

❖

Just for today: I will remember that my honest story is what I share the best. Today, that's enough.

*"We are not going to be perfect. If we were perfect,
we would not be human."*

Basic Text, p. 31

❖

All of us had expectations about life in recovery. Some of us thought recovery would suddenly make us employable or able to do anything in the world we wanted to do. Or maybe we imagined perfect ease in our interactions with others. When we stop and think, we realize that we expected recovery would make us perfect. We didn't expect to continue making many mistakes. But we do. That's not the addict side of us showing through; that's being human.

In Narcotics Anonymous we strive for recovery, not perfection. The only promise we are given is freedom from active addiction. Perfection is not an attainable state for human beings; it's not a realistic goal. What we often seek in perfection is freedom from the discomfort of making mistakes. In return for that freedom from discomfort, we trade our curiosity, our flexibility, and the room to grow.

We can consider the trade: Do we want to live the rest of our lives in our well-defined little world, safe but perhaps stifled? Or do we wish to venture out into the unknown, take a risk, and reach for everything life has to offer?

❖

Just for today: I want all that life has to offer me and all that recovery can provide. Today, I will take a risk, try something new, and grow.

> *"When we were using, our lives became
> an exercise in survival. Now we are doing
> much more living than surviving."*

Basic Text, p. 52

❖

"I'd be better off dead!" A familiar refrain to a practicing addict, and with good reason. All we had to look forward to was more of the same miserable existence. Our hold on life was weak at best. Our emotional decay, our spiritual demise, and the crushing awareness that nothing would ever change were constants. We had little hope and no concept of the life we were missing out on.

The resurrection of our emotions, our spirits, and our physical health takes time. The more experience we gain in *living,* rather than merely existing, the more we understand how precious and delightful life can be. Traveling, playing with a small child, making love, expanding our intellectual horizons, and forming relationships are among the endless activities that say, "I'm alive." We discover so much to cherish and feel grateful to have a second chance.

If we had died in active addiction, we would have been bitterly deprived of so many of life's joys. Each day we thank a Power greater than ourselves for another day clean and another day of life.

❖

Just for today: I am grateful to be alive. I will do something today to celebrate.

> *"Take my will and my life.*
> *Guide me in my recovery.*
> *Show me how to live."*

Basic Text, p. 26

❖

How do we begin the process of letting our Higher Power guide our lives? When we seek advice about situations that trouble us, we often find that our Higher Power works through others. When we accept that we don't have all the answers, we open ourselves to new and different options. A willingness to let go of our preconceived ideas and opinions opens the channel for spiritual guidance to light our way.

At times, we must be driven to the point of distraction before we are ready to turn difficult situations over to our Higher Power. Anxiously plotting, struggling, planning, worrying—none of these suffice. We can be sure that if we turn our problems over to our Higher Power, through listening to others share their experience or in the quiet of meditation, the answers will come.

There is no point in living a frantic existence. Charging through life like the house is on fire exhausts us and gets us nowhere. In the long run, no amount of manipulation on our part will change a situation. When we let go and allow ourselves access to a Higher Power, we will discover the best way to proceed. Rest assured, answers derived from a sound spiritual basis will be far superior to any answers we could concoct on our own.

❖

Just for today: I will let go and let my Higher Power guide my life.

> *"We gradually and carefully pull ourselves*
> *out of the isolation and loneliness of addiction*
> *and into the mainstream of life."*

Basic Text, p. 37

❖

Many of us spent much of our using time alone, avoiding other people—especially people who were not using—at all costs. After years of isolation, trying to find a place for ourselves in a bustling, sometimes boisterous fellowship is not always easy. We may still feel isolated, focusing on our differences rather than our similarities. The overwhelming feelings that often arise in early recovery—feelings of fear, anger, and mistrust—can also keep us isolated. We may feel like aliens but we must remember, the alienation is ours, not NA's.

In Narcotics Anonymous, we are offered a very special opportunity for friendship. We are brought together with people who understand us like no one else can. We are encouraged to share with these people our feelings, our problems, our triumphs, and our failures. Slowly, the recognition and identification we find in NA bridge the lonely gap of alienation in our hearts. As we've heard it said—the program works, if we let it.

❖

Just for today: The friendship of other members of the fellowship is a life-sustaining gift. I will reach out for the friendship that's offered in NA, and accept it.

"We never have to use again, no matter how we feel.
All feelings will eventually pass."

Basic Text, p. 82

❖

It hurts like never before. You get out of bed after a sleepless night, talk to God, and still don't feel any better. "It will pass," a little voice tells you. "When?" you wonder, as you pace and mutter and get on with your day.

You sob in your car and turn the radio all the way up so you can't hear your own thoughts. But you go straight to work, and don't even think about using drugs.

Your insides feel as though they've been torched. Just when the pain becomes unbearable, you go numb and silent. You go to a meeting and wish you were as happy as other members seem to be. But you don't relapse.

You cry some more and call your sponsor. You drive to a friend's house and don't even notice the beautiful scenery because your inner landscape is so bleak. You may not feel any better after visiting your friend—but at least you didn't visit the connection instead.

You listen to a Fifth Step. You share at a meeting. You look at the calendar and realize you've gotten through another day clean.

Then one day you wake up, look outside, and realize it's a beautiful day. The sun is shining. The sky is blue. You take a deep breath, smile again, and know that it really does pass.

❖

Just for today: No matter how I feel today, I'll go on with my recovery.

"The Tenth Step can help us correct our living problems and prevent their recurrence."

Basic Text, p. 42

❖

Our identities, how we think and feel, have been shaped by our experiences. Some of our experiences have made us better people; others have caused us shame or embarrassment; all of them have influenced who we are today. We can take advantage of the knowledge gained in examining our mistakes, using this wisdom to guide the decisions we'll make today.

Acceptance of ourselves means accepting all aspects of ourselves—our assets, our defects, our successes, and our failures. Shame and guilt left unaddressed can paralyze us, preventing us from moving forward in our lives. Some of the most meaningful amends we can make for the mistakes of our past are made simply by acting differently today. We strive for improvement and measure our success by comparing who we used to be with who we are now.

Being human, we will continue making mistakes; however, we need not make the same ones over and over again. By looking over our past and realizing that we have changed and grown, we'll find hope for the future. The best is yet to come.

❖

Just for today: I will do the best I can with what I have today. Each day I'll learn something new that will help me tomorrow.

"... the addict would find from the start as much identification as each needed to convince himself that he could stay clean, by the example of others who had recovered for many years."

Basic Text, p. 88

❖

Many of us attended our first meeting and, not being entirely sure that NA was for us, found much to criticize. Either we felt as though no one had suffered like we had or that we hadn't suffered enough. But as we listened we started to hear something new, a wordless language with its roots in recognition, belief, and faith: the language of empathy. Desiring to belong, we kept listening.

We find all the identification we need as we learn to understand and speak the language of empathy. To understand this special language, we listen with our hearts. The language of empathy uses few words; it feels more than it speaks. It doesn't preach or lecture—it listens. It can reach out and touch the spirit of another addict without a single spoken word.

Fluency in the language of empathy comes to us through practice. The more we use it with other addicts and our Higher Power, the more we understand this language. It keeps us coming back.

❖

Just for today: I will listen with my heart. With each passing day, I will become more fluent in the language of empathy.

*"We weren't oriented toward fulfillment; we focused on
the emptiness and worthlessness of it all."*

Basic Text, p. 89

❖

There were probably hundreds of times in our active addiction
when we wished we could become someone else. We may have
wished we could trade places with someone who owned a nice
car or had a larger home, a better job, a more attractive mate—
anything but what we had. So severe was our despair that we could
hardly imagine anyone being in worse shape than ourselves.

In recovery, we may find we are experiencing a different sort
of envy. We may continue to compare our insides with others'
outsides and feel as though we still don't have enough of anything.
We may think everyone, from the newest member to the oldest
oldtimer, sounds better at meetings than we do. We may think
that everyone else must be working a better program because
they have a better car, a larger home, more money, and so on.

The recovery process experienced through our Twelve Steps
will take us from an attitude of envy and low self-esteem to a place
of spiritual fulfillment and deep appreciation for what we *do* have.
We find that we would never willingly trade places with another,
for what we have discovered within ourselves is priceless.

❖

Just for today: There is much to be grateful for in my life. I will
cherish the spiritual fulfillment I have found in recovery.

> *"If [character defects] contributed to our health
> and happiness, we would not have come to
> such a state of desperation."*

Basic Text, p. 35

❖

Getting started on the Sixth and Seventh Steps isn't always easy. We may feel as though we have so much wrong with us that we are totally defective. We might feel like hiding under a rock. Under no circumstance would we want our fellow addicts to know about our inadequacies.

We will probably go through a time of examining everything we say and do in order to identify our character defects and make sure we suppress them. We may look back at one particular day, cringing at what we're certain is the most embarrassing thing we've ever said. We become determined to be rid of these horrible traits at all costs.

But nowhere in the Sixth or Seventh Steps does it say we can learn to control our defects of character. In fact, the more attention we focus on them, the more firmly entrenched they will become in our lives. It takes humility to recognize that we can't control our defects any more than we can control our addiction. We can't remove our own defects; we can only ask a loving God to remove them.

Letting go of something painful can be as difficult as letting go of something pleasant. But let's face it—holding on is a lot of work. When we really think about what we're holding onto, the effort just isn't worthwhile. It's time to let go of our character defects and ask God to remove them.

❖

Just for today: I'm ready to have my defects removed. I will let go and allow a loving Higher Power to care for me.

"As we begin to function in society, our creative freedom helps us sort our priorities and do the basic things first."

Basic Text, p. 86

❖

No sooner do we get clean than some of us begin putting other priorities ahead of our recovery. Careers, families, relationships—all these are part of the life we find once we've laid the foundation of our recovery. But we can't build a stable life for ourselves before we do the hard, basic work of laying our recovery foundation. Like a house built on sand, such a life will be shaky, at best.

Before we begin putting all our attention to rebuilding the detailed framework of our lives, we need to lay our foundation. We acknowledge, first, that we don't yet *have* a foundation, that our addiction has made our lives utterly unmanageable. Then, with the help of our sponsor and our home group, we find faith in a Power strong enough to help us prepare the ground of our new lives. We clear the wreckage from the site upon which we will build our future. Finally, we develop a deep, working familiarity with the principles we will practice in our continuing affairs: honest self-examination, reliance upon our Higher Power's guidance and strength, and service to others.

Once our foundation is prepared, *then* we can go full steam ahead to put our new lives together. But first we must ask ourselves if our foundation is secure, for without our foundation, nothing we build can stand for long.

❖

Just for today: I will take care to lay a secure foundation for my recovery. Upon such a foundation, I can build for a lifetime in recovery.

> *"The relief of 'letting go and letting God' helps us
> develop a life that is worth living."*

Basic Text, p. 26

❖

In our addiction, we were afraid of what might happen if we didn't control everything around us. Many of us made up elaborate lies to protect our use of drugs. Some of us manipulated everyone around us in a frenzied attempt to get something from them so we could use more drugs. A few of us went to great lengths to keep two people from talking to each other and perhaps discovering our trail of lies. We took pains to maintain an illusion of control over our addiction and our lives. In the process, we kept ourselves from experiencing the serenity that comes with surrender to a Higher Power's will.

In our recovery, it is important to release our illusion of control and surrender to a Higher Power, whose will for us is better than anything we can con, manipulate, or devise for ourselves. If we realize that we are trying to control outcomes and are feeling afraid of the future, there is action we can take to reverse that trend. We go to our Second and Third Steps and look at what we have come to believe about a Higher Power. Do we truly believe that this Power can care for us and restore us to sanity? If so, we can live with all of life's ups and downs—its disappointments, its sorrows, its wonders, and its joys.

❖

Just for today: I will surrender and let a Higher Power's will happen in my life. I will accept the gift of serenity this surrender brings.

> *"We entertained the thought that staying clean*
> *was not paying off, and the old thinking stirred up*
> *self-pity, resentment and anger."*

Basic Text, p. 102

❖

There are days when some of us wallow in self-pity. It's easy to do. We may have expectations about how our lives *should* be in recovery, expectations that aren't always met. Maybe we've tried unsuccessfully to control someone, or we think our circumstances should be different. Perhaps we've compared ourselves with other recovering addicts and found ourselves lacking. The more we try to make our life conform to our expectations, the more uncomfortable we feel. Self-pity can arise from living in our expectations instead of in the world as it actually is.

When the world doesn't measure up to our expectations, it's often our expectations that need adjusting, not the world. We can start by comparing our lives today with the way they used to be, developing gratitude for our recovery. We can extend this exercise in gratitude by counting the good things in our lives, becoming thankful that the world does not conform to our expectations but exceeds them. And if we continue working the Twelve Steps, further cultivating gratitude and acceptance, what we can expect in the future is more growth, more happiness, and more peace of mind.

We've been given much in recovery; staying clean *has* paid off. Acceptance of our lives, just for today, frees us from our self-pity.

❖

Just for today: I will accept my life, gratefully, just as it is.

> *"Quieting the mind through meditation brings*
> *an inner peace that brings us into contact*
> *with the God within us."*

Basic Text, pp. 46–47

❖

As our recovery progresses, we often reflect on what brought us to Narcotics Anonymous in the first place and are able to appreciate how much the quality of our lives has improved. We no longer have to fear our own thoughts. And the more we pray and meditate, the more we experience a calm sense of well-being. The peace and tranquility we experience during our quiet times confirms that our most important needs—our spiritual needs—are being met.

We are able to empathize with other addicts and strengthen our conscience in the process. We learn to avoid judging others and experience the freedom to be ourselves. In our spiritual reflection, we intuitively find "the God within us" and see that we are in harmony with a Power greater than ourselves.

❖

Just for today: I will reflect upon the gift of recovery and listen quietly for my Higher Power's guidance.

*"A lot happens in one day, both negative and positive.
If we do not take the time to appreciate both, perhaps
we will miss something that will help us grow."*

IP No. 8, *Just for Today*

❖

Responsibility, responsibility—the responsibilities of life are everywhere. We're "supposed to" wear seat belts. We're "supposed to" clean our homes. We're "supposed to" do certain things for our spouse, our children, the people we sponsor. On top of all this, we're "supposed to" go to meetings and practice our program as best we can. It's no wonder that, sometimes, we want to run from all these tasks and escape to some far-off island where we're not "supposed to" do anything!

At times like these, when we've become overwhelmed with our responsibilities, we have forgotten that responsibility need not be burdensome. When we have a desire to run away from our responsibilities we need to slow down, remember why we have chosen them, and pay attention to the gifts they bring. Whether it's a job we normally find challenging and interesting, or a partner whose personality we are usually excited by, or a child whom we naturally like to play with and care for, there is joy to be found in all the responsibilities of our lives.

❖

Just for today: Each moment is special. I will pay attention, grateful for my responsibilities and the special joys they bring.

> *"At times during our recovery, the decision
> to ask for God's help is our greatest source
> of strength and courage."*

Basic Text, p. 26

❖

When we take the Third Step, we decide to allow a loving Higher Power to guide us and care for us in our daily lives. We make the decision to allow this guidance and care into our lives. Some of us believe that, once we've made the Third Step decision, God leads us; from that point on, it's just a matter of paying attention to where we are led.

The Third Step decision is an act of faith, and asking for God's help is a way of renewing that act of faith. Putting faith to work in our daily lives gives us all the courage and strength we need, because we know we have the help of a loving Higher Power. We trust that our needs will be met. We can tap into that faith and trust just by asking.

❖

Just for today: I will remind myself that I'm not alone by asking my Higher Power for help each step of the way.

> *"To be truly humble is to accept
> and honestly try to be ourselves."*

Basic Text, p. 36

❖

Humility is a puzzling concept. We know a lot about *humiliation,* but *humility* is a new idea. It sounds suspiciously like groveling, bowing, and scraping. But that's not what humility is at all. True humility is, simply, acceptance of who we are.

By the time we reach a step that uses the word "humbly," we have already started to put this principle into practice. The Fourth Step gives us an opportunity to *examine* who we really are, and the Fifth Step helps us *accept* that knowledge.

The practice of humility involves accepting our true nature, honestly being ourselves. We don't have to grovel or abase ourselves, nor must we try to appear smarter, wealthier, or happier than we really are. Humility simply means we drop all pretense and live as honestly as we can.

❖

Just for today: I will allow knowledge of my true nature to guide my actions. Today, I will face the world as myself.

> *"We believe that our Higher Power*
> *will take care of us."*

Basic Text, p. 58

❖

Our program is based on the idea that the application of simple principles can produce profound effects in our lives. One such principle is that, if we ask, our Higher Power will care for us. Because this principle is so basic, we may tend to ignore it. Unless we learn to consciously apply this spiritual truth, we may miss out on something as essential to our recovery as breathing is to life itself.

What happens when we find ourselves stressed or panicked? If we have consistently sought to improve our relationship with our Higher Power, we'll have no problem. Rather than acting rashly, we will stop for a moment and briefly remind ourselves of particular instances in the past when our Higher Power has shown its care for us. This will assure us that our Higher Power is still in charge of our lives. Then, we will seek guidance and power for the situation at hand and proceed calmly, confident that our lives are in God's hands.

"Our program is a set of principles," our White Booklet tells us. The more consistently we seek to improve our conscious appreciation of these principles, the more readily we will be able to apply them.

❖

Just for today: I will seek to improve my conscious contact with the Higher Power that cares for me. When the need arises, I know I will be able to trust in that care.

*"Sharing with others keeps us from feeling
isolated and alone."*

Basic Text, p. 85

❖

Intimacy is the sharing of our innermost thoughts and feelings with another human being. Many of us long for the warmth and companionship intimacy brings, but those things don't come without effort. In our addiction, we learned to guard ourselves from others lest they threaten our using. In recovery, we learn how to trust others. Intimacy requires us to lower our defenses. To feel the closeness intimacy brings, we must allow others to get close to us—the *real* us.

If we are to share our innermost selves with others, we must first have an idea of what those innermost selves are truly like. We regularly examine our lives to find out who we really are, what we really want, and how we really feel. Then, based on our regular inventories of ourselves, we must be as completely and consistently honest with our friends as we can be.

Intimacy is a part of life, and therefore a part of living clean—and intimacy, like everything in recovery, has its price. The painstaking self-scrutiny intimacy calls for can be hard work. And the total honesty of intimacy often brings its own complications. But the freedom from isolation and loneliness that intimacy brings is well worth the effort.

❖

Just for today: I seek the freedom from isolation and loneliness that intimacy brings. Today, I will get to know "the real me" by taking a personal inventory, and I will practice being completely honest with another person.

❖ ❖ ❖

December

❖ ❖ ❖

> *"We begin to pray only for God's will for us. That way,*
> *we get only what we are capable of handling."*

Basic Text, p. 49

❖

Imagine what might happen if God gave us everything we wanted. A fabulous new car, straight As, a triple salary raise—all ours without effort, just for the asking.

Now imagine the problems that come along with unearned riches, new luxury cars, and unmerited scholastic recognition. What would we do with a huge salary raise that had been granted for no reason? How would we handle our new financial responsibilities? And how would we live up to that raise? Could we ever make it appear that we deserve such pay when we know we don't?

What about that fantastic new car? Most come with expensive insurance premiums and hefty maintenance costs. Are we prepared to care for what we've asked for?

Academic honors? Could we perform like A students after we'd been given high marks we hadn't earned? What would we do if we were exposed as frauds?

When we talk to God, we need to remember that we live in the real world. We earn rewards and learn to handle them as we do. Confining our prayers to requests for knowledge of God's will, the power to carry it out, and the ability to live with the consequences will ensure that we get no more than we can handle.

❖

Just for today: I will pray only for knowledge of God's will and the power to carry that out in the real world.

*"We have to keep our recovery first and
our priorities in order."*

Basic Text, p. 82

❖

Before coming to NA, we used many excuses to justify our use of drugs: "He yelled at me." "She said *this*." "My partner left." "I got fired." We used these same excuses for not seeking help for our drug problem. We had to realize that these things kept happening because we kept using drugs. Only when we made recovery our first priority did these situations begin to change.

We may be subject to the same tendency today, using excuses for not attending meetings and being of service. Our current excuses may be of a different nature: "I can't leave my kids." "My vacation wore me out." "I have to finish this project so I can impress my boss." But still, if we don't make recovery our first priority, chances are that we won't have to worry about these excuses anymore. Kids, vacations, and jobs probably won't *be* in our lives if we relapse.

Our recovery must come first. Job or no job, relationship or no relationship, we have to attend meetings, work the steps, call our sponsor, and be of service to God and others. These simple actions are what make it possible for us to have vacations, families, and bosses to worry about. Recovery is the foundation of our lives, making everything else possible.

❖

Just for today: I will keep my priorities in order. Number One on the list is my recovery.

"Perhaps for the first time,
we see a vision of our new life."

Basic Text, p. 35

❖

In our addiction, our vision of ourselves was very limited. Each day, we went through the same routine: getting, using, and finding ways and means to get more. And that's all we could reasonably expect for the duration of our lives. Our potential was limited.

Today, our prospects are changed. Recovery has given us a new vision of ourselves and our lives. We are no longer trapped in the endlessly gray routine of addiction. We are free to stretch ourselves in new ways, trying out new ideas and new activities. In doing so, we come to see ourselves in a new way. Our potential is limited only by the strength of the Higher Power that cares for us—and that strength *has* no limits.

In recovery, life and everything in it appears open to us. Guided by our spiritual principles, driven by the power given us by the God of our understanding, our horizons are limitless.

❖

Just for today: I will open my eyes to the possibilities before me. My potential is as limitless and as powerful as the God of my understanding. Today, I will act on that potential.

*"We know that if we pray for God's will we will receive
what is best for us, regardless of what we think."*

Basic Text, p. 46

❖

By the time we came to NA, our inner voices had become
unreliable and self-destructive. Addiction had warped our desires,
our interests, our sense of what was best for ourselves. That's
why it's been so important in recovery to develop our belief in
a Power greater than ourselves, something that could provide
saner, more reliable guidance than our own. We've begun learning
how to rely on this Power's care and to trust the inner direction
it provides us.

As with all learning processes, it takes practice to "pray *only* for
knowledge of God's will for us and the power to carry that out."
The selfish, ego-driven attitudes we developed in our addiction
are not cast off overnight. Those attitudes may affect the way we
pray. We may even find ourselves praying something like, "Relieve
me of this character defect so I can look good."

The more straightforward we are about our own ideas and
desires, the easier it will be to distinguish between our own will and
our Higher Power's will. "Just for your information, God," we might
pray, "here's what *I* want in this situation. Nonetheless, I ask that
your will, not mine, be done." Once we do this, we are prepared
to recognize and accept our Higher Power's guidance.

❖

Just for today: Higher Power, I've learned to trust your guidance, yet I still have my own ideas about how I want to live my
life. Let me share those ideas with you, and then let me clearly
understand your will for me. In the end, let your will, not mine,
be done.

"We have seen the program work for any addict who honestly and sincerely wants to stop [using drugs]."

Basic Text, p. 10

❖

How do we know when someone honestly and sincerely wants to stop using drugs? The truth is that we don't know! Because we cannot read minds or know another's motives and desires, we simply have to hope for the best.

We may talk to a newcomer at a meeting and think we'll never see them again, only to find them several years later doing well in their recovery. We may be tempted to give up on someone who keeps relapsing or doesn't get clean right away, but we must not. No matter how unwilling someone may seem, a simple fact remains—*the addict is at a meeting*.

We may never know the results of our Twelfth Step work; it is not up to us to gauge the willingness of a newcomer. The message we carry is a part of us. We carry it everywhere and share it freely, leaving the results to a Power greater than ourselves.

❖

Just for today: I will share my recovery with any addict, any-where, anytime, and under any circumstances. I will leave the results to my Higher Power.

"Relationships can be a terribly painful area."

Basic Text, p. 82

❖

Love is like an elixir for some of us. The excitement of a new lover, the intrigue of exploring intimacy, the sense of release we get from allowing ourselves to become vulnerable—these are all powerful emotions. But we can't forget that we have only a daily reprieve from our addiction. Holding onto this daily reprieve must be the top priority in any recovering addict's life.

We can become too involved in our relationship. We can neglect old friends and our sponsor in the process. Then, when things get difficult, we often feel that we can no longer reach out to those who helped us prior to our romantic involvement. This belief can lay the groundwork for a relapse. By consistently working our program and attending meetings, we ensure that we have a network of recovery, even when we're deep in a romance.

Our desire to be romantically involved is natural. But we mustn't forget that, without our program, even the healthiest relationship will not guard us against the strength of our addiction.

❖

Just for today: In my desire for romance, I will not ignore my recovery.

> *"We use the tools available to us and develop
> the ability to survive our emotions."*

Basic Text, p. 31

❖

"Survive my emotions?" some of us say. "You've got to be kidding!" When we were using, we never gave ourselves the chance to *learn* how to survive them. You don't survive your feelings, we thought—you drug them. The problem was, that "cure" for our unsurvivable emotions was killing us. That's when we came to Narcotics Anonymous, started working the Twelve Steps and, as a result, began to mature emotionally.

Many of us found emotional relief right from the start. We were tired of pretending that our addiction and our lives were under control; it actually felt good to finally admit they weren't. After sharing our inventory with our sponsor, we began to feel like we didn't have to deny who we were or what we felt in order to be accepted. When we'd finished making our amends, we knew we didn't have to suffer with guilt; we could own up to it and it wouldn't kill us. The more we worked the NA program, the better we felt about living life as it came to us.

The program works today as well as it ever did. By taking stock of our day, getting honest about our part in it, and surrendering to reality, we can survive the feelings life throws our way. By using the tools available to us, we've developed the ability to survive our emotions.

❖

Just for today: I will not deny my feelings. I will practice honesty and surrender to life as it is. I will use the tools of this program to survive my emotions.

*"When we see how our defects exist in our lives
and accept them, we can let go of them
and get on with our new life."*

Basic Text, p. 35

❖

Sometimes our readiness to have our character defects removed depends on what we call them. If misnaming our defects makes them seem less "defective," we may be unable to see the damage they cause. And if they seem to be causing no harm, why would we ever ask our Higher Power to remove them from our lives?

Take "people pleasing," for example. Doesn't really sound all that bad, does it? It just means we're nice to people, right? Not quite. To put it bluntly, it means we're dishonest and manipulative. We lie about our feelings, our beliefs, and our needs, trying to soothe others into compliance with our wishes.

Or perhaps we think we're "easygoing." But does "easygoing" mean we ignore our housework, avoid confrontations, and stay put in a comfortable rut? Then a better name for it would be "laziness," or "procrastination," or "fear."

Many of us have trouble identifying our character defects. If this is the case for us, we can talk with our sponsor or our NA friends. We clearly and honestly describe our behavior to them and ask for their help in identifying our defects. As time passes, we'll become progressively better able to identify our own character defects, calling them by their true names.

❖

Just for today: I will call my defects by their true names. If I have trouble doing this, I will ask my sponsor for help.

> *"This ability to listen is a gift and grows as we grow
> spiritually. Life takes on a new meaning when
> we open ourselves to this gift."*

Basic Text, p. 107

❖

Have you ever watched two small children carry on a conversation? One will be talking about purple dragons while the other carries on about the discomfort caused by having sand in one's shoes. We sometimes encounter the same communication problems as we learn to listen to others. We may struggle through meetings, trying desperately to hear the person sharing while our minds are busy planning what we will say when it's our turn to speak. In conversation, we may suddenly realize that our answers have nothing to do with the questions we're being asked. They are, instead, speeches prepared while in the grip of our self-obsession.

Learning how to listen—really *listen*—is a difficult task, but one that's not beyond our reach. We might begin by acknowledging in our replies what our conversational partner is saying. We might ask if there is anything we can do to help when someone expresses a problem. With a little practice, we can find greater freedom from self-obsession and closer contact with the people in our lives.

❖

Just for today: I will quiet my own thoughts and listen to what someone else is saying.

"I started to imitate some of the things the winners were doing. I got caught up in NA. I felt good ..."

Basic Text, p. 153

❖

We often hear it said in meetings that we should "stick with the winners." Who are the winners in Narcotics Anonymous? Winners are easily identified. They work an active program of recovery, living in the solution and staying out of the problem. Winners are always ready to reach their hands out to the newcomer. They have sponsors and work with those sponsors. Winners stay clean, just for today.

Winners are recovering addicts who keep a positive frame of mind. They may be going through troubled times, but they still attend meetings and share openly about it. Winners know in their hearts that, with the help of a Higher Power, nothing will come along that is too much to handle.

Winners strive for unity in their service efforts. Winners practice putting "principles before personalities." Winners remember the principle of anonymity, doing the principled action no matter who is involved.

Winners keep a sense of humor. Winners have the ability to laugh at themselves. And when winners laugh, they laugh with you, not at you.

Who are the winners in Narcotics Anonymous? Any one of us can be considered a winner. All of us exhibit some of the traits of the winner; sometimes we come very close to the ideal, sometimes we don't. If we are clean today and working our program to the best of our ability, we *are* winners!

❖

Just for today: I will strive to fulfill my ideals. I will be a winner.

"No one is forcing us to give up our misery."

Basic Text, p. 29

❖

It's funny to remember how reluctant we once were to surrender to recovery. We seemed to think we had wonderful, fulfilling lives as using addicts and that giving up our drugs would be worse than serving a life sentence at hard labor. In reality, the opposite was true: Our lives were miserable, but we were afraid to trade that familiar misery for the uncertainties of recovery.

It's possible to be miserable in recovery, too, though it's not necessary. No one will force us to work the steps, go to meetings, or work with a sponsor. There is no NA militia that will force us to do the things that will free us from pain. But we do have a choice. We've already chosen to give up the misery of active addiction for the sanity of recovery. Now, if we're ready to exchange today's misery for even greater peace, we have a means to do just that—if we really want to.

❖

Just for today: I don't have to be miserable unless I really want to be. Today, I will trade in my misery for the benefits of recovery.

> *"By working the steps, we come to accept
> a Higher Power's will.... We lose our fear
> of the unknown. We are set free."*

Basic Text, p. 16

❖

Life is a series of changes, both large and small. Although we may know and accept this fact intellectually, chances are that our initial emotional reaction to change is fear. For some reason, we assume that each and every change is going to hurt, causing us to be miserable.

If we look back on the changes that have happened in our lives, we'll find that most of them have been for the best. We were probably very frightened at the prospect of life without drugs, yet it's the best thing that's ever happened to us. Perhaps we've lost a job that we thought we'd die without, but later on we found greater challenge and personal fulfillment in a new career. As we venture forth in our recovery, we're likely to experience more changes. We will outgrow old situations and become ready for new ones.

With all sorts of changes taking place, it's only natural to grab hold of something, *anything* familiar and try to hold on. Solace can be found in a Power greater than ourselves. The more we allow changes to happen at the direction of our Higher Power, the more we'll trust that those changes are for the best. Faith will replace fear, and we'll know in our hearts that all will be well.

❖

Just for today: When I am afraid of a change in my life, I will take comfort from knowing that God's will for me is good.

*"There is only one requirement for membership,
the desire to stop using."*

Basic Text, p. 9

❖

We all know people who could benefit from Narcotics Anonymous. Many people we encounter from all walks of life—our family members, old friends, and coworkers—could really use a program of recovery in their lives. Sadly, those who need us don't always find their way to our rooms.

NA is a program of attraction, not promotion. We are only members when we say we are. We can bring our friends and loved ones to a meeting if they are willing, but we cannot force them to embrace the way of life that has given us freedom from active addiction.

Membership in Narcotics Anonymous is a highly personal decision. The choice to become a member is made in the heart of each individual addict. In the long run, coerced meeting attendance doesn't keep too many addicts in our rooms. Only addicts who are still suffering, if given the opportunity, can decide if they are powerless over their addiction. We can carry the message, but we can't carry the addict.

❖

Just for today: I am grateful for my decision to become a member of Narcotics Anonymous.

*"Addiction is a physical, mental, and spiritual disease
that affects every area of our lives."*

Basic Text, p. 20

❖

Before we started using, most of us had a stereotype, a mental image of what addicts were supposed to look like. Some of us pictured a junkie robbing convenience markets for drug money. Others imagined a paranoid recluse peering at life from behind perpetually drawn drapes and locked doors. As long as we didn't fit any of the stereotypes, we thought, we couldn't be addicts.

As our using progressed, we discarded those misconceptions about addiction, only to come up with another: the idea that addiction was about *drugs*. We may have thought addiction meant a physical habit, believing any drug that didn't produce physical habituation was not "addictive." Or we thought the drugs we took were causing all our problems. We thought that merely getting rid of the drugs would restore sanity to our lives.

One of the most important lessons we learn in Narcotics Anonymous is that addiction is much more than the drugs we used. Addiction is a part of us; it's an illness that involves every area of our lives, with or without drugs. We can see its effects on our thoughts, our feelings, and our behavior, even after we stop using. Because of this, we need a solution that works to repair every area of our lives: the Twelve Steps.

❖

Just for today: Addiction is not a simple disease, but it has a simple solution. Today, I will live in that solution: the Twelve Steps of recovery.

"There is a spiritual principle of giving away what we have been given in Narcotics Anonymous in order to keep it. By helping others to stay clean, we enjoy the benefit of the spiritual wealth that we have found."

Basic Text, p. 49

❖

Time and again in our recovery, others have freely shared with us what was freely shared with them. Perhaps we were the recipients of a Twelfth Step call. Maybe someone picked us up and took us to our first meeting. It could be that someone bought us dinner when we were new. All of us have been given time, attention, and love by our fellow members. We may have asked someone, "What can I do to repay you?" And the answer we received was probably a suggestion that we do the same for a newer member when we were able.

As we maintain our clean time and recovery, we find ourselves wanting to do for others the things that someone did for us, and happy that we can. If we heard the message while in a hospital or institution, we can join our local H&I subcommittee. Perhaps we can volunteer on the NA helpline. Or we can give of our time, attention, and love to a newcomer we are trying to help.

We've been given much in our recovery. One of the greatest of these gifts is the privilege of sharing with others what's been shared with us, with no expectation of reward. It's a joy to find we have something that can be of use to others, and that joy is multiplied when we share it. Today we can do so, freely and gratefully.

❖

Just for today: I have been given much in my recovery, and I am deeply grateful for it. I will take joy in being able to share it with others as freely as it was shared with me.

> *"Complacency is the enemy of members with substantial clean time. If we remain complacent for long, the recovery process ceases."*

Basic Text, p. 84

❖

Recognizing complacency in our recovery is like seeing smoke in a room. The "smoke" thickens when our meeting attendance drops, contact with newcomers decreases, or relations with our sponsor aren't maintained. With continued complacency, we won't be able to see through the smoke to find our way out. Only our immediate response will prevent an inferno.

We must learn to recognize the smoke of complacency. In NA, we have all the help we need to do that. We need to spend time with other recovering addicts because they may detect our complacency before we do. Newcomers will remind us of how painful active addiction can be. Our sponsor will help us remain focused, and recovery literature kept in easy reach can be used to extinguish the small flare-ups that happen from time to time. Regular participation in our recovery will surely enable us to see that wisp of smoke long before it becomes a major inferno.

❖

Just for today: I will participate in the full range of my recovery. My commitment to NA is just as strong today as it was in the beginning of my recovery.

"Everything that occurs in the course of NA service must be motivated by the desire to more successfully carry the message of recovery to the addict who still suffers."

Basic Text, p. xxvi

❖

Our motives are often a surprise to us. In our early days of recovery, they were almost *always* a surprise! We've learned to check our motives through prayer, meditation, the steps, and talking to our sponsor or other addicts. When we find ourselves with an especially strong urge to do or have something, it's particularly important to check our motives to find out what we *really* want.

In early recovery, many of us throw ourselves into service with great fervor before we have started the regular practice of motive-checking. It takes awhile before we become aware of the real reasons for our zeal. We may want to impress others, show off our talents, or be recognized and important. Now, these desires may not be harmful in another setting, expressed through another outlet. In NA service, however, they can do serious damage.

When we decide to serve NA, we make a decision to help addicts find and maintain recovery. We have to carefully check our motives in service, remembering that it's much easier to frighten away using addicts than to convince them to stay. When we show them game-playing, manipulation, or pomposity, we present an unattractive picture of recovery. However, the unselfish desire to serve others creates an atmosphere that is attractive to the addict who still suffers.

❖

Just for today: I will check my motives for the true spirit of service.

*"The fact that we, each and every group,
focus on carrying the message provides consistency;
addicts can count on us."*

Basic Text, p. 68

❖

Tales of our antics in active addiction may be funny. Stories of our old bizarre reactions to life when using may be interesting. But they tend to carry the mess more than the message. Philosophical arguments on the nature of God are fascinating. Discussions of current controversies have their place—however, it's not at an NA meeting.

Those times when we grow disgusted with meetings and find ourselves complaining that "they don't know how to share" or "it was another whining session" are probably an indication that we need to take a good, hard look at how *we* share.

What we share about how we got into recovery and how we stayed here through practicing the Twelve Steps is the real message of recovery. That's what we are all looking for when we go to a meeting. Our primary purpose is to carry the message to the still-suffering addict, and what we share at meetings can either contribute significantly to this effort or detract greatly. The choice, and the responsibility, is ours.

❖

Just for today: I will share my recovery at an NA meeting.

"Words mean nothing until we put them into action."

Basic Text, p. 58

❖

The Twelfth Step reminds us "to practice these principles in all our affairs." In NA, we see living examples of this suggestion all around us. The more experienced members, who seem to have an aura of peace surrounding them, demonstrate the rewards of applying this bit of wisdom in their lives.

To receive the rewards of the Twelfth Step, it is vital that we practice the spiritual principles of recovery even when no one is looking. If we talk about recovery at meetings but continue to live as we did in active addiction, our fellow members may suspect that we are doing nothing more than quoting bumper stickers.

What we pass on to newer members comes more from how we live than what we say. If we advise someone to "turn it over" without having experienced the miracle of the Third Step, chances are the message will fail to reach the ears of the newcomer for whom it's intended. On the other hand, if we "walk what we talk" and share our genuine experience in recovery, the message will surely be evident to all.

❖

Just for today: I will practice the principles of recovery, even when I'm the only one who knows.

> *"In living the steps, we begin to let go*
> *of our self-obsession."*

Basic Text, p. 97

❖

Many of us came to the program convinced that our feelings, our wants, and our needs were of the utmost importance to everyone. We had practiced a lifetime of self-seeking, self-centered behavior and believed it was the only way to live.

That self-centeredness doesn't cease just because we stop using drugs. Perhaps we attend our first NA function and are positive that everyone in the room is watching us, judging us, and condemning us. We may demand that our sponsor be on call to listen to us whenever we want—and they, in turn, may gently suggest that the world does not revolve around us. The more we insist on being the center of the universe, the less satisfied we will be with our friends, our sponsor, and everything else.

Freedom from self-obsession can be found through concentrating more on the needs of others and less on our own. When others have problems, we can offer help. When newcomers need rides to meetings, we can pick them up. When friends are lonely, we can spend time with them. When we find ourselves feeling unloved or ignored, we can offer the love and attention we need to someone else. In giving, we receive much more in return—and that's a promise we can trust.

❖

Just for today: I will share the world with others, knowing they are just as important as I am. I will nourish my spirit by giving of myself.

"Freedom to change seems to come after acceptance of ourselves."

Basic Text, p. 58

❖

Fear and denial are the opposites of acceptance. None of us are perfect, even in our own eyes; all of us have certain traits that, given the chance, we would like to change. We sometimes become overwhelmed when contemplating how far short we fall of our ideals, so overwhelmed that we fear there's no chance of becoming the people we'd like to be. That's when our defense mechanism of denial kicks in, taking us to the opposite extreme: nothing about ourselves needs changing, we tell ourselves, so why worry? Neither extreme gives us the freedom to change.

Whether we are long-time NA members or new to recovery, the freedom to change is acquired by working the Twelve Steps. When we admit our powerlessness and the unmanageability of our lives, we counteract the lie that says we don't *have* to change. In coming to believe that a Power greater than we are can help us, we lose our fear that we are damaged beyond repair; we come to believe we *can* change. We turn ourselves over to the care of the God of our understanding and tap the strength we need to make a thorough, honest examination of ourselves. We admit to God, to ourselves, and to another human being what we've found. We accept the good and the bad in ourselves; with this acceptance, we become free to change.

❖

Just for today: I want to change. By working the steps, I will counter fear and denial and find the acceptance needed to change.

> *"When at the end of the road we find that we can
> no longer function as a human being, either with
> or without drugs, we all face the same dilemma....
> Either go on as best we can to the bitter ends—jails,
> institutions, or death—or find a new way to live."*

Basic Text, p. 87

❖

What was the worst aspect of active addiction? For many of us, it wasn't the chance that we might die some day of our disease. The worst part was the living death we experienced every day, the never-ending meaninglessness of life. We felt like walking ghosts, not living, loving parts of the world around us.

In recovery, we've come to believe that we're here for a reason: to love ourselves and to love others. In working the Twelve Steps, we have learned to accept ourselves. With that self-acceptance has come self-respect. We have seen that everything we do has an effect on others; we are a part of the lives of those around us, and they of ours. We've begun to trust other people and to acknowledge our responsibility to them.

In recovery, we've come back to life. We maintain our new lives by contributing to the welfare of others and seeking each day to do that better—that's where the Tenth, Eleventh, and Twelfth Steps come in. The days of living like a ghost are past, but only so long as we actively seek to be healthy, loving, contributing parts of our own lives and the lives of others around us.

❖

Just for today: I have found a new way to live. Today, I will seek to serve others with love and to love myself.

---

*"We reevaluate our old ideas so we can become
acquainted with the new ideas that lead to
a new way of life."*

Basic Text, p. 94

❖

Learning to live a new way of life can be difficult. Sometimes, when the going gets especially hard, we're tempted to follow the path of least resistance and live by our old ideas again. We forget that our old ideas were killing us. To live a new way of life, we need to open our minds to new ideas.

Working the steps, attending meetings, sharing with others, trusting a sponsor—these suggestions may meet our resistance, even our rebellion. The NA program requires effort, but each step in the program brings us closer to becoming the kinds of people we truly want to be. We want to change, to grow, to become something more than we are today. To do that, we open our minds, try on the new ideas we've found in NA, and learn to live a new way of life.

❖

Just for today: I will open my mind to new ideas and learn to live my life in a new way.

*"The Twelfth Step of our personal program also says
that we carry the message to the addict who
still suffers.... The group is the most powerful vehicle
we have for carrying the message."*

Basic Text, p. 68

❖

When we first come to Narcotics Anonymous meetings, we meet recovering addicts. We know they are *addicts* because they talk about the same experiences and feelings we've had. We know they are *recovering* because of their serenity—they've got something we want. We feel hope when other addicts share their recovery with us in NA meetings.

The atmosphere of recovery attracts us to the meetings. That atmosphere is created when group members make a commitment to work together. We try to enhance the atmosphere of recovery by helping set up for meetings, greeting newcomers, and talking with other addicts after the meeting. These demonstrations of our commitment make our meetings attractive and help our groups share their recovery.

Sharing experience in meetings is one way in which we help one another, and it's often the foundation for our sense of belonging. We identify with other addicts, so we trust their message of hope. Many of us would not have stayed in Narcotics Anonymous without that sense of belonging and hope. When we share at group meetings, we support our personal recovery while helping others.

❖

Just for today: I will reach out to another addict in my group and share my recovery.

> *"The drive for personal gain ... which brought
> so much pain in the past falls by the wayside if we
> adhere to the principle of anonymity."*

Basic Text, p. 76

❖

The word *anonymity* itself means *namelessness,* but there's a larger principle at work in the anonymity of the NA program: the principle of *selflessness.* When we admit our powerlessness to manage our own lives, we take our first step away from self-will and our first step toward selflessness. The less we try to run our lives on self-will, the more we find the power and direction once so sorely lacking in our lives.

But the principle of selflessness does a lot more than just make us feel better—it helps us live better. Our ideas of how the world should be run begin to lose their importance, and we stop trying to impose our will on everyone and everything around us. And when we abandon our "know-it-all" pretensions and start recognizing the value of other people's experience, we start treating them with respect. The interests of others become as important to us as our own; we start to think about what's best for the group, rather than just what's best for us. We start living a life that's bigger than we are, that's more than just us, our name, ourself—we start living the principle of anonymity.

❖

Just for today: God, please free me from self-will. Help me understand the principle of anonymity; help me to live selflessly.

*"As we learn to trust this Power,
we begin to overcome our fear of life."*

Basic Text, p. 25

❖

We are people accustomed to placing all our eggs in one basket. Many of us had one particular drug of choice that was our favorite. We relied on it to get us through each day and make life bearable. We were faithful to that drug; in fact, we committed ourselves to it without reservation. And then it turned on us. We had been betrayed by the only thing we had ever depended on, and the betrayal left us floundering.

Now that we've stumbled into the rooms of recovery, we may be tempted to rely on another human being to meet our needs. We may expect this from our sponsor, our lover, or our best friend. But dependence on human beings is risky. They fall short of perfection. They may be on vacation, sleeping, or in a bad mood when we need them.

Our dependence must rest on a Power greater than ourselves. No human force can restore our sanity, care for our will and our lives, or be unconditionally available and loving whenever we are in need. We place our trust in the God of our understanding, for only that Power will never fail us.

❖

Just for today: I will place my trust in a Power greater than myself, for only that Power will never let me down.

"The process of coming to believe restores us to sanity. The strength to move into action comes from this belief."

Basic Text, p. 25

❖

Now that we've finally admitted our insanity and seen examples of it in all its manifestations, we might be tempted to believe that we are doomed to repeat this behavior for the rest of our lives. Just as we thought that our active addiction was hopeless and we'd never get clean, we might now believe that our particular brand of insanity is hopeless.

Not so! We know that we owe our freedom from active addiction to the grace of a loving God. If our Higher Power can perform such a miracle as relieving our obsession to use drugs, surely this Power can also relieve our insanity in *all* its forms.

If we doubt this, all we have to do is think about the sanity that has already been restored to our lives. Maybe we've gotten carried away with our credit cards; but sanity returns when we admit defeat and cut them all up. Perhaps we've been feeling lonely and want to go visit our old using buddies. Going to visit our sponsor instead is a sane act.

The insanity of our addiction recedes into the past as we begin experiencing moments of sanity in our recovery. Our belief in a Power greater than ourselves grows as we begin to understand that even our brand of insanity is nothing in the face of this Power.

❖

Just for today: I thank the God of my understanding for each sane act in my life, for I know they are indications of my restoration to sanity.

*"We are no longer fighting fear, anger, guilt,
self-pity, or depression."*

Basic Text, p. 27

❖

As addicts, many of us experience depression from time to time. When we feel depressed, we may be tempted to isolate ourselves. However, if we do this, our depression may turn to despair. We can't afford to let depression lead us back to using.

Instead, we try to go about the routine of our lives. We make meeting attendance and contact with our sponsor top priorities. Sharing with others about our feelings may let us know we aren't the only ones who have been depressed in recovery. Working with a newcomer can work wonders for our own state of mind. And, most importantly, prayer and meditation can help us tap the power we need to survive depression.

We practice acceptance and remember that feelings like depression will unquestionably pass in time. Rather than struggle with our feelings, we accept them and ask for the strength to walk through them.

❖

Just for today: I accept that my feelings of depression won't last forever. I will talk openly about my feelings with my sponsor or another person who understands.

> *"When someone points out a shortcoming,*
> *our first reaction may be defensive .... [But] if we truly*
> *want to be free, we will take a good look at*
> *input from fellow addicts."*

Basic Text, p. 36

❖

At some point in our recovery, we come to the awkward realization that the way we see ourselves is not necessarily the way others do. We are probably neither as bad, as good, as beautiful, nor as ugly as we think we are—but we are too close to ourselves to really tell for sure. That's where our friends in the program come in, caring enough to share with us what they see when they look in our direction. They tell us the good things about ourselves we might not know—and they tell us the hard things, too, that we might not be able to see.

We may react defensively to such "help"—and, in some cases, justly so. However, even malicious remarks about our supposed shortcomings can shed light on aspects of our recovery that we cannot see ourselves. Wherever a useful insight comes from, for whatever reason it is offered, we cannot afford to discount it.

We don't need to wait for others to spontaneously offer their insight. When we spend time with our sponsor or other NA members we trust, we can make the first move and *ask* them to tell us what they see about particular areas of our lives to which we are blind. We want a broader vision of our life than just our own; we can have that vision by seeing ourselves through the eyes of others.

❖

Just for today: I seek to see myself as I truly am. I will listen to what others say about me, and see myself through their eyes.

*"... growth is not the result of wishing
but of action and prayer."*

Basic Text, p. 37

❖

Sometimes it seems as if our recovery is growing much too slowly. We struggle with the steps; we wrestle with the same problems; we labor under the same uncomfortable feelings day after day. We wish that recovery would move a little faster so we could find some comfort!

Wishing doesn't work in recovery; this isn't a program of magic. If wishes cured addiction, we all would have been well long ago! What *does* give us relief in recovery is action and prayer.

Narcotics Anonymous has worked for so many addicts because it is a carefully designed program of action and prayer. The actions we undertake in each of the steps bring more and more recovery to each area of our lives. And prayer keeps us connected to our Higher Power. Together, action and prayer keep us well-grounded in recovery.

❖

Just for today: My recovery is too precious to just wish about it. Today is a good day for action and prayer.

*"Working with others is only the beginning
of service work."*

Basic Text, p. 59

❖

We're in recovery now. Through living the program, we've attained some stability in our lives. Our faith in a Higher Power has grown. Our individual spiritual awakening is progressing comfortably. So now what? Do we simply sit still and enjoy? Of course not. We find a way to be of service.

We tend to think of service only in terms of committee service or holding a position at some level, but service goes far beyond this understanding. In fact, we can find opportunities to be of service in nearly every area of our lives. Our jobs are a form of service to our communities, no matter what our occupation. The work we do in our homes serves our families. Perhaps we do volunteer work in our communities.

What a difference our service efforts make! If we doubt this, we can just imagine what the world would be like if no one bothered to be of service to others. Our work serves humanity. The message we carry goes beyond the rooms of recovery, affecting everything we do.

❖

Just for today: I will look for opportunities to be of service in everything I do.

Index

Acceptance, 2, 48, 71, 174, 180, 229, 297, 320, 329

Action, 209, 274

Addiction, 28, 43, 83, 227, 259, 301, 308, 364

Amends, 144, 149, 161, 176, 247, 258

Anonymity, 55, 257, 375

Attitude, 23, 200, 297, 314

Balance, 5, 137, 270

Basics, 7, 28, 36, 66, 72, 83, 118, 147, 160, 164, 191, 208, 225, 227, 294, 304, 313, 366, 372

Benefits of recovery, 7, 20, 42, 60, 64, 146, 167, 169, 171, 204, 221, 228, 236, 266, 332, 353, 360, 361

Change, 25, 27, 56, 110, 168, 173, 185, 199, 253, 315, 362, 371

Commitment, 104

Compassion, 9, 264

Complacency, 1, 69, 104, 187, 238, 240, 276, 352, 366

Courage, 79, 274, 316

Death, 242

Decisions, 52, 98, 230, 245, 296, 306

Defects, 108, 136, 143, 339, 358

Denial, 87, 216, 279, 371

Dishonesty, 214, 224

Emotions, 36, 60, 90, 103, 151, 187, 270, 287, 335, 378

Empathy, 233, 264, 337, 359

Faith, 2, 10, 11, 15, 39, 50, 92, 123, 124, 139, 155, 172, 231, 288, 317, 328, 345, 347, 376

Family, 5, 114

Fear, 15, 63, 79, 115, 123, 141, 173, 328, 362, 371

Fellowship, 4, 16, 33, 35, 37, 77, 87, 96, 99, 109, 119, 130, 132, 147, 165, 192, 201, 217, 225, 273, 281, 290, 304, 320, 379

Forgiveness, 17, 73, 219, 261, 291, 292

Foundation, 188, 340

Freedom, 84, 221

Friendship, 144, 243, 300, 334

God of our understanding, 14, 46, 82, 117, 128, 152, 183, 195, 197, 198, 278

God's will, 3, 54, 91, 142, 213, 246, 307, 323, 325, 341, 354

Gossip, 162, 277

Gratitude, 10, 30, 53, 129, 229, 244, 253, 342

Group, 45, 152, 186, 374

Growth, 8

Guilt, 223

Higher Power, see faith, God of our understanding, Step Two, Step Three, Step Eleven

Honesty, 57, 68, 93, 100, 163, 179, 224, 239, 303, 330

Hope, 92, 170, 282

Humility, 67, 106, 134, 203, 324, 346

Humor, 132, 177

Insanity, 103, 326

Isolation, 24, 41, 77, 99, 146, 150, 156, 175, 211, 214, 239, 267, 300, 334

Journal writing, 135

Judging others, 73, 89, 122, 182, 219, 235, 263, 280, 291

Just for today, 44, 123, 157, 283, 315

Keep it simple, 19, 71, 157, 191, 241

Life on life's terms, 48, 119, 133, 150, 153, 174, 180, 194, 209, 303, 320, 344, 357

Life's wonders, 249

Listening, 233, 264, 337, 359

Meditation, 138, 178, 343

Meetings, 111, 147, 240, 260

Membership, 33, 35, 166, 192

Open-mindedness, 6, 22, 55, 61, 105, 110, 128, 134, 159, 236, 373, 379

Patience, 202

Perseverance, 316

Plans, 167, 327

Powerlessness, 49, 234, 309

Prayer, 163, 275, 302, 323, 351, 354

Priorities, 1, 69, 238, 290, 340, 352

Progress in recovery, 8, 25, 56, 59, 74, 86, 113, 116, 139, 164, 237, 256, 380

Rationalizing, 68

Relapse, 28, 51, 65, 98, 165, 212

Relationships, 76, 95, 182, 205, 218, 272, 295, 348, 356

Remorse, 58, 101, 251

Resentments, 73, 121, 261, 262

Reservations, 51, 268

Responsibility, 40, 52, 118, 176, 230, 296, 306, 310, 344

Secrets, 57, 218, 226, 250, 268

Self, 26, 34, 162, 205, 295, 298, 370

Self-acceptance, 41, 66, 70, 93, 107, 120, 140, 154, 203, 206, 214, 279, 284, 312, 324, 331, 336, 338, 346

Self-will, 38, 184, 213, 289, 293, 309

Service, 127, 367

Serving others, 34, 102, 244, 269, 299, 319, 322, 365, 367, 370, 381

Sharing our recovery, 49, 75, 80, 81, 87, 101, 129, 152, 170, 199, 269, 284, 321, 330, 368

Spiritual awakening, 12, 30, 47, 67, 97, 106, 138, 148

Sponsorship, 9, 40, 75, 88

Staying clean, 51, 65, 98, 165, 212, 249, 290

Step Eight, 58, 196, 205, 251, 292

Step Eleven, 3, 85, 138, 142, 163, 193, 195, 232, 270, 275, 288, 302, 325, 343, 351, 354

Step Five, 250

Step Four, 76, 78, 121, 141, 271, 305

Step Nine, 144, 149, 161, 176, 247, 258

Step One, 13, 29, 83, 210, 234, 309, 364

Step Seven, 112, 339

Step Six, 108, 136, 143, 271, 358

Step Ten, 18, 23, 54, 145, 220, 248, 252, 262, 314

Step Three, 14, 124, 155, 156, 231, 288, 289, 293, 323, 327, 333, 345, 347, 376

Step Twelve, 12, 30, 49, 97, 130, 148, 197, 215, 355, 363, 369

Step Two, 128, 140, 183, 278, 326, 377

Surrender, 13, 33, 103, 181, 211, 216, 265, 329, 333, 361

Tolerance, 89, 112, 122, 182, 194, 219, 235, 263, 277, 280, 291

Tradition Eleven, 96

Tradition Five, 21, 96, 130, 368

Tradition One, 21, 45

Tradition Seven, 84

Tradition Three, 166, 363

Tradition Twelve, 55, 257, 311, 375

Tradition Two, 186

Trust, 31, 217, 225

Unconditional love, 235

Unmanageability, 298

Using dreams, 207

Values, 27, 59, 91, 168, 255, 305

Willingness, 61, 131, 136, 160, 208

Winners, 360

The Twelve Steps of Narcotics Anonymous

1. We admitted that we were powerless over our addiction, that our lives had become unmanageable.

2. We came to believe that a Power greater than ourselves could restore us to sanity.

3. We made a decision to turn our will and our lives over to the care of God *as we understood Him*.

4. We made a searching and fearless moral inventory of ourselves.

5. We admitted to God, to ourselves, and to another human being the exact nature of our wrongs.

6. We were entirely ready to have God remove all these defects of character.

7. We humbly asked Him to remove our shortcomings.

8. We made a list of all persons we had harmed, and became willing to make amends to them all.

9. We made direct amends to such people wherever possible, except when to do so would injure them or others.

10. We continued to take personal inventory and when we were wrong promptly admitted it.

11. We sought through prayer and meditation to improve our conscious contact with God *as we understood Him*, praying only for knowledge of His will for us and the power to carry that out.

12. Having had a spiritual awakening as a result of these steps, we tried to carry this message to addicts, and to practice these principles in all our affairs.

The Twelve Traditions of Narcotics Anonymous

1. Our common welfare should come first; personal recovery depends on NA unity.

2. For our group purpose there is but one ultimate authority —a loving God as He may express Himself in our group conscience. Our leaders are but trusted servants; they do not govern.

3. The only requirement for membership is a desire to stop using.

4. Each group should be autonomous except in matters affecting other groups or NA as a whole.

5. Each group has but one primary purpose—to carry the message to the addict who still suffers.

6. An NA group ought never endorse, finance, or lend the NA name to any related facility or outside enterprise, lest problems of money, property, or prestige divert us from our primary purpose.

7. Every NA group ought to be fully self-supporting, declining outside contributions.

8. Narcotics Anonymous should remain forever nonprofessional, but our service centers may employ special workers.

9. NA, as such, ought never be organized, but we may create service boards or committees directly responsible to those they serve.

10. Narcotics Anonymous has no opinion on outside issues; hence the NA name ought never be drawn into public controversy.

11. Our public relations policy is based on attraction rather than promotion; we need always maintain personal anonymity at the level of press, radio, and films.

12. Anonymity is the spiritual foundation of all our traditions, ever reminding us to place principles before personalities.